moral

Images of Youth

Adolescent
Cultures,
School
& Society

Joseph L. DeVitis & Linda Irwin-DeVitis
General Editors

Vol. 12

PETER LANG
New York • Washington, D.C./Baltimore • Bern
Frankfurt am Main • Berlin • Brussels • Vienna • Oxford

Images of Youth

Popular Culture
as Educational Ideology

EDITED BY
Michael A. Oliker
and Walter P. Krolikowski, S.J.

PETER LANG
New York • Washington, D.C./Baltimore • Bern
Frankfurt am Main • Berlin • Brussels • Vienna • Oxford

Library of Congress Cataloging-in-Publication Data

Images of youth: popular culture as educational ideology /
edited by Michael A. Oliker and Walter P. Krolikowski, S.J.
p. cm. — (Adolescent cultures, school and society; vol. 12)
Includes bibliographical references.
1. Mass media and youth—United States. 3. Popular culture—United
States—History—20th century. 3. Motion pictures and youth—United States.
4. Music and youth—United States. 5. Television and youth—United States.
6. Adolescent psychology—United States. 7. Education—Social
aspects—United States. I. Oliker, Michael A. II. Krolikowski,
Walter P. III. Adolescent cultures, school & society; vol 12.
HQ799.2.M35 I43   302.23'0835'0973—dc21   2001029584
2001   ISBN 0-8204-4519-3
ISSN 1091-1464

Die Deutsche Bibliothek-CIP-Einheitsaufnahme

Images of youth: popular culture as educational ideology /
ed. by: Michael A. Oliker and Walter P. Krolikowski, S.J.
–New York; Washington, D.C./Baltimore; Bern;
Frankfurt am Main; Berlin; Brussels; Vienna; Oxford: Lang.
(Adolescent cultures, school, and society; Vol. 12)
ISBN 0-8204-4519-3

Cover design by Randy Garrett

The paper in this book meets the guidelines for permanence and durability
of the Committee on Production Guidelines for Book Longevity
of the Council of Library Resources.

© 2001 Peter Lang Publishing, Inc., New York

Printed in the United States of America

Contents

Acknowledgments

I wish to express my gratitude to all the contributors to this volume including Randy Garrett who did the cover drawing. Randy's delightful drawings of George Reeves as Superman were brought to my attention by Jim Nolt of Lititz, Pennsylvania, who edits and publishes a George Reeves fan magazine titled *The Adventures Continue.*

I would also like to thank Professors Joe and Linda DeVitis of the State University of New York at Binghamton; Chris Myers of Peter Lang Publishing, Inc.; and my co-editor of this volume, Fr. Walter P. Krolikowski, S.J., of Loyola University Chicago for their assistance in getting this book into print. Because of my acquaintance with Walter I got to know the contributors Fr. Gene Phillips, S.J., Prof. Don G. Smith, and Prof. Phillip L. Smith. I am also grateful to Ruth E. McGugan for the demanding work that she had to do to prepare the camera-ready copy of this book for the publisher.

And additional thanks to the following people:

My wife Marjory Oliker who first called my attention to the work of Prof. B. Lee Cooper after hearing him speak at a meeting for music librarians back in the 1980s.

Ronald R. Morgan, Professor of Educational Psychology at Loyola University Chicago, who first called my attention to the work of Professor Laurence Miller on psychological dimensions of *film noir.*

Peter C. Rollins, Professor of English at Oklahoma State University, who posted my Call for Papers for this volume to the listserv of the Popular Culture Association several years ago. As a result, I obtained the papers by Grant Tracey, Michael Kassel, Bill Osgerby, and Francis N. Njubi.

My father—the late Fredrick B. Oliker—who took me with him to the Triangle News Co. warehouse in Pittsburgh, Pennsylvania, in the early 1950s when I was a little kid. His close friend the late Ben Morton, owner of Triangle News, gave me large amounts of comic books. When I began to become an enthusiast of Superman in the early 1950s, Dad gave me his copy of Philip Wylie's novel *Gladiator* and I quickly noticed similarities between Superman and Hugo Danner (the main character in Wylie's novel). Ms. Marilyn Morton Watson, daughter of Ben Morton, who managed Triangle News for many years after her father's retirement and death, recently chatted with me about her father and the controversies about comics and kids in the 1950s. I am most grateful to her.

I am also grateful to the three teachers who encouraged my interest in research on popular culture back in the 1960s: Dr. Lorraine Harvilla, Professor Emerita of Education at Kutztown State College; Dr. Bruce Underwood, Professor Emeritus of Journalism at Temple University; and Dr. Alan L. Soffin, a filmmaker and adjunct faculty member at Temple. I was especially thrilled when Alan agreed to contribute a chapter to this book. Alan's course "Aesthetics in Education" addressed issues in critical thinking about the fine arts and popular arts. I still regard it as the best course I ever had.

—Michael A. Oliker, Chicago, Illinois, 2001

List of Contributors

B. Lee Cooper is Vice President for Academic Affairs/Dean of the College at Reinhardt College, Waleska, Georgia. He obtained his Ph.D. in history at Ohio State University. Prof. Cooper is an internationally published scholar in the fields of contemporary lyric analysis, popular music bibliography, educational adaptation of popular culture resources, and specialty recordings and is the author of twelve books. His articles, research papers, and reviews have appeared in more than forty periodicals in the United States, Canada, and Great Britain. A notable recent publication is a three-volume work, *Rock Music in American Popular Culture* (Haworth Press, 1994–99).

Michael B. Kassel is Coordinator of the Academic Enrichment Center at the University of Michigan–Flint (UMF) and a Ph.D. candidate in history at Michigan State University. Mr. Kassel has taught history and communications courses at UMF, Baker College, and Mott Community College. His articles have appeared in the journal *Film & History* and Horace Newcomb's *Encyclopedia of Television* (Fitzroy Dearborn, 1977). Mr. Kassel is also the author of a book: *America's Favorite Radio Station: WKRP in Cincinnati* (Bowling Green State University Popular Press, 1993).

Walter P. Krolikowski, S.J. is Professor of Education at Loyola University Chicago and serves the Hispanic community in Chicago as a priest in Holy Rosary Parish. He holds a Ph.D. in philosophy of education from the University of Illinois at Urbana-Champaign. Father Krolikowski has also been a visiting faculty member at the University of British Columbia, the University of San Francisco, Xavier University, and the El Centro campus of Northeastern Illinois University. His publications have appeared in *The Modern Schoolman*, *The Priest*, E. C. Moore and R. S. Robin's *Studies in the*

Philosophy of Charles Sanders Peirce (University of Massachusetts Press, 1964), *Thought, The Jesuit Educational Quarterly, Dialogue* (Australia), *Proceedings of the Philosophy of Education Society, Proceedings of the Midwest Philosophy of Education Society, Educational Theory, Educational Considerations, Theory into Practice, Educational Studies,* and J. J. Chambliss's *Philosophy of Education: An Encyclopedia* (Garland, 1996). He has also edited *Faith and Justice* (Loyola University Press, 1982) and is the author of *An Alphabetical Companion to Philosophy of Education* (published by the author, 1974). In 1994 Father Krolikowski conducted a memorial mass in honor of the late World War II correspondent Ernie Pyle, which was chronicled in the *Chicago Sun-Times* by the well-known Chicago columnist Irv Kupcinet.

Laurence P. Miller is Professor of Psychology at Western Washington University. He attained his Ph.D. at Ohio State University. Prof. Miller's research interest is psychological influences in film and literature. His publications have appeared in *Empirical Studies of the Arts, Journal of Social Behavior and Personality, Film Criticism,* and *Psychological Reports.* Prof. Miller has also presented papers at psychology, film, and literature conferences.

Francis N. Njubi is an Assistant Professor in the Department of Africana Studies at San Diego State University. He has completed requirements to receive his Ph.D from University of Massachusetts at Amherst in September 2001. He has also studied at the University of Notre Dame and the University of Nairobi (Kenya, Africa). Prof. Njubi has taught at Holyoke Community College and worked as a newspaperman in Springfield, Massachusetts, and Seattle, Washington. His publications have appeared in *Africa World Review, African World, African Philosophy, Wajibu: A Journal of Social Concern,* and *Weekly Review.*

Michael A. Oliker is Executive Director of the Midwest Philosophy of Education Society and editor of the MPES *Proceedings.* He has served as an adjunct faculty member at Northeastern Illinois University and Loyola University Chicago and as a part-time librarian at Truman College of the Chicago City Colleges and the Biddle Law Library of the University of Pennsylvania. Dr. Oliker holds a Ph.D. from the Department of Educational Policy Studies at the University of Illinois at Urbana-Champaign. He has taught "Foundations of Education" at Rowan University of New Jersey (formerly Glassboro State College) and Loyola University of Chicago, Library and Information Science at Central Missouri State University, and served as a consultant and researcher for the Lieutenant Governor of Illinois in 1979 and 1980. Dr. Oliker's publications have appeared in *College Press Review, Proceedings of the Philosophy of Education Society, Educational Studies, Journal of Educational Thought* (Canada), *Journal of Thought, Illinois Libraries, Proceedings of the Midwest PES, Educational Horizons,* and J. J. Chambliss's *Philosophy of Education: An Encyclopedia* (Garland, 1996).

Bill Osgerby is Senior Lecturer in Media and Cultural Studies at the School of Social Science at the University of North London in the United Kingdom. He holds a D.Phil. degree in history from the University of Sussex. Dr. Osgerby has also taught at Southampton Institute, the University of Leicester, The Open University, the University of Sussex, the University of East London, and Crawley College of Technology. He has published articles in: Roger Sabin's *Punk Rock: So What?* (Routledge, 1998), Paul Cobley and Adam Briggs's *Introduction to the Media* (Longman, 1997), *Arena Homme Plus,* David Mellor et al.'s *Les Annes Utopias* (Paris, 1996), B. L. Brivati et al.'s *The Impact of the Second World War on the British Polity* (Leicester U. Press, 1993), *Contemporary Record,* and *Bulletin of the British Society of Sports History.* Dr. Osgerby is also the author of *Youth in Britain since 1945* (Blackwell, 1998).

Gene D. Phillips, S.J. is Professor of English at Loyola University Chicago where he teaches courses in fiction and film history. He received his Ph.D. from Fordham University in New York City. Father Phillips has served on special juries at the Cannes, Berlin, Chicago, and Midwest Film Festivals. He has published over a hundred articles on literature and film and is a contributing editor of *Literature/Film Quarterly.* His many books include: *The Movie Makers: Artists in an Industry* (Nelson-Hall, 1973); *Graham Greene: The Films of His Fiction* (Teachers College Press, 1974); *Evelyn Waugh's Officers, Gentlemen, and Rogues: The Fact Behind His Fiction* (Nelson-Hall, 1975); *Ken Russell* (Twayne Publishers, 1979); *Hemingway and Film* (Ungar, 1980); *John Schlesinger* (Twayne Publishers, 1981); *George Cukor* (Twayne Publishers, 1982); *Fiction, Film, and F. Scott Fitzgerald*

(Loyola University Press, 1986); *Fiction, Film, and Faulkner: The Art of Adaptation* (University of Tennessee Press, 1988); *Conrad and Cinema: The Art of Adaptation* (Peter Lang, 1995); *Exiles in Hollywood: Major European Film Directors in America* (Associated University Presses, 1998); *Fiction, Film, and Raymond Chandler: The Art of Adaptation* (forthcoming).

Don G. Smith is Associate Professor of Secondary Education and Foundations at Eastern Illinois University and president of the Midwest Philosophy of Education Society. He received his Ph.D. in philosophy of education from Southern Illinois University at Carbondale. Prof. Smith has published papers in *Poe Studies, Educational Considerations, Proceedings of the Midwest Philosophy of Education Society, Midnight Marquee,* and many other periodicals devoted to film and education. His two books, *Lon Chaney, Jr.: Horror Film Star* (1996) and *The Poe Cinema* (1998), were both published by McFarland and Co. Prof. Smith is currently working on a book, tentatively titled *The Cinema of H. G. Wells.*

Philip L. Smith is Associate Professor of Education at Ohio State University and an intercollegiate hockey referee. Prof. Smith teaches philosophy of education, philosophy of sport, and hockey. He received a Ph.D. in philosophy of education from the University of Michigan at Ann Arbor where his dissertation was titled, "The Development and Formulation of John Dewey's Theory of Mind." Prof. Smith is a past president of the Midwest Philosophy of Education Society, editor of the State University of New York Press Philosophy of Education Series, a former member of the Executive Board of the John Dewey Society. He was Visiting Professor of Philosophy of Education at Harvard University during the 1995–96 academic year. His publications have appeared in *International Philosophical Quarterly, Educational Considerations, Educational Theory, Proceedings of the Midwest Philosophy of Education Society, Proceedings of the Philosophy of Education Society, Journal of Social Philosophy, Philosophy East and West, Harvard Educational Review, Journal of Higher Education, Journal of Genetic Psychology,* and J. J. Chambliss's *Philosophy of Education: An Encyclopedia* (Garland, 1996). Prof. Smith is also the author of two books: *Sources of Progressive Thought in American Education* (University Press of America, 1980) and *The Problem of Values in Educational Thought* (Iowa State University Press, 1982).

Alan L. Soffin is a part-time faculty member at the Center for Learning in Retirement of Delaware Valley College in Doylestown, Pennsylvania. He has served as director of the Institute for International Video Exchange at Temple University and has been a full-time faculty member at Temple and Michigan State universities. Dr. Soffin obtained a Ph.D. in philosophy of education from the University of Illinois at Urbana-Champaign and did post-doctoral work in Communications at the Annenberg School of Communications at the University of Pennsylvania. He has done considerable work in mass media, including managing the Community/School Documentary Television Project for Wissahickon School District and serving as co-owner, producer, and director with Bergman-Soffin Films. Dr. Soffin's work in "videoexchange" has been the subject of articles in *Families, Basic Education, Technology Review,* and *The Christian Science Monitor.* His own publications have appeared in *PSMLA Bulletin, Basic Education,* and *Educational Theory.* In 1972, the Bergman-Soffin Films feature film *Confessor* was awarded a Special Jury Gold Medal at the Atlanta International Film Festival.

Grant Tracey is Assistant Professor of English at the University of Northern Iowa (UNI). He received his Ph.D in English from the University of Illinois at Urbana-Champaign. Prof. Tracey teaches courses at UNI in film and creative writing. His short stories have appeared in *Kansas Quarterly, Aethlon,* and *Farmer's Market.* Prof. Tracey's articles have also appeared in *Literary Magazine Review* and *Statement.* He is editor of *Images: The Journal of Film and Popular Culture* and fiction editor of *North American Review.*

Preface
Adolescents, Popular Culture, Critical Thinking, and Ideology

Michael A. Oliker,
Midwest Philosophy of Education Society

I. Critical Thinking, Ideology, and Popular Culture

This book is intended to demonstrate that critical thinking can be applied to the study of popular culture and to continuing controversies about the influence of popular culture on adolescents and children. My position is contrary to the view that the meaning of popular culture is always obvious and that attempts to think critically about popular culture are a waste of time (Broudy, 210–11). A critical thinker should be aware that both language and images can have multiple meanings. The term for this is "ambiguity." (Israel Scheffler [109, 111–12] has identified both semantic and pictorial ambiguity in a recent paper.) The content of this volume can be subject to multiple interpretations. Since several of the papers deal with historical aspects of the interaction between adolescents and popular culture, I shall discuss the characteristics of different historical narratives (Oliker: 1990, 475–76) and how they might be used to develop an historical theory of adolescents and popular culture. According to Robert H. Ennis, a critical thinker's first reaction to a statement should be to clarify its meaning. Ennis (1967: 117–19) distinguishes among three dimensions of critical thinking: logical, criterial, and pragmatic. The logical dimension of the claim that popular culture can be seen as educational ideology requires a clarification of the terms "educational ideology" and "popular culture" and their connotations or implications. The criterial dimension addresses the grounds for claiming that a statement is true or false. For example: What would be the basis for claiming that the statement "Reading comic books causes juvenile delinquency," is true or false? Finally, in the third dimension of critical thinking, what Ennis would call the pragmatic dimension, he tends to emphasize statements and how they function in a culture. The pragmatic dimension of critical thinking also, I would maintain, requires a knowledge of the historical context of a concept or an image. For example, I recall seeing an old building in Chicago that had a design on its front wall containing a row of swastikas. I wondered if the building had once been owned by Nazis, but I later found out that it had had that design since roughly 1910. If that building ever were occupied by Nazis, it would be an issue for a historian to research. The design itself is not sufficient evidence to claim that the building was once the headquarters of a group of Nazis. In his analysis of the concept of ideology in his 1977 book *Ideology and Education,* Richard Pratte goes beyond language in his discussion of what Ennis would call the pragmatic dimension of an ideology. Pratte (59) states that "ideology has the same kind of consistency that a person's aesthetic and artistic preferences have." So, the pragmatic dimension of an ideology may identify a concept with a certain visual image. The result of this may be what is called typecasting in theater, film, and television (Katz, 1372). An actor who plays villains may become so identified with the role that he will be denied the opportunity to play a hero. And, the public may assume that a man on the street who resembles that actor is himself a villain. As I argued in a review of two of Pratte's books in 1981, Pratte holds that "an ideology is a type of belief system that is subscribed to by some social group and functions as a link between individual belief systems and collective action" (Oliker, 1981: 79). So, if teenage gang members murder their teacher, a possible explanation for their action might be that the victim resembled a character in a film, television show, or comic book who was regarded as a villain. Or, if the same gang treats a morally questionable person as a hero, a researcher might look into whether the person resembles a popular entertainer whose looks identify him or her as a hero to that group. Many of the papers in this volume contain historical accounts of popular culture. The meaning of a concept such as juvenile delinquent, or superman, or progressive education can change over time. I maintain that critical thinking about a popular song, film, comic book, television program, detective story, or the endorsement of a product by a professional athlete requires some knowledge of the historical circumstances in which the item was created. There are a variety of critical questions that can be asked about adolescents and popular culture:

1. How does popular culture influence adolescents, and how do adolescents influence popular culture?

2. What are the predominant images of adolescents in popular culture?

3. Are the images of adolescents in popular culture an influence on, or are they influenced by, educational ideology or educational philosophy?

4. What are the predominant images of education in popular culture?

5. Are these images desirable or undesirable?

Each of the contributions to this volume addresses aspects of some of these questions.

II. The Cover and the Papers in this Volume

A) Garrett's Cover. Both the title of this book and Randy Garrett's cover drawing should be seen as ambiguous. Readers should be aware that Garrett did that drawing exactly the way I asked him to. The phrase "Images of Youth" can mean either "representations of youth" or "the beliefs that youth possess." The phrase "popular culture as educational ideology" can mean "ways in which popular culture influences public beliefs about education" or "ways in which popular culture reflects public beliefs about education." Garrett's drawing illustrates this. If his drawing represented an actual historical incident, it would have taken place in roughly 1951. The drawing shows the great philosopher of education John Dewey and Superman scrutinizing three teenagers watching the actor James Dean, the singer Elvis Presley, and the actress Marie Windsor on television. The three teenagers are all dressed to emulate the styles of the television performers. James Dean (Katz, 339) frequently played young men who rebelled against adult authority. Marie Windsor (Katz, 1468) often played hard-boiled women in the genre called *film noir* who became a threat to men whom her characters were involved with. In 1951, Elvis Presley (Katz, 1099–1100) was only sixteen, but he had already begun to do some performing in high school. So, the image on the screen may be Elvis and the kid in the audience may also be Elvis. Both Dean and Presley appeared on television before making major films. By contrast, Marie Windsor had appeared in many films before appearing on television. By the mid-1950s, Presley's television appearances and Dean's film appearances had established them as symbols of the youth rebellion that began after World War II. Dewey and Superman had become popular figures long before the 1950s. Friedrich Nietzsche's conception of the *ubermensch* (translated as both "superman" and "overman") appeared in the late 19th century (Kaufmann, 21, 115, 124–128). Jerry Siegel and Joe Shuster's comic book character, Superman, appeared nationally in *Action Comics* in 1938 and was a major factor in the comic book displacing the pulp magazine in the late 1940s (Daniels, 10–47). John Dewey became famous for his Laboratory School at the University of Chicago between 1896 and 1904 and remained the leading figure in American progressive educational thought until his death in 1952 (Dykhuizen, 87–98; 301–304; 348: n57). In the cover drawing, they represent the ideals of an older generation worried about the impact of the mass media on youth. But their generation still held the optimistic view that education could overcome popular prejudice. Superman represents an ethical ideal—the superhero— who is able to transcend his environment as well as stimulate a juvenile delinquent to do the same thing in an episode of the 1950s television series *The Adventures of Superman (AOS)*, "The Boy Who Hated Superman" (Bifulco, 82–84). From November 1951 until his death on June 1, 1952, Dewey was unable to walk because of a broken hip (Dykhuizen, 320), so, in the cover drawing, he has the help of Superman to stand up. Those of us who were children at this time will recognize the face of Superman as being that of the actor George Reeves. My paper contains a discussion of several episodes of the 1950s television series that starred George Reeves in the title role. Those who are still fans of the 1950s series may remember an early episode (produced in 1951), "The Mind Machine" (Bifulco, 22–23), in which an invention that resembles an early television set is stolen from its inventor, Professor Stanton, and used by criminals to murder witnesses in a televised trial. The actor who played the part of Stanton was Griff Barnett, who either strongly resembled John Dewey or was deliberately made up to resemble him. Professor Stanton cooperates with Superman to destroy the mind machine because it has fallen into the hands of villains. Superman assures the professor that he does not regard him as a conspirator in the crimes. There are a number of episodes of *AOS* in which Superman must deal with a danger caused by the work of a scientist or professor who is either irresponsible or a criminal. But in this episode, Superman is clearly sympathetic to the efforts of Professor Stanton. (Fans of *AOS* should also be aware that the cast and crew of *AOS* made an extra episode, "Stamp Day for Superman" [Bifulco, 100–102], which was produced by the U.S. Treasury Department and shown in schools to encourage the purchase of government savings stamps. It portrays Superman as an ally of teachers and a school principal!)

B) **Tracey.** The paper by Prof. Grant Tracey discusses James Cagney as a hero of adolescents in the 1930s. Tracey discusses the work of a 1930s sociologist, Henry James Forman, who claimed that Cagney's popularity with adolescents in the '30s was undermining the authority of Protestantism. Forman argued that, because Cagney was himself an Irish-Catholic who played Irish-Catholic gangsters, his characters stimulated "emotional possession" among adolescent audiences that caused them to abandon the "rational norms" of Protestant culture and become criminals. Tracey responds critically to Forman's claims by arguing that, in the early 1930s, James Cagney's character in the film *The Mayor of Hell* attempts to reform juvenile delinquents by reforming a reform school, using an approach to education taught to him by the school's Protestant nurse, Miss Griffith (Madge Evans). Interestingly, Miss Griffith's approach to educational reform has much in common with the democratic approach to school administration advocated by John Dewey (Dykhuizen, 296). A few years later, Cagney played a criminal (Rocky Sullivan) in *Angels with Dirty Faces*. Sullivan is a negative influence on juvenile delinquents who are led down a better path by a Catholic priest (Pat O'Brien), a longtime friend. When the priest begs him to display cowardice on the day he is taken to the electric chair, Sullivan refuses. He is then told that, if he shows courage on his day of execution, the juvenile delinquents (The Dead End Kids) are likely to follow his example and end up in electric chairs themselves. Tracey argues that Cagney's shocking display of cowardice in the execution scene at the end of the film is intended to show the positive consequences of emotional possession because, after Rocky's execution, the boys are shown to have become devoted disciples of the priest. While I like Tracey's paper, I want the reader to know that according to Cagney's biographer John McCabe (165), the actor often said that what he was doing in the execution scene was creating an ambiguity so the audience could not be sure whether Rocky was following the priest's advice and pretending to be cowardly or actually had turned cowardly. But, in the brief post-execution scene, the priest tells the boys that he agrees with the newspaper headline, "Rocky Dies Yellow," but then asks them to join him in a prayer for the dead criminal. They do it! Both these films display an optimistic image of the possibility of the reform of juvenile delinquents. In *Mayor* there is an endorsement of the view that a reformed school environment can reform its students; *Angels* shows that a figure of legitimate authority can enable youth to transcend a corrupting environment.

C) **Phillips.** The paper by Gene D. Phillips contains a critical analysis of the film Dead End (1937) in relation to the concept of juvenile delinquency. The same group of juvenile delinquents who appear in Dead End became known as the Dead End Kids and also appeared in *Angels with Dirty Faces*. In *Dead End,* they are influenced by an evil gangster named Baby Face Martin (Humphrey Bogart) who personified the dark and dirty environment of their riverfront neighborhood. Another character in *Dead End* is architect Dave Connell (Joel McCrea), who seeks to reform their environment in a fashion that Dewey would have approved of. Phillips points out the similarity between the names of the architect in *Dead End* (1937) and the priest in *Angels* (1938), Father Jerry Connelly. Dave Connell kills Baby Face Martin when Martin pulls a gun on him in an alley. He subsequently succeeds in reforming Tommy (Billy Halop), the leader of the juvenile delinquents. But the ending of the film remains somewhat ambiguous. The juvenile delinquents are heard singing, "If I had the wings of an angel, over these prison walls I would fly." This hints that Dave Connell may not have the influence over the juvenile delinquents that Father Connelly does in *Angels*. Phillips shares the optimistic view of the potential of education and believes that a priest can do a better job than an architect. He may be right. In the 1930s, when a priest appeared in a film, he was commonly treated as a symbol of legitimate authority. As I pointed out in my 1993 paper, "On the Images of Education in Popular Film," in the 1930s, it was still common to portray teachers as heroes.

D) **Oliker.** What if juvenile delinquents should encounter someone who has "the wings of an angel?" In the same year that *Angels* appeared on the screen, a man appeared in American popular culture who could fly! In the late 1930s, the beginning of World War II swept the world into a darkness that Dewey feared could not be overcome (Dykhuizen, 290–291). But the man who could fly had come to Earth to save us from self-destruction. He appeared in *Action Comics* in the late 1930s, and was introduced on a Superman radio program and in the Max Fleischer animated cartoons of the 1940s as: "The amazing stranger from the planet Krypton—SUPER-

MAN!!!!." My paper discusses the history of the concept of superman and argues that the version of Superman played by George Reeves in the 1950s represents an ethical ideal who occasionally becomes involved in the moral education of youth. I first discuss an episode of *AOS,* "The Big Squeeze" (Bifulco, 62–63), in which Hugh Beaumont appears in the role of a father who is mistrusted by his son who has discovered the father is an ex-convict who committed a crime as an adolescent. In "The Big Squeeze," Superman and Clark Kent make an effort to show the public and Beaumont's character's family that he has reformed himself and is now a "good guy." In the episode, "The Boy Who Hated Superman," the staff of the Metropolis newspaper, the *Daily Planet* (Editor Perry White, reporters Clark Kent and Lois Lane, and photographer Jimmy Olsen), cooperate to show the juvenile delinquent that Superman did not frame his uncle and to establish the boy's sense of right and wrong by treating one another like a family and treating him like a member of it. In the episode, "Around the World with Superman" (not discussed in my paper, see Bifulco, 98–100), Superman cooperates with a physician to restore a blind little girl's eyesight, flies her around the world so she can see that the world is beautiful, and then reunites her divorced mother and father. Superman's cooperation with the doctor and the little girl reestablishes her sense of reality and unreality. I argue—consistent with the views of Sarah Kozloff (78–82)—that Superman should be seen as a figure of salvation who does transcend the corrupt world of reality. The problem is that, since World War II, we have continued to live in a world of darkness that encourages cynicism about the very possibility of heroism. Although Marie Jean Lederman makes a strong case that Superman exemplifies the Freudian psychologist Otto Rank's ideal of the hero (235–36), these days, an enthusiast for hero-worship is likely to be accused of being a fascist. In his book on the history of psychology, *Scientists of the Mind,* Clarence J. Karier (311–14) makes that accusation against Otto Rank himself despite the fact that Rank was Jewish and a refugee from Nazi-dominated Austria. I hold that Superman stories are not stories about a master race. They are stories about the possibility of salvation from a world of darkness.

E) Miller. The world of darkness emerged in popular culture in a genre of film called film noir ("black film"). Film noir refers to a film with dark scenes that may take place at night, or are photographed at night, or make use of shadow imagery (Katz, 452–453). A film noir often contains dangerous environments and stresses the kind of pessimistic worldview defended in the writings of the 19th century German philosopher Arthur Schopenhauer. Schopenhauer's philosophy is an explicit rejection of the optimistic philosophy of history that originated with his German contemporary G. W. F. Hegel (Gottfried). Again, in my 1993 paper, I pointed out that, in the 1940s, Bela Lugosi, Edward G. Robinson, and Orson Welles appeared in films as teachers who were discovered to be murderers. Laurence Miller's paper discusses portrayals of juvenile delinquency in film noir and other popular films of the 1940s and 1950s. He also displays considerable interest in critical thinking in his attempts to argue for criteria of what a film noir is and is not. Miller discusses four films from the years 1949 and 1959 that can be regarded as paradigms of film noir accounts of the lives of adolescents. He compares those films with three other films of that era that he argues are not examples of the genre. Three of the film noirs about adolescents were made in 1949 when there was considerable controversy about a growing rate of juvenile delinquency. The first two, showing youth being doomed by a corrupt environment, were directed by Nicholas Ray (1911–1979). In *They Live by Night*, a young man and young woman, who are in love, are shown to be corrupted by their families who in turn are dominated by criminals. The young man is played by Farley Granger, who had appeared as a youthful murderer in Alfred Hitchcock's masterpiece, *Rope*. That same year, Nicholas Ray made a shocking film noir entitled *Knock on Any Door*, in which Humphrey Bogart portrays a defense attorney for a young man (John Derek) accused of murder. Bogart's character is shown as a man of integrity who believes that the young man is innocent. But the young man is found guilty, shown to be guilty, and dies in the electric chair. So, the film hints that Bogart's character is being victimized by a corrupt urban environment dominated by juvenile delinquents. The third film noir about adolescents made in 1949, *City Across the River*, was directed by Maxwell Shane. It stresses the corrupt environment in a city that motivates adolescents to become criminals. A fourth film noir, *Cry Tough*, was directed ten years later in 1959 by Paul Stanley. This one emphasized the negative influence of a corrupt urban environment on Hispanic adolescents. Miller points out that *Cry Tough* was the only film noir about adolescents made after the 1940s. He goes on to argue that three well-known films made in the 1930s about adolescents that contained violent scenes and subplots about doomed adolescents should not be regarded as film noirs because, in these films, the adolescents are shown to be justified in their rebellion. In his 1954 film *The Wild One,* the great Marlon Brando played the leader of a teenage motorcycle gang. Brando is able to overcome conflicts with another, clearly criminal, gang, whose leader is played by Lee Marvin, as well as threats from the residents of a town boasting many vigilantes. In 1955, the film *The Blackboard Jungle* portrayed a vocational high school with dangerous students and mean-spirited and incompetent teachers. (One of the teachers is played by the actor Richard Deacon, who later played the role of a mean parent on the television series *Leave It to Beaver,* discussed in a paper in this volume by Michael B. Kassel.) In *The Blackboard Jungle,* Glenn Ford portrays a teacher who is hostile to his students and his colleagues but successful in teaching an African-American student. The student is played by the fine actor Sidney Poitier, and it is hinted that his success in school may enable him to transcend a noir environment dominated by racial discrimination. And, in another 1955 film, *Rebel without a Cause,* James Dean also plays a high school student who successfully rebels against nihilistic environments in his school and in his home. However, there is clearly a bleak aspect to the environment in *Rebel without a Cause.* Dean's character's friend, Plato (Sal Mineo), is gunned down by the local police. It is noteworthy that *Rebel without a Cause* was also directed by Nicholas Ray, who might be properly called one of the grandmasters of film noir.

The papers by B. Lee Cooper, Don G. Smith, Michael Kassel, and Bill Osgerby might be described using the phrase that T. Bailey Saunders used to describe the essays of Arthur Schopenhauer, "Studies in Pessimism" (xxi–xxii, 379). Prof. Cooper discusses the themes in the lyrics of rock music from 1955 until 1980; Don Smith does a careful interpretation of a group of horror films from the late 1950s; Kassel scrutinizes the popular television series of the late 1950s and the early 1960s, *Leave It to Beaver;* and, Osgerby examines themes in British music and adolescent culture of the 1960s that were also popular in the United States. All of them identify aspects of what they are discussing that might be called a noir point of view.

F) **Cooper.** Prof. B. Lee Cooper seems sympathetic to the noir view of the high school that he argues is a major theme of lyrics in rock music in the period of 1955–1980, which he calls the Rock Era. He describes the rock lyricists and singers as "troubadours of contemporary young people." Cooper takes the position that rock lyrics clearly represent reality. According to him, in the Pre-Rock Era of 1906–1950, popular songs about schools were nothing more than expressions of nostalgia. In order to show that rock lyrics are accurate representations of reality, Cooper offers what Robert H. Ennis (1996: 345–346) calls stipulative definitions of ten terms that he uses to describe schooling. Ennis would hold that such a definition is not a description of the use of the term, it is an author's attempt to persuade his reader to accept his use of the term. I am not claiming that Cooper is wrong, but I would suggest that a critical thinker should consult sociological accounts of schools of the Rock Era for evidence about whether he is right or wrong and whether his definitions should be accepted. (For example, I recommend the book *Society's Children* by Carl Nordstom, Edgar Z. Friedenberg, and Hilary A. Gold [1967].) Cooper holds that, because these lyrics generally condemn teachers, they are "sharper" than the traditional nostalgic songs. Rock songs typically describe schools as tyrannical, noisy, and segregated. They praise students for being anti-intellectual and describe teachers as boors. Cooper expresses enthusiasm for the song "Another Brick in the Wall" by the band Pink Floyd, which is especially hostile to teachers. Then he describes the portrayals of parents in rock music as authoritarians, hypocrites, and advocates of conformity to an extreme that undermines the democratic ideal. And, schools are also portrayed as antagonistic to students' intellectual growth and self-discovery. Cooper acknowledges that these songs are nihilistic but claims that they make a legitimate cry for reform of American schooling. A reader who wants to listen to the lyrics in these songs to find out if Cooper is right or wrong will find his extensive discography quite useful. He also includes an extensive bibliography of cultural criticism and writings about rock music.

G) **D. Smith.** Don G. Smith has done extensive research on the history of the horror film. His study of nine horror films from the late 1950s that featured teenage monsters might be evidence for a claim—contrary to Miller's view—that film noirs about adolescence multiplied in the late 1950s and did not decline. But, on the other hand, the teenage monsters may be portrayed in these films as successful because becoming monsters enables them to rebel against oppressive parents, scientists, and teachers. The eight films that Smith discusses were all made between 1957 and 1959. Three were directed by Herbert L. Strock and four were written by Aben Kandel. The first and best known of these teenage monster films was the 1957 production, *I Was a Teenage Werewolf.* Written by Kandel, it starred

Michael Landon in the title role. (Landon later became a very popular television star because of his being cast as one of the stars of the television western series *Bonanza*.) In *Teenage Werewolf,* Landon plays a character who is already an adolescent delinquent but is changed into a werewolf by his doctor. Smith argues that, although the change enables him to rebel against society, and the doctor is portrayed as irresponsible, at the end of the film, when the *teenage werewolf* is killed by policemen, the film seems to hint that he is getting what he deserved. In *Teenage Monster* (1957) a teenager becomes a monster because of the cruelty of adults. A ball of fire comes out of the sky, that changes him into a monster and kills his father. Then, in the remainder of the film, the teenager's mother is sympathetic to him and encourages monstrous behavior. The next three films that Smith discusses were all written by Kandel and directed by Strock. *I Was a Teenage Frankenstein* and *Blood of Dracula* were both produced in 1957. In the Frankenstein film, a teenager again becomes a monster as the result of being an innocent victim of adults. Like the mother in *Teenage Monster,* the character called Professor Frankenstein encourages the teenage monster. In these films, the teenage monsters were all boys, but in *Blood of Dracula,* the teenager who is changed into a vampire by a chemistry teacher is a girl. Smith argues that the female chemistry teacher can be described as a type of feminist who encourages the teenage vampire to attack men. But the teenage vampire, Nancy, kills her teacher and then is herself found dead. Smith's viewpoint seems to be somewhat critical of feminism, but he does not seem to be enthusiastic about teenage monsters. In the 1958 production of the last horror film directed by Strock and written by Kandel, *How to Make a Monster,* a dangerous film makeup artist manages to change some young actors into monsters in order to have them attack studio administrators who object to the makeup man's horror films. In this film, the teenagers are clearly the victims of oppressive adults, and a couple of them are rescued by the police. Another teenage horror film from 1958, *Teenage Caveman,* was directed by the well-known producer-director Roger Corman and features the future film and television star Robert Vaughn in the title role. Smith argues that the title character in this film is not a monster but is regarded as such by an oppressive community. The noir dimension of *Teenage Caveman* is shown at the end of the film to have been caused by a nuclear war. The last two films discussed in Smith's paper were made in 1959. In *Teenage Zombies,* a woman scientist assists a group of zombies in changing a group of teenagers into zombies. Smith argues that the point of view of this film can be described as both paranoid and anti-intellectual. However, the teenagers in *Teenage Zombies* succeed in freeing themselves. In *Teenagers from Outer Space,* a group of teenagers who come to Earth discover that the creature their parents asked them to bring with them changes from a pet into a monster when they reach this planet. Once again, a film shows teenagers who have been corrupted by a noir adult world. Smith concludes that *I Was a Teenage Werewolf* is the only film in this group that shows a teenager who may be somewhat responsible for becoming a monster. In most of the films, Smith argues, the scientists are evil and the teenagers blameless. So, he concludes that the teenage monster films of the late 1950s reflect a growing nihilism among Americans about the value of the transmission of American culture.

H) **Kassel.** The argument of this paper about the television series of the late 1950s and early 1960s, *Leave It to Beaver,* is that it reflects the popular ideology of the time that identified suburbia as the ideal environment to raise children. But Michael B. Kassel is not defending that view. The title "Mayfield after Midnight" and much of the paper suggests that suburbia may have had a noir dimension. The preadolescent character Beaver Cleaver (Jerry Mathers) and his adolescent brother Wally Cleaver (Tony Dow) are shown to encounter threats from corrupt children, adolescents, and adults. Nevertheless, Kassel cites the work of the media sociologist Todd Gitlin whose view is that television networks can generate ideology. *Leave It to Beaver* is generally consistent with Miller's view, in the film noirs he discusses, i.e., that urban environments are generally dangerous while suburban environments are not. Two characters in *Leave It to Beaver* who could be described as counterexamples (see Ennis, 1996: 376–377) to the positive view of Beaver's environment are Wally's adolescent friend Eddie Haskell (Ken Osmond) and the parent, Fred Rutherford, played by Richard Deacon who, as I mentioned previously, played the role of a villainous teacher in *The Blackboard Jungle.* Kassel argues that the form of parenting in a family is often portrayed as more influential on children and adolescents in *Leave It to Beaver* than is their total environment. Fred Rutherford serves as a negative contrast to Beaver's parents, Ward (Hugh Beaumont) and June Cleaver (Barbara Billingsley). Rutherford advocates extensive use of physical punishment, while the Cleavers frequently mention behavioral science as a valuable source of information about raising children. But Kassel also suggests that there is a kind of ambiguity about Ward Cleaver. The character that Hugh Beaumont played on *The Adventures of Superman* was the object of ambivalence from his son until Clark Kent urged the boy to respect his father. Kassel argues that Ward Cleaver can be described as an "Organization Dad." Although Ward is not a doctrinaire believer in conformity, he does sympathize with the psychologists who regarded comic books as a categorically negative influence on the youth of the 1950s (Savage: 95–103). Kassel holds that there are episodes of *Leave It to Beaver* in which Ward and June urge Beaver and Wally to be conformists, but, in those episodes, Beaver and Wally become suspicious of adults, and Beaver is shown to become friendly with the rebellious adolescent Eddie Haskell. Kassel concludes that *Leave It to Beaver* communicates an ideology that stresses a generation gap between adults and children and ambivalence toward suburbia.

I) **Osgerby.** Bill Osgerby is a British historian whose area of expertise is the history of youth culture and mass media in England. But this paper also contains a subtle account of the interaction of British and American youth culture since the phenomenon called Beatlemania also existed in the United States in the 1960s. Osgerby makes a strong case that the Beatles received enthusiasm from both major British political parties. I regard this paper as raising questions relevant to the history of both British and American youth culture from the 1960s until the 21st century. Osgerby argues that the concept of "youth" became important to British political ideology in the 1950s and 1960s. His argument is that youth became identified with cheap labor in Great Britain in that era, but the Beatles became a symbol of affluent youth. Osgerby acknowledges that British youth enthusiasm for rock music and adolescent-oriented films ("teenpics") was originated in Britain by American musicians and filmmakers. (The musicians that Osgerby mentions can all be found in Cooper's discography.) An American film director whom Osgerby regards as highly influential in British youth culture is Roger Corman, whose film *Teenage Caveman* is discussed in Don Smith's paper. Osgerby points out that, since the 19th century, there has been a segment of British culture that uses the term "Americanization" as a condemnation. He goes on to argue that, since the end of World War II, there has been growing outrage in Britain about the Americanization of British youth. In the 1950s in Britain, "Teddy boy" emerged as a pejorative term for adolescent male delinquents. An American film that was regarded as central to the formation of Teddy boy culture was Sam Katzman's 1956 production *Rock Around the Clock,* which featured Bill Haley and the Comets as well as the singing group The Platters, and the influential rock music disc jockey Alan Freed. Osgerby points out that the British stereotype of the Teddy boy was identified with hair and clothing styles. Then, in the early 1960s, the pejorative phrase, Teddy boy, was replaced in Britain by the word, "Mod." Osgerby claims that from 1960 until 1964 a Mod was regarded as an adolescent whose clothes and hair style were offensive but who was also the personification of the degeneration of British youth culture. But, around 1964, when the political leaders of Britain became enthusiastic about the Beatles, "Mod" was replaced in British vocabulary by "teenager," which Osgerby argues was a positive concept with the connotation of affluent youthful consumers. Since the Beatles were distinguished by their long hair styles, the pejorative term for adolescent delinquents became "skinheads" in the 1970s. Although in the early 1960s, an adolescent with long hair was often regarded as a criminal in the United States, the skinhead style has become common among violent and rebellious adolescents in both Britain and the United States in the last thirty years. Osgerby seems to claim that hostility between adolescents and adults has become worse in Britain during that period.

I suspect that that generational hostility may also be happening in the United States. The noir viewpoint would claim—consistent with Arthur Schopenhauer's pessimistic view of education (427–434)—that trends toward doom among youth cannot be overcome. The paper in this volume about African-American adolescent culture and rap music discusses the pessimism and advocacy of violence that is expressed in the type of rap music called gangsta rap. Although the classic film noir about adolescents, *Knock on Any Door,* was based on a novel by the African-American writer Willard Motley, Professor Njubi would oppose a claim that a noir viewpoint should be regarded as universal among African Americans. (I have also been told by African-American teachers that Motley's novels are not highly regarded in African-American literature.) The doomed adolescent who is sent to the electric chair in the film noir *Knock on Any Door* is white, not African American. Although there are some black actors and writers involved with films, novels, and music in the noir style, I certainly do not regard the word "noir" as categorically referring to African-American youth culture.

J) **Njubi.** According to Francis N. Njubi, one term that refers to African-American youth culture is Hip Hop. Rap music is a product of Hip Hop culture. Njubi acknowledges that there is a form of rap music that glorifies violence, guns, and drugs. He also points out that there are three major types of rap music. The type of rap that glorifies violence, guns, and drugs is gangsta rap, and its audience is not limited to African Americans. Njubi claims that gangsta rap developed considerable appeal for white adolescents in the last thirty years of the twentieth century. The other kinds of rap music that Njubi identifies are Message Rap and Pop Rap. Message Rap reflects a Black Nationalist ideology but does not glorify guns, violence, and drugs; Pop Rap is entirely dance music with no ideological content. Although lyrics to rap music often expresses the desirability of nonconformity, Njubi explains why Gangsta Rap can be termed nihilistic. But he also agrees with W. E. B. DuBois that African-American music in the entire twentieth century has been a valuable gift to American culture as a whole. The rock music performed by such white entertainers as Elvis Presley and the Beatles originated in African-American culture but has become popular in both America and Europe. Njubi argues that another aspect of the impact of Hip Hop culture is what the distinguished African-American cultural critic Henry Louis Gates calls "signifying." The popularity of rap music is commonly accompanied by the popularization of rappers' styles of clothing, talking, and walking. Njubi argues that a negative aspect of Hip Hop culture is the nihilism that black gangsta rappers and white skinheads have in common. He also observes that gangsta rappers and skinheads share a "hard masculinism." (In a recent essay Charise Cheney emphasizes the same point.) Njubi and Osgerby both characterize adolescent culture as having a commodity orientation. Njubi points out that this was a factor in alienating youth in poor gang-oriented neighborhoods in New York City in the 1970s. The poor youth who could not obtain the turntables, recordings, videotapes, and video players that were regarded as essential possessions by the higher classes of Hip Hop culture have become enthusiasts for Gangsta Rap since the 1990s. Njubi holds that poverty-stricken urban neighborhoods have become even more dangerous since the 1990s because the expressions of the desirability of violence in Gangsta Rap have been a factor in stimulating drive-by shootings by adolescent gangs in the last decade. Njubi also makes the observation that, in recent years, television has replaced schooling as the primary window to society among adolescents in poor neighborhoods. He argues that the mass media have been a factor in encouraging the pessimistic worldview that is popular these days among both black and white adolescent fans of Gangsta Rap. Njubi does not endorse a noir viewpoint himself. He argues that, in the past, oppressed groups in America have always produced intellectuals who have opposed both racist and capitalist ideologies. He asserts that the revival of intellectual criticism in oppressed communities will result in a revival of the form of popular music called message rap. Njubi asserts that message rap still exists. Perhaps that claim should be taken as the basis for optimism that the violent youth culture that has been encouraged by both the gangsta rap version of Hip Hop culture and the commodity orientation encouraged in the mass media will be overcome in the 21st century.

The last three papers in this volume all take the optimistic view that youth can be and should be taught to think about popular culture from critical and ethical perspectives. Father Krolikowski argues that the genre he calls the didactic novel can be valuable for that purpose. Dr. Soffin discusses what I would call the noir aspect of the influence of endorsements by celebrities in advertisements and the domination of popular culture by what he calls a positivist ideology. Finally, Prof. Philip Smith argues that, while popular culture is often antagonistic to standards of objective truth, one aspect of popular culture that should not be trivialized by high culture is sports because learning to participate in sports requires learning rule-governed behavior.

K) **Krolikowski.** Father Walter P. Krolikowski begins his paper with a brief history of novels that are versions of Jean Jacques Rousseau's classic novel *Emile,* which was first published in 1762. In the final paragraph Krolikowski uses the phrase "didactic novel" to describe the type of text that he is writing about. His thesis is that Robert B. Parker's 1981 detective story *Early Autumn* should be regarded as a variation on Rousseau's *Emile.* Like *Emile, Early Autumn* deals with the education of an adolescent boy. But Krolikowski argues that, although the boy named Paul in Parker's novel does get a type of education from the hard-boiled detective Spenser, his education has some disturbing limitations. I would suggest Parker's novel shows that Paul has grown up in a noir world which he cannot transcend. Spenser cannot do for Paul what Father Connelly did for the *Dead End Kids* or what Superman did for Frankie in "The Boy Who Hated Superman." When Spenser first meets Paul, he realizes the boy is in need of an education. Spenser also realizes that Paul hates his parents and lacks the self-control to benefit from schooling. Although Spenser was hired by Paul's mother to help Paul, he is a believer in what might be called Autonomous Individualism. So Spenser concludes that Paul should not be educated to conform to his parents' desires. Krolikowski makes a case that Paul's parents married for money, not love, and are called consumerists by Spenser. Because Spenser takes Paul from Boston to a cabin in rural Maine and teaches him skills in carpentry, cooking, fighting, bodybuilding, and acting, Krolikowski concludes that, while Spenser is teaching Paul how to make autonomous rational choices that will enable him to abandon his parents, Spenser is also teaching Paul a viewpoint that could be called Proportionalist Utilitarianism or Neo-Weberian. According to Krolikowski, both of those viewpoints treat questions of value as subjectivist. So, Spenser's viewpoint is an advocacy of doing what you want to do and not doing the right thing. Krolikowski claims that both Parker and Rousseau see cities as corrupt environments in which adolescents cannot benefit from education. He concludes that Rousseau and Parker would agree that a rural area is the best place for a teacher to educate a student and points out that both Rousseau and Parker tend to regard physical education as more important than intellectual education and see indoctrination as having a role in education. Because Spenser can be described as a hired gunman or hardboiled in the tradition of detective fiction established in America by Dashiell Hammett and Raymond Chandler, Rousseau would not regard Spenser as the proper person to be a teacher. So, although Krolikowski is slightly more sympathetic to Rousseau than Parker, he appears to be opposed to the cynical view shared by Rousseau and Parker that education in urban areas cannot be successful. I suspect that Krolikowski and Njubi would agree that we should continue the effort to create a successful form of education for urban adolescents and not accept the nihilistic view common in noir popular culture.

L) **Soffin.** Alan L. Soffin takes the position that the use of celebrity endorsements in advertising and the popularity of a positivist ideology in popular culture are factors in the decline of morality in the United States. But Soffin does not endorse Schopenhauer's noir pessimism that there is nothing that can be done about these problems. I suspect that he takes the position that, if we can learn to think critically about celebrity endorsements and positivist ideology, the noir worldview can be overcome and that ideals of morality and personal honor can be revived. Soffin identifies Positivism as an ideology that treats scientific research as the only source of truth. A Positivist denies that science can verify claims such as, "It is immoral to do X." Soffin then claims that the fictional mad scientist Dr. Frankenstein personifies the positivist viewpoint, but he also seems to reject the view that a fictional character can serve as a moral exemplar. His position is that a moral exemplar should be a person who does work worthy of respect and expresses opinions which are based on expertise about the topic. Soffin makes a strong case that the use of celebrity endorsements in advertising is damaging to ethical thinking. He points out that the reader will find many endorsements of products by celebrity athletes in sports magazines and cites research that supports his claim that adolescents tend to be more impressed by endorsements by a celebrity than by a person whose expertise can support a claim that "This product will enable you to do X." Soffin also points out that that there is evidence that celebrity endorsements encourage adolescents to become heavy drinkers of alcohol. He then gives several absurd fictional examples of unethical celebrity endorsements. If we were to see an advertisement in which a product was endorsed by the Pope, a leader of social reform like Martin Luther King, or a president of the United States, such an advertisement should be seen as baiting viewers to a product. Doing such an advertisement, he argues, would undermine public respect for the person. Soffin concludes that a celebrity who sells his or her word is doing something that is "devoid of personal honor." He also observes that an actor who portrays a variety of characters in dramas is doing something worthwhile, but an actor who appears in commercials is not doing something worthy of respect. For the record, I think it is appropriate to mention that during the years that George Reeves was appearing in *AOS* as Superman and Clark Kent, he appeared in several commercials for Kellogg's cereals in his Superman costume. When I was a child, I often tried the product that Superman endorsed because I liked having cereal for breakfast. But, I regarded those commercials as humorous and not expressions of expertise about breakfast food. Because I had a relative who was a professional cook and was close to my mother and grandmother, I regarded their judgments about food as more reliable than the claims made in commercials. And, because my grandfather was in the movie business, I became aware at an early age that Superman was a fictional character and that a film of George Reeves in the role of Superman was drama and not a newsreel.

M) P. Smith. The short philosophical essay by Prof. Philip L. Smith urges commitment to the distinction between high culture and popular culture and argues for the Platonic view of high culture as representations of objective truth and popular culture as reflections of the biases of ordinary people. Smith takes the position that popular culture these days reflects the animosity to higher authority that is common among adolescents and is being accepted by the public in general. He also asserts that popular culture encourages the view that social conventions are never prudent and that value judgments are entirely subjective. So, Smith and Soffin seem to agree that popular culture reflects a positivist ideology, and both seem sympathetic to a revival of a Platonic approach to ethics. The distinguished ethical theorist and historian of ethics Alasdair MacIntyre summarizes Plato's view as "if anything is to be a good, and a possible object of desire, it must be specifiable in terms of some set of rules which might govern behavior" (32). Smith also claims that contemporary enthusiasm for popular culture has contributed to the decline of institutions associated with high culture, such as schools that stress philosophy and theology, opera halls, museums, and libraries. However a type of activity that may be regarded as popular culture, but is defended by Smith as consistent with Platonic ethics is sports. He argues that sports puts individuality to good use because the games that athletes play are socially constructed, rule-governed behavior. The rules of a game can serve as the basis of practices that require integrity. And, in sports, a person who ignores the rules of a game can be and should be excluded. So, Smith concludes that sports should not be regarded as trivial by high culture.

III. Conclusion

This book, as a whole, can be understood as containing aspects of a history of the interaction among adolescents, popular culture, and education. In a paper that I published in 1990 on the future of librarianship (Oliker, 1990), I discussed the four narrative patterns that Richard Angelo (229–35) takes from the work of the late literary critic Northrop Frye's book *Anatomy of Criticism* (162–239) and applies to the critical analysis of historical writing about education. So, I pose the question: Which of these four narrative patterns would be the most accurate representation of the history of the interaction of adolescents, popular culture, and education in the twentieth century? The four narrative patterns are: romance, irony, comedy, and tragedy. Each of the four can be seen as implying different relationships among the past, the present, and the future.

A romance is an optimistic view that regards the present as an improvement over the past and expresses confidence that the future will be an improvement over the present. In his 1899 book *The School and Society,* John Dewey (6–29; 150–159) urges elementary school teachers to teach history to children from a viewpoint that emphasizes progress in history. That viewpoint, often called Progressivism, uses a romance narrative to encourage optimism among children. (Dewey did not insist that all historians or history teachers conform to that viewpoint.) A romance narrative often includes an account of the success in life of a hero. A hypothetical example of a romance narrative of the history of adolescents, education, and popular culture might hold that youth have always had their interest in art stimulated by religious institutions. Then, since the establishment of public schools in the 19th century and the inclusion of courses in art, music, and literature in the curriculum, more and more teenagers have become artists, musicians, or poets. And then in the 20th century, the popularity of comic books and rock music among adolescents resulted in the expansion of schools that enabled students to study the arts as well as the expansion and improvement of the quality of art-oriented professions. (I am not claiming that this is true!) The papers by Tracey, Phillips, and myself all suggest that popular culture can have positive influences, but none of us offers a romance historical narrative that makes a case that it has in the past, does in the present, and will in the future.

An ironic narrative has a plot structure that is the reverse of romance. In an ironic narrative, the past is portrayed as undesirable; the present, as worse than the past; and the view of the future is pessimistic. So, I would hold that an ironic narrative would be the basis for what I have called a noir account of history or some aspect of history. A hypothetical example might be that, before the 20th century, many cultures designated an ethnic group as slaves. But in the 20th century, slavery was abandoned and replaced by genocide or ethnic cleansing. So, an historian who subscribed to an ironic viewpoint might claim that, in the future, genocide will be regarded as a normal practice of the public or of government. The papers by Cooper, Don Smith, Kassel, and Osgerby all suggest that adolescent culture is deteriorating and that, in the last fifty years of the 20th century, popular culture reflected the negative impact of schools and parents on adolescents.

A comic historical narrative would claim that the desirable practices of the past have degenerated into the undesirable practices of the present. But a comic narrative is optimistic about the overcoming of today's world in the future. In the fourth edition of his book *The Imperfect Panacea,* the historian Henry J. Perkinson treats American faith in education in roughly the last two hundred years as a delusion that resulted in the establishment of public education. Perkinson (153–198) argues that a positive consequence of the creation of television is that it has revealed the negative influence of education on the public and that public schools should be abandoned and replaced by a free market system of education (193–198; 213). The papers by Miller and Njubi seem to express different versions of a comic view of the history of adolescent education and popular culture. Miller expresses sympathy for the characters in films who are adolescents rebelling against the dominant culture and rejecting the delusions that their parents and teachers attempt to impose on them. Njubi takes the position that, for many years, schools imposed a slave mentality on African Americans, and that there are aspects of popular culture that encourage African Americans to behave in ways consistent with the white-racist stereotype that African-American youth want to be criminals. Although Njubi seems to believe that Gangsta Rap music is a factor these days in encouraging both white and black youth to become criminals, he holds that a revival of Message Rap can be a factor in encouraging both black and white youth to overcome the noir environment. (Charise Cheney holds that a revival of religion can also have that consequence.) Again, the comic view of history holds that the delusions of the present will be overcome in the future.

An historical narrative can be called tragedy if it is the reverse of a comedy. If there were a historian who regarded the events that Perkinson discusses as tragedy, he or she might argue that the ancient and medieval view of education, as solely the privilege of the leaders of society or the rich upper classes, was undesirable. Although Perkinson (22) refers to Horace Mann as "a pompous and self-righteous windbag," a tragic history of American education might regard Mann as Nietzsche's *ubermensch.* Mann was able to convince Americans to transcend the view that education was solely the privilege of aristocrats. Because Mann also advocated the abolition of slavery, he took the position that education should be available to everyone and that the profession of teaching should not be restricted to white males. An historian who advocated a tragic viewpoint might regard the period from 1838 (when Horace Mann became the first secretary of the Massa-chusetts Board of Education) (Gutek: 94–98) until 1968 (when the first alumnus of a state teachers college to become president of the United States—Lyndon B. Johnson—was convinced to leave the White House) as a high point in the history of American education and the last thirty years of the 20th century as a period when faith in education has been aban-doned. The advocate of a tragic viewpoint would then argue that the hos-tility of youth to adults and teachers (possibly traceable to the influence of the noir era of the 1940s and 1950s) might have been a factor in the hos-tility to President Johnson that cost him the presidency in 1968 (Gutek: 294–297). An advocate of tragedy in the history of American education would probably regard a free market system of education as a return to the undesirable educational ideology of the ancient and medieval eras. So, a tragic view could share the pessimistic view of the future that is held by the ironists. A tragic view of history might be called conservative because it regards the events of the present which seek to abandon a desirable tradi-tion as undesirable. I would suggest that an appropriate response to a tragic outlook would be a revival of the romance view that the culture of the recent past was superior to that of the distant past and that, in the future, we can overcome the shortcomings of the present. Perhaps it is possible that, in the future, a Superman will appear who will find a way to overcome the present. The forms of moral education advocated by Krolikowski, Sof-fin, and Philip Smith may all be useful ways to overcome pessimism about the future. The didactic novels discussed by Krolikowski may be useful in encouraging the public to believe that education can succeed. The critical response to the use of celebrity endorsements in the mass media advocated by Soffin could be a basis for establishing critical thinking as a necessary part of education and education as essential to youth culture. Philip Smith's view that participation in sports can enable youth to regard rule-governed behavior as central to ethics might be a desirable basis for understanding that the claim that an athlete is guilty of unsportsmanlike conduct can be supported by evidence and that that accusation by an umpire or a referee is not always just an expression of personal bias against an athlete.

Reader: which of these views would you endorse?

Bibliography

Angelo, Richard. "Myth, Educational Theory, and the Figurative Imagination." In *Philosophy of Education 1978*, edited by Gary D. Fenstermacher, 227–238. Champaign, Ill.: Philosophy of Education Society, 1979.

Bifulco, Michael J. *Superman on Television*. 10th Anniversary ed. Grand Rapids, Mich.: Michael Bifulco, 1998.

Broudy, Harry S. *Enlightened Cherishing: An Essay on Aesthetic Education*. Urbana: University of Illinois Press, 1972.

Cheney, Charise. "Representin' God: Masculinity and the Use of the Bible in Rap Music." In *African Americans and the Bible: Sacred Texts and Social Textures*, edited by Rosamond C. Rodman and Vincent L. Wimbush, 804–16. New York: Continuum, 2000.

Daniels, Les. *Superman: The Complete History*. San Francisco, Calif.: Chronicle Books, 1998.

Dewey, John. *The Child and the Curriculum and The School and Society*. Chicago: University of Chicago Press, 1956.

Dykhuizen, George. *The Life and Mind of John Dewey*. Carbondale: Southern Illinois University Press, 1978.

Ennis, Robert H. "A Concept of Critical Thinking: A Proposed Basis for Research in Teaching and Evaluation of Critical Thinking Ability." In *Psychological Concepts in Education*, edited by B. Paul Komisar and C. J. B. Macmillan, 114–148. Chicago: Rand McNally, 1967.

———. *Critical Thinking*. Upper Saddle River, N.J.: Prentice-Hall, 1996.

Frye, Northrop. *Anatomy of Criticism*. New York: Atheneum, 1966.

Golightly, Cornelius and Israel Scheffler. "'Playing the Dozens': A Note." *Journal of Abnormal and Social Psychology* 43 (January 1948): 104–105.

Gottfried, Paul. "Arthur Schopenhauer as a Critic of History." *Journal of the History of Ideas* 36 (April–May 1975): 331–338.

Gutek, Gerald L. *Education in the United States*. Needham Heights, Mass.: Allyn and Bacon, 1991.

Haywood, Richette. "Eartha Kitt at Sixtysomething. Entertainer, Who Was First Catwoman, is Older and Better." *Ebony* 48, no. 12 (October 1, 1993): 112.

Karier, Clarence J. *Scientists of the Mind: Intellectual Founders of Modern Psychology*. Urbana: University of Illinois Press, 1986.

Katz, Ephraim. *The Film Encyclopedia*. 2nd ed. New York: HarperCollins Publishers, 1994.

Kaufmann, Walter, ed. *The Portable Nietzsche*. New York: Viking Press, 1954.

Kozloff, Sarah. "Superman as Savior: Christian Allegory in the Superman Movies." *Journal of Popular Film and Television* 9, no. 2 (Summer 1981): 78–82.

Lederman, Marie Jean. "Superman, Oedipus, and the Myth of the Birth of the Hero." *Journal of Popular Film and Television* 7, no. 3 (1979): 235–245.

MacIntyre, Alasdair. *A Short History of Ethics*. New York: Macmillan, 1966.

McCabe, John. *Cagney*. New York: Knopf, 1997.

Nordstrom, Carl, Edgar Z. Friedenberg, and Hilary A. Gold. *Society's Children: A Study of "Ressentiment" in the Secondary School*. New York: Random House, 1967.

Oliker, Michael A. "The Deprofessionalization Story and the Future of Technical Services." *Illinois Libraries* 72 (September 1990): 472–478.

———. "On the Images of Education in Popular Film." *Educational Horizons* 71 (Winter 1993): 72–75.

———. "Reason to Believe." (Review of Pluralism in Education and Ideology and Education, by Richard Pratte) *Journal of Educational Thought* 15 (April 1981): 77–81.

Perkinson, Henry J. *The Imperfect Panacea: American Faith in Education.* 4th ed. New York: McGraw-Hill, 1995.

Pratte, Richard. *Ideology and Education.* New York: David McKay Co., 1977.

Savage, William W. *Comic Books and America. 1945–1954.* Norman: University of Oklahoma Press, 1990.

Scheffler, Israel. "Pictorial Ambiguity." *The Journal of Aesthetics and Art Criticism* 47, no. 2 (Spring 1989): 109–115.

Schopenhauer, Arthur. *Essays of Arthur Schopenhauer.* Translated by T. Bailey Saunders. New York: A. L. Burt Co. Publishers, (1902?).

1
Youth and the History of American Popular Culture: 1930 to 1980

Chapter 1
Scripting the Narrative of "Emotional Possession": James Cagney's Appeal to Immigrant Youth in the 1930s

Grant Tracey,
University of Northern Iowa

Popular writers and sociologists in the 1930s indicated with consistent alarm actor James Cagney's appeal to immigrant juvenile delinquents. Pop-sociologist Henry James Forman, in his bastardized version of the Payne Fund Studies, pointed to Cagney as a negative influence on second-generation immigrant youth:

"Who's your favorite actor," the investigator asked of a boy.

"Jim Cagney." His answer shot out virtually as the question ended.

"You like the way he acts?"

"I eat it. You get some ideas from his actin.' You learn how to pull off a job, how he bumps off a guy, an' a lotta t'ings" (263).

This Italian-American's interview responses played into the fears of conservative watchdogs who feared the powerful hold film had on immigrant youth. By informing the public about this problem of overidentification with media images, Forman had hoped to rally public pressure on Jewish producers to change the tenor of Hollywood films.

In 1934, sociologist Paul G. Cressey wasn't interested in Forman's moralizing agenda, but he did also list Cagney as one of the major stars having an impact on the lives of New York City boys (511). Cressey contended that, by watching a star such as Cagney, adolescent boys acquired his onscreen personality patterns, standards of dress and conduct, and even philosophy or way of life (512). Moreover, in his previously unpublished manuscript, "The Community—A Social Setting for the Motion Picture," Cressey, in a very advanced contextual approach, convincingly argues that the neighborhood kids erroneously saw Cagney and fellow Warner Bros. star Edward G. Robinson as two of their own: "Their conviction that these two actors are products of the local community is abetted by the feeling that their acting is a perfect depiction of styles of conduct approved among the street boys of the community" (Jowett, Jarvie, and Fuller, 181).

David Riesman, a functional sociologist, suggests further links between media and second-generation immigrants. In *The Lonely Crowd*, Riesman argues that by 1950, America has become an "other-directed" culture, sensitized to the expectations and preferences of others (9). First-generation immigrants, according to Riesman, tend to be inner-directed and loyal to past customs and beliefs, but their children succumb to peer pressure and the need for other-directed approval. Cities, the schoolyard, and media (film, newspapers, books) all play a strong role in creating cultural conformity. As a star on the Warner Bros. lot, Cagney's post-*Taxi!* films did their to part to encourage immigrant children to assimilate, "to be regular," to play by the rules.

Beginning with *Taxi!* (1932), Warner Bros. used Cagney's image to help immigrants conform to a hegemonic norm. A New Deal studio during the ascendancy of Franklin Delano Roosevelt, Warner Bros. promoted a national image of collective unity, and producer Darryl F. Zanuck constructed Cagney as an immigrant icon. In a memo to Warner Bros. scriptwriters, Zanuck defined the star around certain working-class, city-boy stereotypes: "He has got to be tough, fresh, hard-boiled, bragging—he knows everything, everybody is wrong but him—everything is easy to him—he can do everything and yet it is a likable trait in his personality" (Sklar, 43).

In the opening to *Taxi!*, a Jewish-American speaks Yiddish to an Irish-American cop (Robert Emmet O'Connor), and the baffled cop, only able to understand "Ellis Island, Ellis Island" stands back, lost. Cabbie Matt Nolan (James Cagney in his third starring role) jumps into the confusion and comfortably converses in Yiddish, asking the man, "Where do you want to go?" Nolan discovers that the man wants to pick up his wife and three children arriving from Russia, and he tells him to hop in. Bewildered by Cagney's command of Yiddish, the cop strolls to his cab, shakes his head, and skeptically arches his eyebrows. "Nolan, eh? What part of Ireland did your folks come from?" Cagney, comfortable in his own ethnicity and the polyglot tongues of New York, replies with a thick Irish brogue, "Delancey Street thank you."

The studio's scripting of Cagney as a swaggering ego-ideal for immigrants was profitable. On the West Coast, his films grossed above average; in the Middle West, fair; in the South, poor; but in New York, where, according to the 1930 census report on heads of households, the foreign-born white population (largely Italians, Jews, Poles, Slavs) dominated the "native" population 54.1 percent to 41.1 percent, first-week runs were often well over $30,000 and clobbered the competition in the neighborhood theaters. *Taxi!* ran three weeks at the Strand and grossed $51,000, $40,000, and $26,000. It was a huge and unexpected success for the studio, and Warner Bros., it appears, subsequently assigned Irish-Catholic Cagney in response to these numbers. In eight subsequent films, the studio cast Cagney as an ambiguous, but ultimately status-quo, figure, both a part of and apart from Anglo-Saxon society. He begins as an outlaw, a character who doesn't want to conform to the dictates of WASP society, but, through the love of a WASPish woman (Madge Evans in *Mayor of Hell* [1933]) or the demands of an authoritative Pat O'Brien (a priest in *Angels with Dirty Faces* [1938]), Cagney's characters either integrate or sacrifice their energies to communal good.

The cultural codes within Cagney's persona mirrored the apparent social role of Irish Catholics. Irish Catholics were ethnic in-betweens, an earlier immigrant group who had experienced prejudice and Anglo-conformity pressures, and had tried to assimilate by gaining prominence in city politics; however, even with their political power, they weren't fully integrated into the dominant mainstream. Separate schooling had kept them outside the hegemonic Protestant norm, and the resounding defeat, in 1928, of Irish-Catholic presidential hopeful Al Smith to Herbert Hoover (87 electoral votes to 444) made their differences and lack of real acceptance alarmingly clear.

In 1949, sociologist Milton L. Barron proposed that the Irish had represented the middle-ground between "new" immigrants and Anglo-Saxon society (259). They spoke English, the norm, but like Italians and Poles, many were Catholic, an "outsider" religion in the Protestant United States. For immigrant newcomers, the socially mobile Irish and stars like the red-headed Cagney represented the American success story.

Thus, by correctly gauging the audience's reception over Cagney's city-boy films, Warner Bros. gave New Yorkers an exciting star who spoke not only to the large mass from Eastern Europe but had his greatest influence on immigrant youth. Playing characters who were simultaneously inside and outside the mainstream connected Cagney with the confusions youth felt in their conflict between following the advice of their old-world parents while seeking their own futures in new world America.[1]

Mayor of Hell (1933): "C'mon, Fella. Be Regular"

During *Mayor of Hell*'s preproduction phase, America was still gripped by a strong, virulent Anglo-conformity movement whose origins went back to World War I. Protestants strongly distrusted immigrants' loyalties and commitment to "American" ideals, and they mostly feared losing their hegemonic power over Catholics and Jews (Gordon, 98). The passing of the Volstead Act in 1919 and the pressure on Hollywood to clean up its films were last gasp efforts of a Midwest majority to maintain Protestant control. By the late 1920s, the conformity discourse had a new fear: second-generation immigrants were rejecting parental authority and becoming Americanized through movies. In 1916, phenomenologist Hugo Munsterberg first suggested that "The intensity with which the plays take hold of the audience cannot remain without strong social effects" and the more "vividly the impressions force themselves on the mind, the more easily must they become starting points for imitation" (95). This fear of "imitation" would, in 1932–33, be coined "emotional possession" by Herbert Blumer and Philip M. Hauser. These two Chicago sociologists, working for the Payne Fund, studied the direct and indirect influences films had on youth. Blumer and Hauser contended that gangster movies influenced juvenile delinquency (1), and indirectly stimulated desires for fast money and sexual pleasure in male spectators (46).

Within this context of a larger Anglo-conformity movement, a fear of emotional possession, and a desire to control spectatorial response, Hollywood altered its filmic content. Warner Bros., a studio run by Jewish immigrants, sought to maintain Cagney's ties to his New York immigrant audience, while also appeasing reformers by de-emphasizing Cagney's gangster-icity, displacing it onto other genres. Following 1931, Cagney's in-between ethnicity would remain a strong residual component of his image, but he would no longer represent the explosively lost-world loser of *Public Enemy*

(1931). Cagney's Tom Powers was opposed to assimilation. He didn't want to fit in and wind up like his brother, a "ding-ding on a streetcar." Instead, Powers followed the crooked ladder to success and eventual disaster. But with *Taxi!*, the studio reconfigured Cagney's immigrant connection. He was no longer rebellious or challenging to the Protestant norm. Instead, Cagney's Matt Nolan crossed over into the collective, checking his hot temper, and committing to the responsibility of marriage. And with the Payne Fund study on the horizon, the cultural codes in the *Mayor of Hell* indirectly responded to Cagney's social critics. In a tough reform school story, Warner Bros. and writer Edward Chodorov didn't apologize for Cagney's popularity, but, instead, scripted it positively. In response to those who feared that Cagney encouraged delinquency, Warner Bros. created a New Deal allegory with Cagney at the forefront, welcoming immigrants into the mainstream. Cagney's Patsy Gargan encourages assimilation and assuages society's fear of emotional possession by representing it as a tool for positive growth.

Wayward, living in the streets, committing petty crimes, and running a car protection extortion racket, the boys in *Mayor of Hell* need someone to guide them. And, the film's opening shot suggests a glaring absence of a positive socializing agency in their lives. As the camera tilts up and tracks back, seven city boys watch Jimmy Smith (Frankie Darro) touch up a chalked sketch of an Irish police officer. "How's that?" The boys, a polyglot mix of European, Jewish, Italian and African-American origins, nod with approval. Living lawlessly, the boys, strangely, admire the sketch of an Irish cop who controls lawlessness. Instinctively, Smith draws the figure that Patsy will step into, the in-between Irish-American, Warner Bros.' class ideal for collective action.

Smith's sketch hints at his desires for an ego-ideal, a role model, and reaffirms a culturally defined myth of Irish-Americans as mediators. After Patsy foils yet another attempt by the evil Thompson (Dudley Digges, as the reform school's vicious warden) to ruin the school's credibility, he sits Smith down and indirectly inscribes himself as the boys' role model. Patsy asks what's wrong, and Smith sketches but doesn't answer. Nurse Dorothy Griffith (Evans) snatches the portrait, looks at it, and the film's opening motif is repeated: Smith has drawn the profile of an Irish-American police officer. Dorothy says it's pretty good, and Patsy asks Jimmy to draw him. Smith meets the challenge, and an elliptical edit reveals Patsy and Dorothy now looking at a sketch of Patsy. The two profiles—Irish cop and Patsy—

are conflated. Thus, allegorically, the film suggests that, as Irish street cops define mainstream institutions for immigrants, Cagney, as the new reform school director, eases second-generation boys into social responsibility and encourages them to assimilate and become American.

But before the narrative can earn this allegory of assimilation, the film's cultural codes must position Cagney as one of the boys, so that the immigrant kids in the film and those sitting in the movie theater can identify with him. The film establishes Cagney as an ego-ideal early. When he first arrives at the school, he witnesses Thompson sadistically whipping young Jimmy against a fence. Patsy intervenes, tells Thompson to leave the boy alone, and, in the aftermath, they have a telling exchange. Thompson suggests that there's no hope for Jimmy because he comes from the worst environment in the world, the city slums. Cagney, surprised by Thompson's prejudice, sneers, "That's where I come from. There's nothing a matter with me, is there?" Thompson, dumbfounded, struggles to find apologetic words, but Cagney dismisses him: "Aw nuts." His shrugged shoulders, tucked-in chin, and barbarous words align Cagney/Patsy in background (lower-East-side slums) and disrespectful attitude ("Aw, nuts") with the kids.

Chodorov's script further identifies Cagney with immigrant spectators by foregrounding his doubleness. Cagney's Patsy is simultaneously established law (one of the leaders of a new experiment, The Juvenile Republic) and hoodlum outsider (a ward heeler who forces voters into line for a city machine). His confusing persona (social reformer and shady racketeer) allegorically mirrors the confusion immigrant youths felt between their old world parents and a new world America. Moreover, his outlaw status may have been appealing because Cagney's criminality represented something outside of a supposed norm, a sort of periphery status that echoed the peripheries that many immigrants, with their different cultural customs and languages, found themselves living in. Cagney's outlaw status is established early, when he first swaggers into Thompson and Walters' office. He appears uncommitted and irresponsible: "Now listen. I want to get everything straightened out before tomorrow morning. I want to get out of here. What do I have to do to make things look regular?" He sits, drinks from his flask, and is only concerned in collecting favors from the city machine. He even asks Thompson and Walters to oversee operations: "Well, say, about these reports I'm supposed to turn in? I don't know anything about that. You could make them out for me, couldn't ya? How about it?"

For Patsy to become part of the norm, he will, like the immigrant spectator, have to change his outsider, nonconformist ways. And easygoing self-interest does give way once he falls for the WASPish heroine, nurse Dorothy. Reformed through love, he commits to the collective and Dorothy's vision for the boys' future, a Juvenile Republic in which the youth largely govern themselves. Deciding to play by the rules, Cagney/Patsy then encourages the kids to follow his example. "Why don't you smarten up? You're in now. Make the best of it," he tells the reluctant Jimmy.

But his commitment to Nurse Griffith and institutional power remains locked within Barron's notion of "structural intermediacy." While operating the school, Patsy maintains his gangland ties. And, as a reformer, he continues to represent an in-between. During the "mayor of hell" scene in which the boys are first introduced to the concepts of the republic and elect officials, the boys defer to Patsy, and Patsy defers to Dorothy. She frequently fills in his ellipses and encourages his discussion of the rules. As they discuss positions for public office, Patsy leans in her direction for guidance. His reliance on her knowledge shows that he doesn't fully understand the workings of a city, and she does. He needs her as the foundation for the society's principles, and she needs him as the man of action enacting those principles. For example, during elections, Butch Kilgore (Mickey Bennett), unhappy about Smith's nomination for mayor, rolls up his sleeves and threatens to fight. Dorothy, wanting to foster communal spirit, nominates Kilgore as chief of police and asks Jimmy to second. Smith, still smarting from Kilgore's threats, hesitates, and Patsy pushes Smith, "C'mon fella, be regular." The push works, as Smith raises a deferential hand, and Kilgore congenially acknowledges Smith. Patsy smiles at Dorothy, leans over, and whispers, "That was close."

The above sequence establishes a troubling, essentializing hierarchy of Protestant institutions (the Juvenile Republic as the brainchild of Miss Griffith) mediated by an Irishman (Cagney) for the education of an immigrant mass (the reform school boys). Moreover, in telling Smith to be "regular," Patsy espouses a thinly disguised Americanizing movement. Interestingly, earlier in Thompson's office, Patsy had wanted others to do the work for him, to make things "look regular." Now, he is no longer shirking his duty.

He has reformed, mediating Dorothy's dreams. Patsy no longer wants things to merely "look regular," but, in fact, he wants the boys to "be regular."

Ultimately, the narrative codes in *Mayor of Hell* suggest that, contrary to the fears of Forman and Anglo-conformers over emotional possession, immigrant youth need characters like Patsy Gargan and film stars like James Cagney. And, as a final punctuation, the film concludes with Patsy/Cagney saving the boys from destroying themselves. Following a riot, in which the boys indirectly kill the tyrannical Thompson and set the school ablaze, Patsy, who had left to attend to a gangland problem in the city, returns at Dorothy's urging. He tells the boys that he had disappeared because he had shot "a rat," confesses that it may mean the "chair" if he's caught, and demands that they put out the fire. He shows that he is willing to sacrifice himself for them. In turn, he asks that they surrender their rebellious spirit and accept the system. He stresses a call to action for the boys in the film and immigrant youth in the audience. The riot is quelled, and, in Mayor's fantasy ending, both Patsy and the boys beat their "raps." The ending affirms an egalitarian utopia as Patsy and Dorothy, under the approving eye of Judge Gilbert (Arthur Byron), stay on at the school, furthering their experiment in self-actualizing education.

Angels with Dirty Faces (1938): "Don't Encourage Them to Admire You"

In 1938, following two years of independent work at Grand National, James Cagney returned to Warner Bros. In his second film after the hiatus, the studio realigned his screen image to his gangster past with the socially responsible, budgetarily upscale *Angels with Dirty Faces. Angels,* a much more romanticized portrait of the gangster than *Mayor of Hell,* continues to present a sociological argument that environment shapes the juvenile delinquent. The film's opening shots boom around a tenement slum to reveal a cityscape, as women beat rugs, people crowd streets, and vendors trade wares. A second long take booms up to a balcony where young Rocky and Jerry, products of this environment, nonchalantly smoke and spit. Several sequences later, Rocky, now a parolee, returns home, and another boom traverses the same area, the same beaten rugs, the same dilapidated fruit carts, and crowded streets to imply a fixed, stratified society.

To climb out of that fixed position, *Mayor of Hell* suggested that, in the absence of strong responsible fathers, immigrant youth could be led to self-autonomy and legitimacy through the actions of a reformed city boy, aided and abetted by a woman of institutional knowledge. In *Angels,* the message is paradoxically similar. The boys, whose parents are never seen, will be led to reform by the actions of two surrogate fathers, a gangster and a priest, but the boys' assimilation into the mainstream will be brought about through a deliberate misunderstanding. Whereas Patsy directly asked the kids to follow his lead, in *Angels,* Rocky play-acts the coward in order to encourage the Dead End Kids not to follow him. Moreover, *Mayor of Hell* primarily articulated elements of Irish-American ethnicity within one character—Cagney as the insider/outsider figure and ethnic in-between—to connect with second-generation immigrants. Five years later, *Angels* splits Cagney's simultaneity (the hoodlum reformer) into two separate characters, gangster Rocky Sullivan (Cagney as the bad boy with a gentle streak) and Father Jerry Connelly (Pat O'Brien as a powerful reformer and man of principle). This bifurcation away from Cagney as the central nexus of meaning incorporates the Catholic Church into the battle against juvenile delinquency and suggests that Catholicism is no longer on the margins but in the center of institutional control as a socializing agency of normative behavior

This shift in Irish signification neatly counteracts Forman's fears of emotional possession by providing the male spectator with a viable alternative to the hoodlum. Father Jerry Connelly represents, in Robert Ray's terms, an official hero to Rocky's outlaw hero. Ray sees within popular narratives an American myth circulating around these two types. The outlaw hero, Ray argues, is self-reliant, free from entanglements (59), and represents the norm of our romantic male traditions, from Huck Finn to Frederick Jackson Turner's frontier thesis (56). The official hero (teacher, lawyer, family man) represents America's belief in collective action (59). Whereas Jerry rode a bus and felt the call to join the priesthood, Rocky's bus ride got him six years. Perhaps Warner Bros. gave us the priest as heroic figure, because pressured by the Legion of Decency and the Roman Catholic Church, they felt the need to present piety as power (Keyser and Keyser, 62). Or perhaps, as Nick Roddick has shown, in the post-1935 period, an era when Warner Bros. was making its first profits since 1930, the studio could no longer use the Depression as an explanation for a wayward hero (121). A change in the economic and cultural climate demanded a foil for the outlaw.

No doubt, in scripting the Church as combating juvenile delinquency, Warner Bros. did appease reformist rhetoric from both Catholics and Protestants, but the representation of O'Brien in this film is very positive and not mere window dressing. O'Brien's Father Jerry "agitates for sweeping reforms, not just cosmetic touches" (Keyser and Keyser, 67). He wants to build a recreation center, a home for wayward boys to learn American values, such as self-sacrifice and teamwork, through playing basketball. To make the center safe inside and outside, he seeks to destroy the corrupt political machine that gangsters Mac Keefer (George Bancroft), Frazier (Humphrey Bogart), and his boyhood friend Sullivan dominate; however, he cannot protect his boys and dismantle the criminal machine without the help of his childhood pal. It is in helping the boys that *Angels with Dirty Faces* fully addresses Cagney's screen image. The film's central opposition revolves around the battle of two father figures, Connelly and Sullivan, and emotional possession. Who will ultimately influence the boys?

Cagney seems to have the upper hand. In the presence of the Dead End Kids (a swarthy-looking but watered-down version of *Mayor's* polyglot), Cagney explodes with dynamic energy. He is an ego-ideal that rearticulates Blumer and Hauser's concept of emotional possession. Early in the film, the Dead End Kids rob Rocky in the street without knowing who he is. Rocky, noting his missing wallet, grins knowingly, and follows the kids to their boiler-room hideout. There, Cagney parodies his Public Enemy persona. He places a hand in his pocket and slowly says, "Stick em up." His pursed lips, cocked hat, and clipped bark, "Collect that dough and fast," illustrate his domination. After he kicks Soapy (Billy Halop) in the rear end, the scene lightens. Rocky reveals that his gun was only a stick of gum and then waves them over to a wall to show them his initials. They discover that Rocky's old hangout is now theirs. The suggested parallel between the boys and Rocky resonates the ongoing problem of juvenile delinquency and social stratification. And, moreover, when the kids are impressed with their link to the notorious gangster, Cagney affectionately winks and offers them two lessons: "Next time you roll a guy for his poke, make sure he don't know your hideout," and "Never bother anybody in your own neighborhood." The kids in the filmic world and inside the movie theater are attracted to Cagney's charm. The boyish wink makes him one of their pals, an equal, and his fatherly advice constructs him as their knowledgeable leader.

Cagney's in-between status (boyish friend and man of streetsmart wisdom) is fully articulated in the basketball sequence. Rocky, at the behest of Father Jerry, has encouraged the boys to play a basketball game at the gym. The boys cheat, tackle opponents, shove, and flagrantly travel with the ball. Jerry appears frustrated, unable to control them. He calls "Foul" to no avail. Numbed, Jerry says, "Now you boys know better than that. You've been committing technical fouls and personal fouls. Now stop it." As the fouls mount, Rocky grabs a loose ball, gives Laury (Ann Sheridan) his hat and tells her, "Here, now watch this." As referee, Rocky becomes one of the kids, but bigger; he cheats as they cheat. He trips them with a knee, slaps them around, stomps on their feet, and lets fly a few elbows. And, with a finger in their faces, he sends a clear message of assimilation, "Now you play by the rules," he raises an arm, "or I'll slap some sense into ya." The boys get his point and are briefly assimilated into the communal values of sport, coerced into playing by the rules. Thus, Rocky uses streetsmart tactics, but he works for the establishment, represented by the priest.

Because Rocky "assimilates" the boys through coercion, his effectiveness as an Americanizing agent is minimized. Whereas Patsy Gargan in *The Mayor of Hell* took on a positive adult role, representing the Irish-American as intermediate ideal who teaches reform school boys communal values and the belief in the American Republic, Rocky represents brute force, the desire not to educate but intimidate. He is the dark side of the hoodlum/cop, Irish dialectical myth. As a role model to the boys, he embodies what Henry James Forman most feared in the screen gangster: false Americanization. Initially, Cagney's Sullivan seems to send a message that says the quickest way to making it in America is the crooked way.

The priest, as official hero, needs to supplant Rocky as the boys' father figure. He loves Rocky and desires for him to "square himself with God," but, nonetheless, a quiet tension builds between them across several scenes. Rocky may have ruled on the basketball court, but, later in his apartment, we see the ill effects of his guidance. Rocky, after Soapy helped him hide $100,000 from the police, gave each of the boys $50.00 to spend any way they liked. While the boys are gone, the priest visits Rocky to find out "What it's all about"—the rumors of his tie-in with gangsters Frazier and

Keefer. Rocky diverts the conversation, avoiding direct answers, and Father Jerry quietly acquiesces. "You know, with them, it's kind of a hero worship," he says, sending subtle signals about the battle between them. Cagney grins mischievously and says, "Well you can't blame them for that, can ya?"

The audience can't blame the kids because we, too, admire Cagney's charm. He is fast-talking and daring in his dealings with Frazier and Keefer, always holding an upper hand, but following Cagney's puckish grin to the priest, the narrative undercuts Rocky, blaming him for the boys' sordid behavior. Rocky's girlfriend, Laury, enters the rusty tenement and tells Father Jerry that the boys are throwing bills around and giving "beer to all the kids in the neighborhood." The former Public Enemy is now a public threat to children.

The priest attempts to correct Rocky's influence by visiting the boys at the pool hall, but he fails. He asks them to play that return basketball game at the church, but they, with some trepidation, refuse. He then asks sternly, "What makes you think that hanging around pool rooms, spending this kind of money with a lot of hoodlums will get you any place but jail?" Their response, rearticulated in Rocky-like antiestablishment terms, "Aw, Father, there ain't no future in playing basketball," denies Jerry's legitimacy. Although he seeks to keep the Dead End Kids out of jail, he is losing the battle of two fathers, a battle of emotional possession. The boys take Rocky's way, what the priest disconsolately refers to as "quickest way with a racket or a gun." As Father Jerry leaves the pool hall, O'Brien elides his image with Cagney's by slugging a bystander who made a crack about the kids not ascending to heaven.

The slugging gesture doubles the priest with Rocky and suggests a common toughness that blurs distinctions between them. It also clearly establishes Father Jerry as a fighter for the kids. He takes his fight to the newspapers and radio, and, although he fails to get the boys out of the pool hall, he attempts to win the bigger battle by raising indicting questions about Keefer, Frazier, and Sullivan. His campaign is a top-down attack on corrupt city bosses, police officials, and lawyers who wield power over the city. When he confronts Rocky at his nightclub, he aggressively returns the $10,000 donation and directly promises to go after him and all the criminals who the boys "look up to and revere and respect and admire and imitate." His hard-hitting approach intersects with the call of the Catholic action committees and the Legion of Decency's pledge to undercut false role models and break their hold over immigrant youth. Aware of Rocky's position with the boys, he warns, "Don't encourage them to admire you." Cagney, in medium close-up, mischievously grins, "All right, I'll do that." Given the previous pool hall scene and the problem of underage drinking, Cagney's grin appears insincere. The priest responds accordingly: "Sure you will."

Ultimately, however, O'Brien's role is somewhat minimized in the narrative's final effect. He can't reach the boys on his terms. He needs the intervention of the reluctant hero, as Ray puts it, to step in on the official hero's behalf (66). It is Rocky who saves Jerry from Keefer and Frazier's guns; it is Rocky who, in the courtroom, names names, ridding the city of corrupt officials; and it is Rocky who, in his "killer turned coward" performance, gets the boys to transfer their admiration from him to the priest.

In his autobiography, Cagney claimed that, over the years, little kids would see him on the street and ask about his death-row walk in *Angels,* "'Didya do it for the Father, huh?'" Cagney always argued that he had played the death-row scene with deliberate ambiguity to let the spectator make his own choice on whether Rocky gave in to the priest's final request or truly died afraid (76). But, as the anecdote attests, Cagney's popularity with his fans probably wouldn't allow the scene to be read ambiguously at all.

The film's finale wonderfully moves from story text (Rocky and the Dead End Kids) to immigrant context (Cagney and immigrant spectators). When Rocky tells Jerry that the boys will be "a lot easier to handle with me out of the way, won't they?" he speaks in a double-voice, text-to-context, aware of the role Sullivan has played in their lives and self-reflexively aware of the role Cagney has played with immigrant audiences. And, during the visit, ambiguity is finely layered into the performance, as Cagney says with false bravado that he's not afraid to die, because, to be afraid, you have to have a heart, and "mine got cut out a long time ago." The comment is unconvincing. Rocky showed heart by protecting the priest and killing Keefer and Frazier, who had ordered Father Jerry's assassination. Rocky has also shown fear.

Just prior to Jerry's arrival, he had attempted to disguise that fear. As he sits on the edge of a cot, he nervously taps his cigarette. After a prison guard (Edward Pawley) taunts him, "Did you enjoy your dinner, Mr. Sullivan?" Rocky reclines on the cot and violently shifts the signification of the cigarette prop from distilled fear to dominant aggression. He barks back with a grimaced face, "Yeah, it was pretty good, only the meat was kinda burnt, and I don't like burnt meat. Do you?" He snaps the cigarette at the guard's face. The tension within the not-so-tough tough continues as the guard sadistically comments, "Listen, big shot, you've got only ten minutes to go, so don't try stalling with that priest pal of yours." Cagney lurches forward and spits at him. "Ten minutes to that hot seat. I'm gonna tell the electrician to give it to you slow and easy, wise guy." Cagney, constrained by the prison bars, punches at the guard and screams, "Somebody get this screw outta here, willya?" Later, he will slug the guard on the way to the chair, but the aggressiveness of Cagney's actions belie the fear motivating them.

Opposed to these subtle signs of fear are textual cues in Cagney's death-row walk that strongly acknowledge a performance-within-a-performance about to take place. As he is led to the chair, the mise-en-scene, a series of spotlights, throw circles of light on the floor, grimly telling us, James Naremore has shown, to expect a Cagney star turn, a dramatic exit (171). Moreover, the last visible image of Rocky is an extreme close-up of his face, a shock of hair dangling over his brow, lips tightly pursed. The look echoes the aggressive image of a rain-lit Cagney, idling past the camera in *Public Enemy*, hands in pockets, as he readies to gun down Matt Doyle's killers. Rocky may die screaming offscreen, his stubby hands clutching the radiator as a life support system, but the final onscreen image reinscribes the tough.

Despite these textual contradictions, it is probable that, contextually, 1930s immigrant youth viewed Cagney's breakdown as an unambiguous performance. Self-sacrifice was a character trait that Cagney's audience was predisposed to look for. William Lewin's interviews with 1930s high-school students revealed that, for them, the most admirable character trait for a screen star was self-sacrifice, listed by 77.3 percent of those interviewed (19). As a social value, self-sacrifice was held in high regard by American culture; it is a theme in many of Cagney's films, and it was a theme permeating the civics texts of the day. Moreover, if Rocky's breakdown isn't read as self-sacrifice, then those fans asking Cagney through the years if he did it for the Father must painfully realize the breakdown of Cagney's persona, and that just might be too hard to confront, given our existing presuppositions about masculinity.

For those viewing the death-row walk as a performance, the film's final effect is doubled. Rocky's "cowardice" undercuts him in the eyes of the Dead End Kids and transfers their allegiances to the tough priest. But, for the immigrant boys sitting in the theater, Rocky becomes a Christ figure, taking on their sins. The ending paradoxically questions Cagney's screen image, self-reflexively critiquing its influence through the years on immigrant youth, but ultimately affirms it. In *Mayor of Hell's* utopian fantasy and call to collective action, outsider Cagney beats the rap and assimilates into the Protestant norm through marriage and a socially responsible job. By contrast, in the ending to *Angels,* Cagney can't beat the rap and pays the ultimate price to society for his lawlessness. His alter ego, Father Jerry Connelly, remains on the inside, assimilating the boys to communal good. But outsider Rocky Sullivan's self-sacrifice legitimizes James Cagney's persona and justifies his 1930s films as being, indeed, moral.

Endnote

1   For more on the cultural intersections of Warner Bros.' publicity campaigns, James Cagney's persona, and the controversy surrounding the Payne Fund study and its analysis of immigrant desires, see Grant Tracey's "'Let's Go Places With Jimmy': James Cagney as 1930s Immigrant Icon" in The Journal of Film and Video Vol. 50, No. 4 (Winter 1998–99), 3–17.

Bibliography

Angels with Dirty Faces. Dir. Michael Curtiz. Perf.: James Cagney, Pat O'Brien, and Billy Halop. Warner Bros., 1938.

Barron, Milton L. "Intermediacy: Conceptualization of Irish Status in America." *Social Forces* 27 (March 1949): 256–63.

Blumer, Herbert and Philip M. Hauser. *Movies, Delinquency and Crime.* New York: Arno Press, 1933, 1970.

Cagney, James. *Cagney by Cagney.* New York: Doubleday, 1976.

Cressey, Paul G. "The Motion Picture as Informal Education." *The Journal of Educational Sociology* 7.8 (April 1934): 504–15.

Forman, Henry James. *Our Movie Made Children.* New York: MacMillan Co., 1933.

Gordon, Milton. *Assimilation in American Life.* New York: Oxford University Press, 1964.

Jowett, Garth S., Ian C. Jarvie and Kathryn H. Fuller. *Children and the Movies: Media Influence and the Payne Fund Controversy.* New York: Cambridge University Press, 1996.

Keyser, Les and Barbara. "Crime Movie: Immigration, Gangsters and Guns." *Hollywood and the Catholic Church: The Image of Roman Catholicism in American Movies.* Chicago: Loyola University Press, 1984. 41–76.

Lewin, William. *Photoplay Appreciation in American High Schools.* New York: D. Appleton-Century Co., 1934.

Mayor of Hell. Dir. Archie Mayo. Perf.: James Cagney, Madge Evans, Frankie Darro, and Dudley Digges. Warner Bros., 1933.

Munsterberg, Hugo. *The Film.* New York: Dover Publications Inc., 1916, 1970.

Naremore, James. "James Cagney in *Angels with Dirty Faces* (1938)." *Acting for the Cinema.* Berkeley: University of California Press, 1988. 157–73.

Public Enemy. Dir. William Wellman. Perf.: James Cagney. Warner Bros., 1931.

Ray, Robert B. *A Certain Tendency of the Hollywood Cinema, 1930–80.* Princeton, N.J.: Princeton University Press, 1985.

Riesman, David. *The Lonely Crowd: A Study of the Changing American Character.* New Haven: Yale University Press, 1950.

Roddick, Nick. *A New Deal in Entertainment: Warner Brothers in the 1930s.* London: British Film Institute, 1983.

Sklar, Robert. *City Boys: Cagney, Bogart, Garfield.* Princeton, N.J.: Princeton University Press, 1992.

Taxi. Dir. Roy Del Ruth. Perf.: James Cagney and Loretta Young. Warner Bros., 1932.

U.S. Department of Commerce. *Fifteenth Census,* 1930. Washington, D.C.: Government Printing Office, 1933.

Chapter 2
A Profile of Adolescent Delinquents:
Dead End as Play and Film

Gene D. Phillips, S.J.,
Loyola University Chicago

I

Sidney Kingsley's social protest drama, *Dead End,* opened at the Belasco Theater on Broadway in October 1935 to rave reviews. At the end of each performance, the cast received an enthusiastic ovation, and the play had a successful run of sixty-five weeks. In March 1936, film director William Wyler saw the play in the company of independent producer Samuel Goldwyn. Immediately afterwards, Wyler told Goldwyn that he thought *Dead End* would make a great movie, and Goldwyn responded by engaging Wyler on the spot to direct the film version of the drama.

Wyler, after all, had recently directed a fine film for Goldwyn which was derived from another Broadway play: *These Three,* adapted from Lillian Hellman's *Children's Hour.* "I suppose I have adapted more plays to the screen than novels," Wyler said some years later. "The reason is that I used to go to New York every year and see the new plays; and, when I saw one I liked, I got the urge to film it," as was the case with *Dead End.* "After all, it is a simpler process to film an established play than to start from scratch with an untried idea and develop it into a script."[1]

Wyler's interest in filming a play like *Dead End,* dealing as it does with juvenile delinquents, was fueled by his earlier involvement with two other projects which focused on troubled teenagers. In 1932 he had made *Tom Brown of Culver* about a moody, rebellious youth named Tom Brown, a cadet at Culver Military Academy. The film deals with Tom's problems in adapting to the discipline and regimentation of the academy's training program. Universal Pictures obtained the academy's permission to film on campus by promising that the movie would show how young Tom matured by coping with the challenges he faced both on the playing fields of the school and in interacting with the other cadets in the normal course of dormitory life.

Because the fictional Tom's father was awarded the Congressional Medal of Honor for bravery in World War I, the American Legion puts the boy through Culver. Since Tom's father is presumed dead, the posthumous medal is presented to Tom by an army officer prior to Tom's entering Culver. "Try and buy grub with it," Tom sneers. His sarcastic remark clearly identifies him as an underprivileged lad who, until now, has lived a destitute existence in Depression America.

When Tom arrives at Culver, he observes a group of cadets drilling to an officer's commands. Wyler thus implies that Tom will have to learn to accept the regimentation and discipline of military school, which is reflected in the cadets who are being drilled into uniformity on the parade ground.

Tom has a chip on his shoulder when he arrives at Culver and soon goads his roommate into a fistfight. But, eventually, the camaraderie Tom develops with Bob and some of the other cadets leads him to shape up. In essence, the film portrays Tom's conversion from a rebellious delinquent to a first-class cadet.

In light of the film's success, Wyler decided to make another movie about boys; but, this time, it was about a group of adolescents a couple of steps down the social ladder from the cadets at Culver. He collaborated on a screenplay with screenwriter (later director) John Huston about the many teenaged boys who were victims of the Depression. A number of them had run away from home because their parents could not support them; they were outcasts, riding the rails in boxcars.

Huston later recalled that, in order to research the film, he and Wyler took to the roads themselves, "like hobos." In cities like Fresno they discovered homeless boys living on Skid Row, scrounging for food just to stay alive. Moreover, Wyler had a studio researcher sift through the files of the *Los Angeles Examiner* for news stories about youngsters arrested for committing crimes. He even arranged for Huston and himself to attend night sessions in the juvenile court.[2] But the screenplay, which was entitled *The*

Forgotten Boys, went unproduced. Wyler was, accordingly, delighted to be able to make *Dead End,* a socially relevant film about the plight of troubled boys like Tom Brown and the youngsters in *The Forgotten Boys.*

II

I shall first consider Kingsley's play as a work of drama in its own right; for it is only in appreciating the play itself, as the playwright originally conceived it, that we can properly grasp the relative merits of the film derived from it.

One of the things that impressed Wyler about the Broadway production of *Dead End* was the elaborate set which designer Norman Bel Geddes had constructed on the stage of the Belasco Theater: "A narrow tenement street dead-ended at the East River and ran smack up against a swanky new high-rise," writes Jan Herman. "Filthy mattresses hung on ghetto fire escapes; clotheslines sagged with torn garments." The grim atmosphere "burned under a harsh, white sky" in the daytime, "and sulked with gaslight in the evening."[3] Gregory Black adds, "A sturdy masonry wall, guarded by a row of spikes on top, separates the wealthy residents of the East River Terrace apartment building from the squalid tenement buildings that line the other side of the street." Black concluded, "Into this environment are thrust the characters whose lives will be, or have been, determined by which side of the wall they live on."[4]

One of the characters who lives on the side of the wall that is in the slums is Gimpty; he contracted rickets while growing up in the disease-ridden slums and is crippled for life. Gimpty belonged to a street gang as a youngster but still managed to finish both high school and college. Although Gimpty earned a degree in architecture, the Depression has left him working at menial jobs, for which he is decidedly overqualified. Nevertheless, he dreams of tearing down the tenements and building public housing in their place. Surveying the wretched environment in which he is forced to live, Gimpty bitterly reflects at one point, "The place you live in is awfully important. When I was in school, they used to teach us that evolution made men out of animals. They forgot to tell us it can also make animals out of men."[5]

But the play's real center is the youth gang headed by Tommy. He and the foul-mouthed hoodlums in his gang fritter away their time by playing truant from school, swimming in the scummy East River, playing cards, committing petty thefts, and brawling with rival gangs. While the boys appear essentially harmless at this stage, Black observes, "it is clear that these lads have little education and no skills, and are destined to live in the slums; only a miracle will save them from a life of crime."[6]

By the same token, the high-class apartment building, which borders their slum area, symbolizes the world of affluence from which they are excluded. In short, they are in training to become criminals. Tommy's parents are dead, so he is being raised by his older sister Drina, who has little control over the defiant boy. At present, Drina is participating in a strike for higher wages at her place of employment, where she and her fellow strikers have been brutally beaten by the police. "The real villain of the play is the environment," Black points out, "but its personification is Baby Face Martin," a notorious racketeer and murderer wanted by the police, who pays a visit to the slum that spawned him to see his mother and his former girlfriend, Francie.[7] Gimpty remembers Martin from their boyhood days; and he eventually turns Martin in for the reward money, whereupon Martin is killed in a gun battle while trying to escape capture.

One episode in particular illuminates the hopelessness of life in the slums for youngsters like Tommy. When Mr. Griswald, the father of a rich boy who lives in the nearby luxury apartment building, confronts Tommy for roughing up his son, Tommy pulls a penknife on him, grazes his hand with it, and gets away from him. After Tommy is captured by the police, Gimpty begs Griswald to forgive the boy and give him a chance to go straight.

In pleading for Tommy, Gimpty points out that Martin was a notorious killer and deserved to die. Nevertheless, Gimpty says that he remembers Martin as a youngster who was brave and honest—until he joined a street gang and got into trouble. Martin was sent to reform school, where the brutal treatment he endured made him tough and mean. Consequently, Gimpty continues, by the time Martin got out of the reformatory, he was well on his way to becoming a hardened criminal. Gimpty concludes that he does not want a similar fate to overtake Tommy.

But Griswald remains adamant about pressing charges against the lad; and the drama ends with the police taking Tommy into custody, just as Gimpty promises Drina that he will use the reward money to get Tommy a competent defense lawyer. Black observes that the audience is left to draw its own conclusion as to Tommy's subsequent fate. Perhaps Tommy's lawyer will get him off, and he will move in with Gimpty and Drina when they are married; or "the system could crush another life, sentencing Tommy to reform school, so that he could become the next Baby Face Martin."[8] On this uncertain note, the curtain falls.

III

Goldwyn was enthusiastic about producing Wyler's film version of Kingsley's drama, not only because it was a hit play, but because, during the Depression, films with significant social themes were proving quite popular with the mass audience. Besides Wyler's own *Tom Brown of Culver,* there was William Wellman's *Wild Boys of the Road* (1933), with a plot similar to Wyler's unrealized film, *Forgotten Boys.* Frank Thompson notes that "the wild boys" of the title are ordinary youngsters who see their dreams of success "stripped away by the worsening economic conditions, until they are forced to live on the run, stealing or begging to provide themselves with food and shelter."[9] Like *Wild Boys of the Road, Dead End* dealt with the effect of the Depression on people's lives, and, hence, Wyler's film seemed to fit the temper of the times. Moreover, in both *Wild Boys* and *Dead End,* the young delinquents are "disturbed by their status as poor slum dwellers," Ralph Bauer comments.[10] Indeed, the chief concern of both movies is that the rebellious boys will grow up to be gangsters.

Movies with thought-provoking social themes had been thriving at the box office since the beginning of the Depression. For example, in gangster films like *Little Caesar* (1930), *Public Enemy* (1931), and *Scarface* (1932), notorious racketeers are shown to be the product of "the corruption and impersonality of the modern city," as Bauer notes.[11] In Wellman's *Public Enemy,* we watch Tom Powers (James Cagney) start out as a tough boy in the neighborhood and graduate from petty thievery to big-time racketeering and murder as he gets older.

According to Bauer, these gangster pictures give us a vision of the underside of American life, as represented by tawdry poolrooms, stale cigarette smoke, naked light bulbs, and dark alleys. It is the grim world that produced criminals like Tom Powers. Similarly, social criticism of this sort is strong in both Kingsley's *Dead End* and the Wyler film adapted from it, as Cormack indicates: "Poor housing is seen as the cause of crime. Reform schools are seen as schools of crime." [12]

Film historian Jerry Vermilye states that films of social conscience, such as those I have just mentioned, were box office successes because they "mixed critical commentary with entertainment. . . . The fact that these stories were basically melodramas helped attract moviegoers. And sometimes they raised enough public consciousness to effect reform"—as, we shall shortly see, *Dead End* certainly did.[13] In summary, Wyler's film is very much a part of the cycle of Depression-era films that were imbued with serious social themes.

Goldwyn entrusted the screenplay for *Dead End* to Hellman, who had written the script for the film version of her own play, *The Children's Hour*, retitled *These Three*. The producer instructed her to fashion a screenplay that would pass muster with the industry's film censor, Joseph Breen. The censor had already advised Goldwyn that the film should be less emphatic than the play "in showing the contrast between conditions of the poor in tenements and those of the rich in apartment houses," and on some other points as well.[14] Hellman recalled later that Goldwyn, accordingly, told her to "clean up the play"; but what he really meant was "to cut off its balls."[15]

Hellman set out, in consultation with Wyler, to bring her script in line with the industry's censorship code (while still retaining as much of the play's unvarnished realism as possible), so that the censor would grant the film the industry's official seal of approval. Hellman purged the obscenities from the vulgar street language of Tommy and his gang; she also deleted explicit mention in the dialogue of the fact that Baby Face Martin's ex-girl-friend, who has since become a prostitute, has syphilis—though it is still suggested in the dialogue. In addition, Hellman transformed Gimpty, the embittered cripple of the play, into Dave Connell (Joel McCrea), a conventional Hollywood leading man, no longer a cripple. He provides love interest for Drina, Tommy's sister (Sylvia Sidney). There was no such love relationship between them in the play.

Withal, Black rightly remarks, "The startling point of the film is not how much of the play was removed from the film, but how much of the social commentary survived both Samuel Goldwyn and Joseph Breen." For example, although there is no direct reference to venereal disease in the film, Black affirms that "only the very young and the extremely naive would fail to understand what Francie suffered from."[16] Furthermore, Drina is pre-

sented as a social activist in the film, as she was in the play: someone who
is committed to fighting for a better life for herself and her younger
brother. In fact, she is committed to social action to the point of striking
for better wages—and standing up to police brutality in the bargain. In
sum, her role as a socially committed heroine, Mike Cormack writes, "is
without equal in Thirties Hollywood."[17]

By the same token, the film follows the play in boldly dramatizing the
social inequities existing between the occupants of the elegant high rise on
one side of the street and the occupants of the tawdry tenement on the
other side of the street. Furthermore, Dave could be called the social conscience of the film, to the extent that he does what he can to encourage
Tommy and his buddies to rise above their slum environment and become
law-abiding citizens. Hence, Andrew Bergman endorses the screen version
of *Dead End* in these terms: "There had been nothing like *Dead End*'s high
voltage class tension in any Depression film."[18]

Since Wyler's film version of *Dead End* has sometimes been criticized
for diluting the social implications of its literary source, I have been at pains
to summon the testimony of film scholars who recognize how Wyler's
movie radiates social consciousness to an exceptional degree. As for Hellman, she was personally impressed with the fine film that Wyler, one of the
more liberal-minded Hollywood directors of his time, fashioned from her
screenplay.

IV

Wyler wanted to film Kingsley's social drama in the New York slums where
it takes place. "I asked Sam Goldwyn if I could make the film on location
in New York, because the background was so integral to the plot," Wyler
recalled, "but he said, 'I'll build you a pier on the East River and some tenements right here on a Hollywood sound stage.'" Goldwyn, it seems, was
against extensive location shooting in principle, since it meant that he
would have less control over a director while he was filming away from the
studio. "Everyone marveled at the huge waterfront set, which was constructed as the principal setting for the film," Wyler continued, "but to me
it looked very phony and artificial. I heard later that *Dead End* was instru-
mental in getting new legislation to clean up the slums in New York City,
because these kids needed better surroundings to grow up in. That was a
pleasant surprise to me, because the slums depicted in the film never looked

like the real thing to me." Few critics agreed with Wyler that the film's gigantic riverfront set, designed by Richard Day, looked artificial; in fact, several reviewers praised the authentic look of the set.

"My approach to filming a play was to retain the basic construction of the original—while at the same time lending the story the illusion of more movement than took place on the stage," Wyler explained. For example, *Dead End* originally took place in one central waterfront setting. Wyler extended the action in the film by principally staging it throughout the slum tenement, from the basement to the roof. "The constant movement back and forth among these various playing areas kept the film from becoming static, while retaining at the same time the tight construction of the play," he concluded.

Dead End, like most of the films Wyler made under Goldwyn's aegis, was photographed by Gregg Toland (*Citizen Kane*), one of the foremost cinematographers of his time. Wyler and Toland would always discuss in detail each scene in a film, in order to determine how it could best be photographed, before going on the studio floor to shoot it. "When photographing a scene, Toland wanted to catch the mood," Wyler explained. "He and I would discuss a picture from beginning to end. The style of photography would vary" from one film to the next, he said. Thus, in *Dead End*, they often employed flat, harsh lighting: "We didn't try to make anybody look pretty." Furthermore, the action of the story takes place within the span of a single day. Hence, the early scenes in the movie, which take place in daytime, are photographed with bright lighting, while the later scenes, which take place in the evening, are photographed in a shadowy style. As Mike Cormack says, "As the plot darkens, so does the lighting. The darkest scenes are the narrative's most extreme and dangerous conflicts."[19] Thus the fight to the death between Martin and Dave, which comes late in the film, is particularly dark and shadowy.

Wyler, in consultation with Toland, made expert use of camera movement in *Dead End*. In fact, "the general impression of *Dead End* is of a film with a fairly mobile camera," Cormack comments. "The reason for this impression is that the traveling shots are very noticeable."[20] Since the film was derived from a play, Wyler explained, "I employed several long takes in the film, in order to allow the camera to move around and thus keep the film from looking static and stagey."

The movie contains a number of extended takes, in which Wyler cleverly works his camera around the actors as it unobtrusively glides about the set, so that the pace of the action never falters. Wyler employs the procedure known as "precutting the film inside the camera" by closing in at times for a close shot to emphasize a key gesture or to capture a significant facial expression, and then falling back for a medium shot as the action continues. Because Wyler rarely opted to interrupt these unbroken takes by the insertion of other shots when the footage was finally cut together, he virtually eliminated the need for any editing in these particular scenes. The film's opening shot is an extraordinary example of a long take in which there is a great deal of adroit camera movement, as we shall shortly see.

V

The movie opens with a printed prologue:

> Every street in New York ends in a river. For many years the dirty banks of the East River were lined with the tenements of the poor. Then the rich, discovering that the river traffic was picturesque, moved their houses eastward. And now the terraces of these great apartment houses look down into the windows of the tenements.

The film proper begins with the kind of traveling shot Cormack referred to above. To be specific, the camera starts out with a panoramic shot of the New York skyline, after which it pans down to the waterfront below. Finally, the camera zeroes in on the film's elaborate principal setting; as in the play, it is a slum street which comes to a dead end at the waterfront. A luxury apartment building has been erected where the slum frontage has been cleared, so that the apartment complex adjoins a tawdry tenement on the waterfront. The film's action takes place in and around the high rental apartment building and its neighboring slum dwelling. Edith Lee calls this slum tenement one of the seediest sets in Hollywood history: Day's expression of poverty includes "every crack in the wall, thick coats of dust, peeling paint . . . and stairways that creak."[21]

This tenement is where the members of the local juvenile gang live. As the camera explores the narrow corridors and cramped living quarters within the tenement in the course of the film, the viewer gets a sense of the confinement which the boys who live there must endure. This slum dwelling is what Michael Anderegg terms a "labyrinthine trap."[22] Moreover, the tenement is located on a dead-end street, which symbolizes how the boys have already reached a dead end; i.e., they have no prospects for a promising future. In brief, unless something dramatic happens to change the course of their lives, these boys seem destined either for lives of poverty or lives of crime.

One of the many arguments Wyler had with Goldwyn during the making of this picture concerned the look of the East River set. Goldwyn wanted all of his films to look beautiful; consequently, the sets in his pictures often looked more handsome than the story really called for. For his part, Wyler wanted the slum neighborhood to look as squalid and grubby as possible, in order to heighten the realistic atmosphere of the film. The day before shooting began, however, Goldwyn showed up on the set, took one look at the garbage littering the street, and shouted, "This set is filthy! Clean it up! I won't have it!" Wyler absolutely refused to do so, since he wanted to reproduce the squalid slum area as realistically as possible.[23]

A former inhabitant of the riverfront slum, Baby Face Martin (Humphrey Bogart), comes back for a nostalgic visit to his old stomping grounds. He is now a major figure in the New York underworld. Martin runs into Dave, whom he remembers as one of the young hoodlums he grew up with. He scoffs at Dave for going straight: "I'm glad I'm not like you saps; working and slaving for what?" By contrast, says Martin, he learned that "you have to take what you want" to get ahead in this world.

The members of the youth gang idolize Martin. "He is the future, as far as these youngsters are concerned," writes Graham Greene; furthermore, Martin's early life as a juvenile delinquent growing up in this shabby neighborhood "is there before your eyes in the juvenile gangsters."[24]

Yet, even though Martin is a tough mobster, he is "just sentimental enough to want to return to his past," notes James Neibaur. Martin has come home to see his mother and his old girlfriend; but his meeting with both women proves to be a disaster. He first spies his mother (Marjorie Main) from a distance; and "he calls after her excitedly," says Neibaur, "like a child with a good report card." "Mom!" he shouts as he runs toward her. Her hostile response to his greeting is to slap him across the face as she spits out her words at him: "Don't call me Mom!" She tells him that she despises him and everything he stands for and calls him a "no-good tramp" for good measure. But, as Neibaur comments, her words are "barely audible," coming from "a beaten woman."[25] Then she dejectedly turns her back on him and walks away.

Martin's encounter with Francie, his erstwhile girlfriend (Claire Trevor), is equally painful for him. He happens upon her on the street and invites her to rekindle their old relationship by coming away with him. She replies pathetically, "Look at me good—I'm not what I used to be." Francie steps out of the dark doorway in which she has been standing and into the sunlight. Cormack notes that Wyler lights Francie in a "harsh and unflattering" way at this point.[26] Wyler's remark, cited earlier, that he and his cinematographer "didn't try to make anybody look pretty," in this film, holds true especially for Francie.

The glaring light of day mercilessly exposes Francie as the miserable, diseased prostitute she has become. With deep revulsion, Martin cries out, "Why didn't you starve first?" "Why didn't you?" is Francie's anguished reply. Martin slips her a few bills and turns away from her, thereby recalling how his mother had turned away from him earlier. Martin's sidekick, Hunk (Allen Jenkins), who has accompanied him on his trip back to the old neighborhood, advises Martin, in the wake of his two bitter confrontations with the past, "Never go back; always go forward."

Wyler's skillful handling of Bogart in these two scenes are reason enough to justify the critical opinion that, in *Dead End*, Bogart gives one of the finest performances of his career. For Bogart, under Wyler's deft direction, skillfully suggests to the filmgoer that this gangster's tough exterior hides a sensitivity that still yearns for the love of both his mother and his old flame. Unfortunately, he finds neither of these love objects still waiting for him when he returns home.

Martin's sole satisfaction, while he is back in the old neighborhood, is to bask in the adulation of Tommy's gang of tough kids on the block, who admire him for making good in the rackets uptown. Tommy (Billy Halop), the ring leader of the gang, looks up to Martin more than the others. Thus, Tommy, in particular, takes to heart Martin's advice always to carry a knife, since, as Martin says, "You never know when you will have to use it." Consequently, when Mr. Griswald accuses Tommy of beating up his boy, Tommy stabs Griswald's hand with a knife and makes his getaway. Drina, who constitutes the only family he has, is distraught when she learns that her kid brother is being pursued by the police at Mr. Griswald's behest.

Two scenes in the film at this juncture are noteworthy for Wyler's use of visual imagery. There is, first of all, the scene in which Tommy cowers in a shadowy basement stairway as he hides from the police. As Cormack observes, Wyler shows us "Tommy's face in close-up, crushed" by the shadow of the prison-like bars of the stairway railing.[27] This image implies that Tommy is already imprisoned by his wretched life in the cruel and indifferent world of the slums.

Another scene in which Wyler's use of visual symbolism stands out is that in which Dave Connell, Drina's boyfriend, has a confrontation with Martin in an alley while Hunk is standing by. Dave warns the mobster to stay away from the neighborhood kids because he is a bad influence on them. The pair get into a scuffle; Martin then pulls a gun on Dave and retreats down the alley. Dave, in turn, grabs Hunk's gun and pursues Martin up a fire escape; Dave fires upward at Martin, who falls into the alley below and soon dies. The image of Martin's ignominious fall from the top of the fire escape to the ground below symbolizes that he has been knocked off the pedestal on which Tommy and the other boys had placed him. As the film draws to a close, Dave assures Drina that he will bail Tommy out of jail with the reward money that is his due for bringing down Baby Face Martin, who had a price on his head. He thereby saves Tommy from going to reform school—in contrast to the play, where Tommy's future remains in doubt.

In *Dead End*, the theme which pervades Wyler's films clearly surfaces; i.e., that an individual can become a better person by enduring the sufferings which life inflicts. In the present case, this theme is reflected in Tommy. In the wake of his brush with the law, Tommy turns over a new leaf. In fact, Tommy begins to mature as a person as a direct result of his rejecting the likes of Baby Face Martin, a vicious criminal, as his role model, and choosing instead a decent, honest man like Dave to serve as a model for his future growth. The hardworking Dave will provide a good home for Tommy, once he and Drina are married.

But the film's closing scene implies that the rest of Tommy's gang will not be as lucky. As the boys disappear into a dark alley, Wyler photographs them through a fence, reminding us once again that these delinquent boys are imprisoned together in the harsh, grim world of the slums. They feel they must stick together for survival.

Graham Greene terms *Dead End* "a magnificent picture of the environment that breeds the gangster."[28] That is why Joseph Breen, the industry censor, stressed that the film offered "a strong plea for slum elimination and better housing" as a means of crime prevention.[29] (In fact, the ads for the movie aptly referred to "Dead End, cradle of crime.") An editorial in *The New York Post* echoed Breen's sentiments: "The best thing that could have been done at the last session of Congress would have been to show the film *Dead End*" (August 31, 1937). Breen accordingly issued *Dead End* the film industry's official seal of approval (seal number 3596), which meant that Hellman had successfully fulfilled Goldwyn's mandate to keep her screenplay in harmony with the industry's censorship code. In addition, the movie was popular with both the critics and the mass audience.

VI

For the record, Tommy and his gang of ruffians were referred to in publicity layouts for the film as the Dead End Kids, though they are never called that in the movie itself. The young actors who played the gang members continued to be billed as the Dead End Kids in the major films which they made together after *Dead End* for the next few years, in order to cash in on the huge success of the film. They appeared in several Warner Brothers films, starting with *Angels with Dirty Faces* (1938), with James Cagney as Rocky Sullivan, replacing Bogart as the gangster they idolize.

In *Dead End*, film historians Les and Barbara Keyser observe, "the kids dream wistfully of escape from their ghetto prison 'on the wings of an angel,'" a reference which is no doubt the basis for the otherwise unexplained title of the later movie. Like *Dead End*, *Angels with Dirty Faces* "explores the question of the causes of crime . . . and confronts the whole issue of juvenile delinquency." In this movie, Father Jerry Connelly (Pat O'Brien) fights Rocky Sullivan's influence over these young street toughs, just as Dave Connell (whose last name, significantly, is similar to Father Jerry's) sought to counteract Baby Face Martin's influence over the boys in *Dead End*.

Father Jerry "pillories the inequities of the American system," the Keysers continue. Father Connelly muses: "What earthly good is it for me to teach that honesty is the best policy when all around, these boys see that dishonesty is a better policy, that the hoodlum and gangster is looked up to with the same respect as the successful businessman?" The film's attitude toward juvenile delinquency thus presupposes that "new heroes can save ghetto youth from a life of crime," as the Keysers conclude.[30] Hence, at the climax of *Angels with Dirty Faces*, Frank Miller writes, Sullivan is sentenced to die for murder, and "Father Jerry begs him to turn yellow at the end, so the kids will stop looking up to him."[31] Sullivan obliges by acting cowardly when he is executed, and this scene provides a powerful dramatic highpoint in the film.

The six films the Dead End Kids made for Warners in 1938–39 continued to portray the boys as youthful rebels who view their elders as comprising an impersonal "establishment" which ignores their needs and aspirations. Between 1938 and 1943 some of the original Dead End Kids made a series of low-budget movies at Universal. They were billed as the "Dead End Kids and the Little Tough Guys," since the first film in this series was entitled *Little Tough Guy* (1938). Graham Greene termed this film "very nearly as good as *Dead End*." He added that the film's social theme was the same as *Dead End* as well: The youngsters were again presented as defiant outsiders rejected by a society that does not care to understand or accept them.

In *Little Tough Guy,* the father of Johnny Boylan (Billy Halop) is unjustly sent to prison, and the whole family is forced to move into the slums, where Johnny becomes the leader of a street gang. In the suspenseful climax, says Greene, Boylan and his henchman (Huntz Hall) "are brought finally to bay in a small grocer's shop with guns in their immature hands and an armed police cordon across the road."[32] Later entries in the Dead End Kids-Little Tough Guys series did not pack the punch of this film. At all events, the group went on to make a series of twenty-two routine programmers at Monogram as the East Side Kids (1940–45); later, as the Bowery Boys, they made another forty-eight low-budget pictures at the same studio (1946–58). There were, of course, changes in the cast members who made up the group along the way.

The cast of "aging delinquents" developed "a camaraderie that was to make them enduringly popular," says Leonard Maltin.[33] Be that as it may, one cannot but agree with Anderegg that Billy Halop and the others gave their best performances under Wyler's capable direction in his superior film about adolescent delinquents. Indeed, they "would never recapture the vibrancy and sheer animal spirits they exhibited for Wyler."[34]

Endnotes

1   Unless specifically noted otherwise, any quotations from William Wyler in this essay are from the author's personal interview with him.

2 Jan Herman, *A Talent for Trouble: The Life of Hollywood's Most Acclaimed Director, William Wyler* (New York: Putnam's, 1996), p. 109.

3 *Ibid.*, p. 140.

4 Gregory Black, *"Dead End,"* in *Hollywood Censored: Morality Codes, Catholics, and the Movies* (New York: Cambridge University Press, 1994), pp. 274–75.

5 Sidney Kingsley, *Dead End* (New York: Random House, 1936), p. 50.

6 Black, *"Dead End,"* in *Hollywood Censored*, p. 278.

7 *Ibid.*, p. 276.

8 *Ibid.*

9 Frank Thompson, *William Wellman* (Metuchen, N.J.: Scarecrow Press, 1983), p. 137.

10 Ralph Bauer, "When the Lights Went Out: Hollywood, the Depression, and the Thirties," in *Movies as Artifacts; Cultural Criticism of Popular Film*, ed. Michael Marsden, John Nachbar, and Sam Grogg, Jr. (Chicago: Nelson Hall, 1982), p. 37.

11 *Ibid.*, p. 39. On the social themes in Depression-era films, see also Louis Giannetti, Scott Eyman, *Flashback: A Brief History of Film*, rev. ed. (Englewood Cliffs, N.J.: Prentice-Hall, 1996), pp. 143–45; Gerald Mast, Bruce Kawin, *A Short History of the Movies*, rev. ed. (Boston: Allyn and Bacon, 1996), pp. 244–47.

12 Mike Cormack, *Ideology and Cinematography in Hollywood, 1930–39: Dead End and Other Films* (New York: St. Martin's Press, 1994), p. 12. On the gangster films of the period, see Frank Walsh, *Sin and Censorship: The Catholic Church and the Motion Picture Industry* (New Haven: Yale University Press, 1996), pp. 71–72.

13 Jerry Vermilye, *The Films of the Thirties* (New York: Carol, 1993), p. 87.

14 Carl Rollyson, *Lillian Hellman* (New York: St. Martin's Press, 1988), pp. 102–103.

15 Scott Berg, *Goldwyn: A Biography* (New York: Knopf, 1989), p. 290.

16 Black, *"Dead End,"* in *Hollywood Censored*, p. 278.

17 Cormack, *Ideology and Cinematography in Hollywood*, p. 126.

18 Andrew Bergman, *We're in the Money: Depression America and Its Films* (New York: New York University Press, 1971), p. 155.

19 Cormack, *Ideology and Cinematography in Hollywood*, pp. 131; 134.

20 *Ibid.*, p. 128.

21 Edith Lee, "Richard Day," in *International Dictionary of Films and Filmmakers: Writers and Production Artists*, ed. Grace Jeromski, rev. ed. (Detroit: St. James Press, 1996), vol. 4, 185.

22 Michael Anderegg, *William Wyler* (Boston: Twayne, 1979), p. 63.

23 Herman, *A Talent for Trouble: William Wyler*, p. 169.

24 Graham Greene, *The Graham Greene Film Reader: Reviews, Essays and Interviews*, ed. David Parkinson (New York: Applause Theater Books, 1995), pp. 240–41.

25 James Neibaur, *Tough Guy: The American Movie Macho* (Jefferson, N.C.: McFarland, 1989), pp. 76; 77.

26 Cormack, *Ideology and Cinematography in Hollywood*, p. 132.

27 *Ibid.*, p. 18.

28 Greene, *Film Reader*, p. 427.

29   Black, *"Dead End,"* in *Hollywood Censored,* p. 280.
30   Les and Barbara Keyser, "The Crime Movie," in *Hollywood and the Catholic Church: The Image of Roman Catholicism in American Movies* (Chicago: Loyola University Press, 1984), p. 70; p. 63; p. 65; p. 72.
31   Frank Miller, *Movies: 100 Classics* (Atlanta: Turner, 1996), p. 17.
32   Graham Greene, *Film Reader,* pp. 160–61.
33   Leonard Maltin, ed., *Movie Guide* (New York: New American Library, 1998), p. 156; see also Frank Miller, "Evolution of a Bowery Boy," in *Movies: 100 Classics,* p. 19.
34   Anderegg, *William Wyler,* p. 64.

Bibliography

Anderegg, Michael. *William Wyler.* Boston: Twayne, 1979.

Bauer, Ralph. "When the Lights Went Out: Hollywood, the Depression, and the Thirties," in *Movies as Artifacts: Cultural Criticism of Popular Films.* Edited by Michael Marsden, John Nachbar, and Sam Grogg, Jr. Chicago: Nelson Hall, 1982.

Berg, Scott. *Goldwyn: A Biography.* New York: Knopf, 1989.

Bergman, Andrew. *We're in the Money: Depression America and Its Films.* New York: New York University Press, 1971.

Black, Gregory. *Dead End in Hollywood Censored: Morality Codes, Catholics, and the Movies.* New York: Cambridge University Press, 1994.

Cormack, Mike. *Ideology and Cinematography in Hollywood, 1930–39: "Dead End" and Other Films.* New York: St. Martin's Press, 1994.

Giannetti, Louis, and Scott Eyman. *Flashback: A Brief History of Film,* rev. ed. Englewood Cliffs, N.J.: Prentice-Hall, 1996.

Greene, Graham. *The Graham Greene Film Reader: Reviews, Essays and Interviews.* Edited by David Parkinson. New York: Applause Theater Books, 1995.

Herman, Jan. *A Talent for Trouble: The Life of Hollywood's Most Acclaimed Director, William Wyler.* New York: Putnam's, 1996.

Keyser, Les and Barbara. "The Crime Movie," in *Hollywood and the Catholic Church: The Image of Roman Catholicism in American Movies.* Chicago: Loyola University Press, 1984.

Kingsley, Sidney. *Dead End.* New York: Random House, 1936.

Lee, Edith. "Richard Day," in *International Dictionary of Films and Filmmakers: Writers and Production Artists.* Edited by Grace Jeromski, rev. ed. Detroit: St. James Press, 1996.

Maltin, Leonard, ed. *Movie Guide.* New York: New American Library, 1998.

Mast, Gerald, and Bruce Kawin. *A Short History of the Movies,* rev. ed. Boston: Allyn and Bacon, 1996.

Miller, Frank. *Movies: 100 Classics.* Atlanta: Turner, 1996.

Neibaur, James. *Tough Guy: The American Movie Macho.* Jefferson, N.C.: McFarland, 1989.

Rollyson, Carl. *Lillian Hellman.* New York: St. Martin's Press, 1988.

Thompson, Frank. *William Wellman.* Metuchen, N.J.: Scarecrow Press, 1983.

Vermilye, Jerry. *The Films of the Thirties.* New York: Carol, 1993.

Walsh, Frank. *Sin and Censorship: The Catholic Church and the Motion Picture Industry.* New Haven: Yale University Press, 1996.

Wyler, William. Interview by the author.

Chapter 3
The Boy Who Hated Superman:
Ethical Ideals, Metaphysical Confusion, and Popular Culture

Michael A. Oliker,
Midwest Philosophy of Education Society

I. Superman as an Ethical Ideal

In introducing the 1950s television series *The Adventures of Superman* (starring George Reeves and henceforth referred to as *AOS*), the announcer always said that Superman stood for "Truth, Justice, and the American Way." Those words are carved into the base of the 15-foot-high statue of Superman in the town square in Metropolis, Illinois (Perlman), which, in recent years, has established a "Super Museum," and has been promoting itself as "The Home of Superman," and holding an annual get-together in early June for fans of Superman. On *AOS*, Superman was not just a tough guy who could beat up people and monsters; he was the personification of ethical ideals. In *AOS*, his ethical obligations always took priority over whatever personal desires the character might have had. In the episode of *AOS* called "Panic in the Sky," Superman temporarily loses his memory, but, when he realizes that he (and only he!) has the power to save the world from an approaching meteor, he quickly concludes that he must act. That episode defines what a superhero is. A being with the power and the obligation to devote his life to heroism is a model case (Wilson, 28) of a superhero. I am inclined to argue that the version of the character portrayed by Christopher Reeve in the film *Superman II* as someone who is willing to give up his powers and obligations for an evening of lovemaking with Lois

Lane is not a superhero but merely a being with ordinary desires who has super powers.

Our minds should be exposed to ideals that can inspire us to actually do the right thing. A familiarity with the actions of superheroes and their reasons for those actions may serve as a valuable part of moral education. Unfortunately, since the attacks on comic books in the late 1940s by Frederic Wertham, Gershon Legman, and others, we have lived in an age of cynicism, where the very idea of a hero tends to be mocked and ridiculed. An actor who plays the part of a superhero may be attacked by violent children. This actually happened to George Reeves (Grossman, 53). Parents and educators should be teaching children about the ideal of heroism. The version of Superman in the 1950s *AOS* series continues to be a model that can be used for that purpose.

Superman's ethics may be described as either Aristotelian or Kantian. If Superman must act because he is the only individual in his universe with the power to take the necessary action, his obligations—as Aristotle might argue—come from his particular virtues. No other superheroes appeared on *AOS,* but, should there be others in his universe with the power to take such actions (as there were and still are in comic books), we would have the basis for a Kantian ethic of the superhero in which there are moral rules that all superheroes should be expected to follow.[1] From an Aristotelian view, a superhero's ethics depend on the nature of his or her powers. Superman's powers are superhuman, but the powers of some other superheroes such as The Spectre, Captain Marvel, and Thor are supernatural. If a meteor had been sent toward Earth by Satan, Superman might be incapable of stopping it. Captain Marvel possesses the powers of Solomon, Hercules, Atlas, Zeus, Achilles, and Mercury (a/k/a The Power of SHAZAM!). The Spectre is a murdered policeman sent back to Earth by the archangel Michael with the power of the wrath of God to avenge the deaths of murder victims. And Thor does not just have the powers of a god, he is a god. While Captain Marvel, The Spectre, and Thor all have the power to substitute for Superman, they also have broader ethical obligations. Zeus, God, and Odin might very well obligate them to go into combat with Satan himself, but, while Superman would have the moral obligation to save the world from an approaching meteor or a megalomaniac such as his own nemesis Lex Luthor or a Hitler, he would not have a moral obligation to combat Satan, because his powers are from the natural, not the supernatural, universe. So, a fan of superheroes should be able to think critically about what a superhero's appropriate obligations are. A superhero should not be admired if he is only shown to be able to overpower his enemies. It must be clear that the superhero has appropriate moral obligations and that his opponents are seeking to achieve evil goals.

This paper does not argue that the ideal of the hero should be taught in a dogmatic uncritical fashion. I agree with Harvey Siegel that an aim of education is the teaching of critical thinking. There is, however, a continuing controversy over whether critical thinking can be taught outside the context of a well-established academic discipline. The "disciplinarian" viewpoint on this issue would exclude materials from the curriculum that are not considered reputable by authoritative writers within the traditional disciplines. So, the late Harry S. Broudy (210–11) would have argued that an English teacher can teach students to think critically about the works of Shakespeare or Herman Melville, but that there is no point in teaching critical thinking about comic books. The job of persuading disciplinarians that popular culture is worthy of critical thought will certainly be a difficult one. It may even be a job for Superman! Another educational theorist whose views on education are often labeled conservative is the literary critic E. D. Hirsch. It is noteworthy that Hirsch's list of information that he considers necessary for the educational goal of cultural literacy includes several comic book characters. The one character central to the comic book industry to whom he devotes a paragraph in his book *Cultural Literacy* is Superman. Hirsch refers to Superman as a mythical figure who "is likely to be used allusively in all sorts of writings" (138). (The notion of a mythical hero alludes to the work of the literary critic Northrop Frye, who will be discussed later in this paper.)

Teaching students to think critically about popular culture is especially important in the case of adolescents. The culture of adolescence, as I. C. Jarvie argues (74), is increasingly a separate culture. John R. Palmer (147–49)—drawing from the work of the psychologist Kenneth Keniston—argues that the alienated adolescents of the 1960s created a negative, cynical mythology that separated the cultures of adolescence and adult society even further. Lawrence Grossberg describes teaching a class on popular music in which students became hostile when he asked them to give reasons for their preferences in popular music. He gives the impression that he abandoned any attempt to encourage critical thinking in his class for fear of

becoming an unpopular teacher (178–82). For many writers, critical thinking and the creation of myth are necessarily conflicting activities. Myth is
taken to be the equivalent of illusion, which necessarily involves falsehoods.
Critical thinking is often identified with the search for truth. So, from the
perspective of a dichotomy between myth and critical thinking, the task of
a critical thinker is to shatter illusions and deprive us of our myths in order
to see reality naked. Cynical views of Superman, such as those of Frederic
Wertham (394–406) and Rose Reissman (18), claim that he is really a law-
breaker, an uncritical American nationalist, or even a Nazi. While I am an
advocate of critical thinking, I agree with John M. Stephens (187–88) that
a belief in critical thinking should not be seen as a justification for cynicism
or negativity.

II. Adolescents and Children in AOS

In the late 1940s and the early 1950s, when Superman first appeared
in a medium other than comic books or animated cartoons, a common type
of film was film noir. The paper by Laurence Miller in this volume is an
insightful discussion of this genre. A film noir about adolescents or children
treats juvenile delinquency as the inevitable outcome of society's treatment
of children. Many of the horror films discussed in Don Smith's paper in this
volume have plots that are consistent with the idea of *film noir*. Smith
points out that, in many horror films of the 1950s, adults were portrayed
as responsible for children growing up to be monsters. So, a cynical, and
pessimistic view of youth was becoming common in the 1950s.

The papers in this volume by Grant Tracey and Gene Phillips discuss
films of the 1930s in which it was still possible for a "good guy" to rescue
children and adolescents from a corrupt environment. In *AOS,* there are
several episodes in which Superman encounters corrupt youth. Some of
these episodes do have some of the characteristics of film noir since they
show the youth's family as responsible for his or her corruption. But Superman is *always* portrayed as being able to rescue youth from corruption.
Before I give the reader an account of how Superman succeeds in reforming corrupt youth in several episodes of *AOS,* I want to acknowledge that
there is a kind of ambiguity in *AOS.* The need for Superman to step in to
prevent an adolescent from doing "X" can be interpreted as reinforcing the
cynical view that no one other than a superhero can prevent an adolescent

from doing such a thing. Unlike the radio version of Superman in the 1940s, the version of Superman in the *AOS* television series is never shown to contact a fellow superhero for help. So in *AOS*, Superman is the only superhero but Superman is *not* the only good guy. The staff of the *Daily Planet*—the newspaper that Superman works for in his secret identity as reporter Clark Kent—is frequently shown to assist Superman when he encounters a corrupt youth who must be reformed. It is a mistake, then, to regard *AOS* as evidence that social problems cannot be solved by anyone other than a superhero.

An episode of *AOS*, "The Boy Who Hated Superman," is an illustration of this point. The forty-third episode of *AOS*, it was written in 1953 by David Chantler, who wrote more episodes of *AOS* than any other writer. The director was George Blair, whose twenty-six directed episodes were second only to the thirty-six episodes directed by Tommy Carr. The episodes produced in 1953 were *all* directed by either Carr or Blair. Thus, I suggest that the episodes of 1953 can be regarded as typical of the *AOS* series. The Princeton philosopher Alexander Nehamas argues that a single episode of a television series or of a comic strip can only be adequately understood if it is seen in the context of the series as a whole (161). So, before my analysis of Episode 43 of *AOS*, I shall offer some comments on another episode.

The educational ideology of *AOS* is rather ambiguous. Characters called "Professor" often assist criminals or make inventions that have negative consequences for Superman to deal with. By contrast, adolescent criminals are treated as people who can be reformed, and Superman is not treated as the only person who can do so. In Episode 28, "The Big Squeeze" (directed by Tommy Carr and written by David Chantler), Perry White and Clark Kent are planning to give the *Daily Planet*'s "Man of the Year" award to a hard-working and responsible father named Dan Grayson, who is discovered to have spent time in jail as an adolescent when he was part of a teenage gang convicted of stealing cars. There is a brief dispute between Perry White and Clark Kent when Perry insists that a newspaper editor must not disagree with public opinion that a man convicted of a crime should be regarded as a criminal for the rest of his life. Kent expresses his conviction that Grayson is reformed and should be regarded as a good man. Kent soon discovers that Grayson's former fellow gang members are trying to pressure him into returning to a life of crime. Since Kent is convinced that that is not what Grayson wants to do, Superman rescues him from the gang and, as Kent, arranges for Grayson to be given the award on television. In a subplot of considerable significance, Grayson's son, Tim, briefly becomes hostile to his father after finding out that he is an ex-convict. In the last scene of the episode, Kent gives Grayson the award on television and assures Tim that his father is not a criminal and should be forgiven for the wrong things he did as an adolescent. The significance of that subplot is that it may have been a factor in getting Hugh Beaumont (the actor who played the part of Dan Grayson) the part of Beaver Cleaver's father, Ward Cleaver, in the late 1950s and early 1960s television series *Leave It to Beaver*. In the chapter on *Leave It to Beaver* in this volume Michael B. Kassel claims that there is a sort of ambiguity in the Ward Cleaver character, and there may be a basis for viewer criticism of Ward's parenting.

While Dan Grayson is an adult who has decided to abandon his life of crime as an adolescent, the character called Frankie Harris in "The Boy Who Hated Superman" is clearly a juvenile delinquent at the beginning of the episode. The story, however, demonstrates how a group of adults can cooperate successfully to educate an adolescent to have a sense of right and wrong. The episode begins in the office of a judge of a juvenile court. Judge Allen tells Frankie that, because he is a minor, he needs to have a suitable guardian. Frankie denies the judge's claim and refers sneeringly to his deceased father as a square. He asserts that his ability to succeed in life is due to his close relationship with his Uncle Duke, who is now in prison because of the indefensible behavior of both Clark Kent and Superman. Frankie claims that he hates both Kent and Superman because they framed his uncle. Then Kent walks into the judge's office and expresses his willingness and the support of the staff of the *Daily Planet* to function as Frankie's guardians. Kent makes the assertion that "loyalty is a fine thing when it is not misplaced." But, at this point, Frankie chooses to ignore Kent's offer and requests the judge's permission to visit Uncle Duke in jail. Judge Allen agrees with Frankie that he does have the right to visit his uncle but suggests that he consider Kent's offer.

In the next scene, Frankie is in the visitors' room in the jail and is being urged by Duke to accept Kent's offer. By staying in Kent's apartment, Frankie may get his hands on the evidence that was used to convict his uncle. Duke is aware that the cub reporter Jimmy Olsen is currently staying with Kent and suggests that Frankie might be able to convince Jimmy to help get him released from prison.

Next, Frankie shows up at Kent's apartment and is permitted to move in with Clark and Jimmy. Frankie assures Clark and Jimmy that he would like them to help him become a reporter. Clark and Jimmy briefly seem to accept Frankie's lies. In the next scene, Frankie is visiting Duke's fellow criminals, Fixer and Babe, who are playing chess. Their chess game seems to symbolize the fact that they are criminal warriors. Fixer tells Frankie that he will have to pay a down payment of $5000 for them to help him get Duke out of jail. And, once they do free Duke, Frankie will be under an obligation to pay them more. Next, Frankie is visiting Clark, Jimmy, and Lois Lane at the *Daily Planet*. Clark assures Frankie that there is ready cash at the office, and Frankie deceptively asks Clark for a job.

That evening, Frankie and Jimmy are at Clark's apartment where Frankie tells Jimmy that Clark is a "square" and temporarily persuades Jimmy that merely having a job will not guarantee a person the expensive clothes that Frankie wears. When he persuades Jimmy that he should want similar clothing, the plot suggests that Frankie and Jimmy may be about to become fellow criminals. After Jimmy falls asleep, Frankie goes through some documents in Clark's living room and finds the file containing the evidence that was the basis for the arrest of his Uncle Duke. Frankie then calls Fixer on Clark's telephone and urges him to send Babe over to Clark's apartment. He promises Fixer he will throw the documents out the window so Babe can pick them up on the street. Suddenly, Clark is shown to be in his bedroom and, with his x-ray vision, sees Frankie throw the files out the window. Babe heads to Fixer's place in his car, but Clark changes his clothes, and Superman flies out the bedroom window and across the dark streets of Metropolis. Moments after Babe arrives at Fixer's apartment, Superman crashes through Fixer's window and takes away the stolen documents.

The next day, Perry White, the editor of the *Daily Planet,* expresses his irritation to Clark that Jimmy "is acting like a kid again." Later, when Lois and Clark invite Jimmy to accompany them to Tony's restaurant for lunch, Jimmy scorns the suggestion and demeans Tony's restaurant. The significance of Jimmy's remark must be understood in relation to *AOS* Episode 41: "My Friend Superman," which was also written by David Chantler. Tony's is a working-class restaurant that is threatened by juvenile delinquents and gangsters. His friendship with Lois and Clark enables Tony to become friendly with Superman, who is willing to protect Tony and the restaurant from its threatening environment. So it is obvious to regular viewers of *AOS* that, if Clark were to quit having lunch at Tony's, Tony would be in serious danger, and Clark would be abandoning Superman's moral obligations. Clark begins to question Jimmy about Frankie's demands. Frankie is then shown to be in another office forging Clark's signature on a form for obtaining ready cash. But then, Frankie walks out into the hallway and overhears the conversation between Clark and Jimmy. Jimmy admits to Clark that Frankie wants Jimmy to become the partner of both Frankie and Duke. And Jimmy also admits to Clark, "I am beginning to hate myself!"

In the next scene, Babe, Frankie, and Jimmy are in an alley where Babe attempts to attract their loyalty to him and away from Duke. Babe tells Frankie and Jimmy about a robbery he and Fixer are planning on Frankie's birthday, which will provide them with more money. He then tells Frankie how Duke had deliberately arranged for Frankie to be beaten up by a gang that was in conflict with Fixer. In addition, Babe tells Frankie that, although Frankie and Duke were planning to move to South America after Duke had acquired the money from his robbery, Duke had purchased only one airline ticket to South America. So, Babe assures Frankie that Duke was setting him up to be a "patsy." Jimmy and Frankie both punch Babe and leave him in his car in the alley.

Finally, Perry, Lois, and Jimmy are giving Frankie a birthday party in Clark's apartment. Frankie is delighted and says, "I have never had anything like this before!" Then Clark walks in, carrying a birthday cake with lit candles. Frankie makes a birthday wish that implies he hopes that Babe and Fixer will be prevented from committing the robbery they have planned at the Metropolis stadium. When Frankie blows out the candles, Clark goes into the bedroom, and we see Superman fly through the Metropolis sky again and land in an alley where Fixer and Babe are climbing out of a manhole. Superman pushes them back down with the manhole cover and then drags a parked car onto the manhole cover to make Frankie's wish come true. When Clark returns to Frankie's party, Frankie admits joyfully that he no longer hates Superman. Clark assures Frankie that Superman will be glad to know that.

So, in this episode, Superman can be described as a figure of salvation who rescues Frankie from the mentality and lifestyle of a criminal. But the birthday party also establishes for Frankie a sense that there are people who care about him. I would argue that the moral teaching of this episode is that, if there are people in the world who care about you, you have an ethical obligation to care about them and not just yourself. But the sort of doctrinaire loyalty that Frankie expresses at the beginning of this episode is shown to be misguided. It is noteworthy that a reworking of the story line from this episode of *AOS* was published as a children's book entitled *I Hate Superman!* in 1996. The author, Louise Simonson, has written many Superman stories for DC Comics in recent years. The message of Simonson's book is that a little boy who hates Superman because Superman has his brother arrested is not justified in these feelings if his brother *did* participate in a robbery. Again, Superman should be regarded as an object of faith. If Superman arrests your brother or your uncle, you should be certain that your brother is guilty.

III. The History of Superman

In this paper, I am using *AOS* as a case study in the critical analysis of popular culture. Since he first appeared in *Action Comics* in 1938, Superman has appeared on a radio program (played by Bud Collyer), in theatrical animated cartoons, in a newspaper comic strip, in two movie serials (played by Kirk Alyn), in five feature films (played by George Reeves in one and Christopher Reeve in four), in two television series (played by George Reeves and Dean Cain), in one Broadway play (played by Bob Holliday), and in many, many television cartoons. Why did Superman become such a popular figure? Superman was not just an innovation that popularized comic books. Variations on the notion of a superhero have appeared in English literature since the Middle Ages.

The late literary critic Northrop Frye (33–35) has identified various types of protagonists who appear throughout the history of Anglo-European literature. Roger Rollin makes a strong case that Frye's archetypes are relevant to the critical analysis of comic books and that the medieval hero Beowulf has much in common with comic book superheroes (434–36). Frye identifies five archetypes of heroic narratives: myth, romance, high mimetic, low mimetic, and ironic and asserts that "European fiction, during the last fifteen centuries, has steadily moved its center of gravity down the list" (34). Rollin argues that only mythic, romantic, and high mimetic narratives can be found in comic books (434). Frye would assert that the mythic hero has not appeared in "high culture" literature since the first five centuries of Christianity; Rollin would disagree.

(1) A *myth* features a hero who is superior in kind to human beings. Frye identifies this kind of hero as a divine being or a god (33). I have suggested that in comic books there are two kinds of mythic heroes: supernatural mythic heroes and superhuman mythic heroes. The Marvel Comics hero Thor is a model of a supernatural mythic hero since he does not just have the powers of a god; he *is* a god. The DC Comics character The Spectre is also supernatural because his powers come from God Himself. Other supernatural mythic heroes include Captain Marvel, his sister Mary Marvel, and his disciple Captain Marvel, Jr., who have superpowers they have acquired from ancient Greek gods and the Old Testament hero King Solomon. Roger Rollin identifies Superman as a model of a mythic hero (435). Superman's powers are superhuman, but can be described as having powers that are the result of interaction with his environment. Because Superman is a survivor of the planet Krypton, the gravity of Earth and the rays of our yellow sun make him superior in kind to human beings and enable him to serve as a figure of salvation for the human race. So Superman *is* a godlike figure.

(2) A *romance* features a hero who can do things that many human beings cannot do but is still clearly identifiable as a human being. Rollin identifies Batman as a model case of a romantic superhero.

(3) A *high mimetic* narrative features a hero who is a leader among human beings and has some superior abilities but does not transcend the natural characteristics of human beings. Rollin identifies the old comic strip character Steve Canyon as a high mimetic hero because of his military leadership to victory in war stories.

(4) A *low mimetic* hero is an ordinary person who is shown to perform a heroic act but is not identified as having superior abilities or any tendency to heroism.

(5) An *ironic* hero is a person with inferior abilities and inclinations toward incompetence rather that heroism, but one who is somehow able to triumph in a particular situation. In the delightful comedy *Abbott and Costello Meet Frankenstein,* Bud Abbott and Lou Costello play marginal lower-class workingmen who are able to defeat the Frankenstein monster (Glenn Strange), the Wolf Man (Lon Chaney, Jr.) and Count Dracula (Bela Lugosi). However, their brief encounter at the end of the film with the

Invisible Man (Vincent Price) suggests that their problems may get worse in the future!

Rollin traces the history of the romantic hero back to the medieval text *Beowulf* (436–39). Like Batman, Paladin, and The Lone Ranger, Beowulf is a "stranger-hero," who enters a community that is about to be destroyed, and he must use violence to restore a moral social order. Both Beowulf and Batman become committed to being "resident heroes" in a particular community and are committed to making violent responses to the criminal element there. Rollin (438) argues that "the community in both epic and pop romance is not only a social unit but a quasi-religious one. It is that which nurtures, controls, and protects the non-heroes who comprise it: the community giveth and the community taketh away. Its wars are holy wars and its champions . . . become quasi-religious figures." Rollin also suggests that the mythic hero may have originated in the epic poem by Edmund Spenser (1552–1599), *The Fairie Queen*. A character in that poem, Prince Arthur—Rollin argues, quoting a letter by Spenser—has virtues that make him superior in kind to all human beings. According to Rollin, Prince Arthur can be correctly seen as having the characteristics of both Batman and Superman (441–42).

The word "superman" did not appear in the English language until the early 20th century. Friedrich Nietzsche's conception of the *ubermensch* (translated as both "superman" and "overman") appeared in the late 19th century (Simpson and Weiner, vol. 17., 232). George Bernard Shaw's 1903 play *Man and Superman* translated Nietzsche's term into English, but Shaw's play can easily be understood as a parody of the notion of superman (Crane). The word "superman" began to appear in articles in scholarly journals soon after the publication of Shaw's play. In 1915, the influential literary and social critic H. L. Mencken published a book in the United States on the philosophy of Nietzsche that stressed the idea of superman as central to Nietzsche's philosophy. Today, many contemporary scholars object to the idea that Nietzsche's notion of *ubermensch* should be translated as "superman" (Ansell-Pearson). In 1930, the science fiction novelist and social critic Philip Wylie published the novel *Gladiator*, which tells of a scientist who injects his pregnant wife with chemicals that give their baby superhuman powers. But, as the young man—Hugo Danner—grows up, he finds that his superhuman abilities as a football player and soldier produce resentment, not admiration. Toward the end of the novel, Danner becomes increasingly depressed and embittered. In the final scene, he climbs to the top of a mountain and denounces God for making the human race the way it is. He is then killed by a bolt of lightning.

A few years later, a copy of *Gladiator* came into the hands of two Cleveland adolescents, Jerry Siegel and Joe Shuster. Siegel was an aspiring writer and Shuster an aspiring artist. They wanted to be able to use their interests to make a living. So, they created a character who was a heroic version of Hugo Danner and sold the idea to a New York publisher who had just started a line of comic books (Steranko). In 1938, their character—Superman—appeared in issue #1 of *Action Comics.*

By the early 1940s, Superman was appearing in several comic books, a nationally broadcast radio program, a newspaper comic strip, and in animated cartoons. In a 1943 World War II film about army nurses, *So Proudly We Hail,* the head nurse (Claudette Colbert) and her subordinates are shown reading Superman comics to war orphans. The head nurse's boyfriend, a combat soldier, was played by a muscular ex-prizefighter turned actor named George Reeves. In the late '40s, two Superman movie serials were made starring actor and dancer Kirk Alyn. At that time, the movie serial was a declining genre. So, when the producer of the Superman radio series, Robert Maxwell, was approached by Kellogg's cereals about doing a Superman film as a pilot for a television series, he rejected Kirk Alyn and chose George Reeves for the part.

In his book *Superman: Serial to Cereal,* Gary Grossman writes that, after a year of producing *AOS,* Robert Maxwell was replaced as producer by Whitney Ellsworth (82–87). The episodes produced by Maxwell treated *AOS* as an adult-oriented show about a crimefighter who often had to step into situations when his friends found themselves confronted by vicious criminals who could not be stopped by conventional means. The later episodes produced by Ellsworth cut back on the film noir atmosphere in Metropolis and emphasized stories that supposedly appealed to children. I will argue in the next section that treating Superman solely as a character for children has had some negative consequences that I call "metaphysical confusion." Adults and children should learn to engage in an analysis of popular culture that enables all of them to discuss and evaluate the ethical ideals that fictional heroes represent.

IV. Metaphysical Confusion and Cynicism

The recent book *Hollywood Kryptonite* (Kashner & Schoenberger) bears the subtitle "The Bulldog, The Lady, and The Death of Superman." The book is about the death of George Reeves, but also about the "Superman" who had broken his neck in a fall from a horse: Christopher Reeve (who portrayed Superman in four films of the 1980s). At the annual Superman Celebration in Metropolis, Illinois, in 1996, Dr. Jeff Anderson of Cleveland, Texas, told me he was assisting Kirk Alyn in preparing a revised edition of his autobiography. Although Alyn died in 1999, I have no doubt that, if Anderson publishes the book, a headline will appear somewhere saying, "Superman Publishes Autobiography." And should Dean Cain (who played the part of Superman in the recent TV series *Lois and Clark: The New Adventures of Superman*) somehow become engaged to a famous woman, tabloid headlines all over the world will scream "MS. X TO MARRY SUPERMAN!"

What is going on here? I would call it metaphysical confusion. When the mass media refer to actors who have played Superman by the name "Superman," they are reinforcing ignorance about the difference between fact and fiction.

Fortunately for me, I learned about the difference between a movie and a documentary when I was a small child. My maternal grandfather managed movie theaters during the entire first half of the 20th century. So, I saw my first movie when I was roughly two years old. I actually remember walking into my grandfather's theater in Beaver Falls, Pennsylvania, with my grandmother and seeing a huge image of cowboys in a gunfight on the screen. My grandmother said with a tone of anxiety, "Oh dear, they're feuding, fussing, and fighting. Let's go to your grandfather's office instead!" She took me to many movies but was not a fan of violence. I became aware, before my grandfather's death in 1949, when I was three years old, that the movies he showed were not pictures of actual events but stories in which the characters were portrayed by actors and actresses. When I saw a couple of horror movies with Bela Lugosi in the early 1950s just before his death, my grandmother recalled having met the actor in the 1920s when he played the part of Dracula on stage in one of my grandfather's theatres. She assured me that Lugosi was a nice man and not like the characters he played in horror movies. I recall watching *AOS* religiously—again, see Kozloff on Superman as a religious figure (78–82)—after my parents bought a television set. Today, as a middle-aged man I have retained my enthusiasm for *AOS*. Andrew Lotterman would probably claim that I am still at a preadolescent stage of moral development (496–98). Maybe, but I do know the difference between fiction and reality. As a kid, I had seen both George Reeves and John Hamilton (who played Perry White on *AOS*) appear in other TV series. I remember Reeves singing country and western songs on Tony Bennett's TV show and Hamilton appearing on the anti-Communist television series *I Led Three Lives* as Herb Philbrick's boss in Philbrick's 9–5 job. So, I knew that George Reeves and John Hamilton were actors. Grossman reports that, not long after George Reeves began shooting the child-centered version of *AOS* under the supervision of Whitney Ellsworth, he made a personal appearance in a Detroit store in 1953. There, he was confronted by a child brandishing a real gun loaded with real bullets (53). Reeves acted heroically, coolly talking the kid into handing over the gun because, he said at the time, although the bullets could not hurt Superman, they might hurt others when they bounced off Superman. I suspect that Reeves did not quite have the same enthusiasm for personal appearances after that incident. Yet the phenomenon of metaphysical confusion has continued.

In "Lucy Meets Superman" (1957) it should be noted that neither "George Reeves" nor "Clark Kent" is ever mentioned during the program. Who then is the guest star? Well, it is Superman, but it does not seem to be the same Superman who appeared on *AOS*. It is a character called Superman who stars on a children's program that Lucy's son, Little Ricky, is a fan of and whom her husband, Ricky Ricardo, "once met in Hollywood." The program is full of cynical remarks from Lucy and her friend Ethel Mertz such as "If he's really Superman, why is he taking an airplane to Terre Haute, Indiana?" With the exception of the brief film clip from *AOS* that Little Ricky is shown watching at the beginning of "Lucy Meets Superman," Superman is never shown doing any of the kind of superhuman heroic stunts that he did regularly on *AOS*. In short, the character called Superman who appears on *I Love Lucy* would seem to be a vaguely untrustworthy entertainer who is taking advantage of the gullibility of Ricky and Little Ricky, but is easily seen to be what he really is by Lucy and Ethel. (Ethel's husband, Fred Mertz (William Frawley), who usually has strong opinions, remains strangely neutral in the matter.)

Of course, we would regard anyone who told us that he really could fly and pick up a locomotive as either lying, joking, or delusional. But should we meet Christopher Reeve or Dean Cain and hear them mention that they were Superman, would we then be justified in calling a psychiatrist or the police? Or, would we be justified in pulling out a gun and saying with a cynical grin, "I'm going to show the world that you aren't really Superman?" Certainly not! But that seems to be the way some people, especially some children, would react. Although Superman differed from most other visitors from outer space in the mass media of the 1950s in that he was a hero and not a threat to the world, the atmosphere in the real world of the 1950s was that of suspicion and distrust. Watching *AOS* during the 1950s was a vacation from a world in which we kids were being subjected to drills in the schools to prepare us for a possible nuclear attack. I can remember watching the Army-McCarthy hearings and *I Led Three Lives* on TV and becoming suspicious of an old man in my neighborhood who acted rather peculiarly. I feared that he might be a Communist and expressed my worries to my father, an attorney who worked as a prosecutor for the U.S. Treasury Department. Dad warned me that accusing someone of being a Communist was a very serious matter and asked me if I had evidence that Mr. X was a Communist or that Mr. X had committed a crime. I admitted that I didn't. Although my parents had given me the usual warnings about not getting into a car with a stranger, I learned from that incident that there was an important difference between being careful and being suspicious. My father was a firm believer in the legal concept of due process of law. From that perspective, a prosecutor must have evidence that Mr. X has committed a crime before the prosecution can begin.

When Lucy got stuck on the ledge near the end of "Lucy Meets Superman," it was Superman who unhesitatingly went out on that ledge and rescued her. Even if that character was a con man and did not have superpowers, his rescue of Lucy was still a heroic act. The program ends with Superman making a demeaning remark about Lucy to Ricky. Feminists will deplore the wisecrack, but Lucy's cynicism in this episode should also be deplored. The script reinforces metaphysical confusion by giving the impression that an actor who played Superman was a con man who wanted the public to think that he really was Superman. Children should be taught that an actor who plays a hero may or may not really be a hero, and an actor who plays a villain may or may not really be a villain. Declaring a real person to be a hero or a villain should be based on knowledge of what the person has actually done. Real people do both good and bad things in their lives. When George Reeves so skillfully disarmed the gun-brandishing child in a Detroit store, he was not really Superman, but he was capable of heroic action. He was also capable of lying to the boy if the lie might convince the boy not to commit murder. This is the only incident that I know about when Reeves actually went along with someone's view that he was really Superman. There is no evidence for the oft-repeated rumor that George Reeves's tragic death in 1959 resulted from his suffering from the delusion that he really was Superman. And, there is growing evidence that Reeves was murdered and did not commit suicide.

Superman is a fictional character, but a fictional or mythical character can be the object of a kind of faith. An actor who plays the part of Superman may deserve considerable admiration if he makes a conscious effort to play Superman as an exemplar of moral behavior. That is exactly what George Reeves did. A producer or director or comic book writer who reduces Superman to being just a man does Superman's audience a serious disservice.

Endnote

1   For this point, I am indebted to Prof. Frederick Rauscher of the Department of Philosophy at Michigan State University.

Bibliography

Ansell-Pearson, Keith. "Who is the *Ubermensch*? Time, Truth, and Woman in Nietzsche." *Journal of the History of Ideas* 53, no. 2 (April–June 1992): 309–331.

Aristotle. "Nicomachean Ethics." In *Introduction to Aristotle,* edited by Richard P. McKeon. New York: The Modern Library, 1947.

Broudy, Harry S. *Enlightened Cherishing: An Essay on Aesthetic Education.* Urbana, Ill.: University of Illinois Press, 1972.

Crane, Gladys. "Shaw's Comic Techniques in *Man and Superman*." *Educational Theatre Journal* 23, no. 1 (March 1971): 13–21.

Frye, Northrop. *Anatomy of Criticism: Four Essays* (1957). New York: Atheneum, 1965.

Grossberg, Lawrence. "Teaching the Popular." In *Theory in the Classroom,* ed. Cary Nelson, 177–200. Urbana, Ill.: University of Illinois Press, 1986.

Grossman, Gary H. *Superman: Serial to Cereal.* New York: Popular Library, 1976.

Hirsch, E. D. *Cultural Literacy.* New York: Vintage Books, 1988.

Jarvie, I. C. *Concepts and Society.* London: Routledge & Kegan Paul, 1972.

Kant, Immanuel. *Fundamental Principles of the Metaphysics of Morals.* Trans. by Thomas K. Abbott. Indianapolis, Ind.: Bobbs-Merrill Co., 1949.

Kashner, Sam and Nancy Schoenberger. *Hollywood Kryptonite: The Bulldog, The Lady, and the Death of Superman*. New York: St. Martin's Press, 1996.

Kozloff, Sarah. "Superman as Savior: Christian Allegory in the Superman Movies." *Journal of Popular Film and Television* 9, no. 2 (Summer 1981): 78–82.

Legman, Gershon. *Love and Death* (1949). New York: Hacker Art Books, 1963.

Lotterman, Andrew. "Superman as a Male Latency Stage Myth." *Bulletin of the Menninger Clinic* 45, no. 6 (November 1981): 491–498.

Mencken, H. L. *Friedrich Nietzsche* (1913). New Brunswick, N.J.: Transaction Publishers, 1993.

Nehamas, Alexander. "Serious Watching." *South Atlantic Quarterly* 89, no. 1 (Winter 1990): 157–180.

Nietzsche, Friedrich Wilhelm. *The Portable Nietzsche*; edited by Walter Kaufmann. New York, Viking Press, 1954.

Palmer, John R. "Theories of Social Change and the Mass Media." *Journal of Aesthetic Education* 5, no. 4 (October 1971): 127–149.

Perlman, Ellen. "Little Cash Cows on the Prairie." *Governing* 8, no. 4 (January 1995): 26.

Reissman, Rose. "Crimebusters or 'Rightsbusters.'" *Update on Law-Related Education* 15, no. 2 (Spring-Summer 1991): 18–19.

Rollin, Roger B. "Beowulf to Batman: The Epic Hero and Pop Culture." *College English* 31, no. 5 (February 1970): 431–449.

Shaw, Bernard. *Man and Superman* (1903). Baltimore: Penguin, 1952.

Siegel, Harvey. "Critical Thinking as an Educational Ideal." *Educational Forum* 45, no. 1 (Nov. 1980): 7–23.

Simonson, Louise. *I Hate Superman!* Boston: Little, Brown, 1996.

Simpson, J. A. and E. S. C. Weiner. *The Oxford English Dictionary*. 2nd ed. Oxford: Clarendon Press, 1989.

Stephens, John M. *The Psychology of Classroom Learning*. New York: Holt, Rinehart and Winston, 1965.

Steranko, James. *The Steranko History of Comics*, Vol. 1. Reading, Pennsylvania: Supergraphics, 1970.

Wertham, Fredric, M.D. "The Curse of the Comic Books: The Value Patterns and Effects of Comic Books." *Religious Education* 49 (1954), 394–406.

———. *Seduction of the Innocent*. New York: Rinehart, 1953.

Wilson, John. *Thinking with Concepts*. Cambridge: Cambridge University Press, 1963.

Wylie, Philip. *Gladiator* (1930). Westport, Conn.: Hyperion Press, 1974.

Additional Bibliography

Anderson, Patrick D. "From John Wayne to E.T.: The Hero in Popular American Film." *American Baptist Quarterly* 2, no. 1 (1983): 16–31.

Anderson, Richard W. "Biff! Pow! Comic Books Make a Comeback." *Business Week*, September 2, 1985, pp. 59–60.

Beniger, James R. "Far Afield." *Communication Research* 20, no. 5 (June 1993): 494–500.

Bifulco, Michael J. *Superman on Television.* Tenth Anniversary ed. Grand Rapids, Michigan: Michael Bifulco, 1998.

Brown, Slater. "The Coming of Superman." *The New Republic,* September 2, 1940, p. 301.

Chang, Gordon H. "'Superman Is about to Visit the Relocation Centers' and the Limits of Wartime Liberalism." *Amerasia Journal* 19, no. 1 (Winter 1993): 37–60.

Collins, Bradford R. and David Cowart. "Through the Looking-Glass: Reading Warhol's Superman." *American Imago* 53, no. 2 (Summer 1996): 107–137.

Connor, John W. "Superman on Main Street: The Schizophrenic Hero in America." *Journal of Psychoanalytic Anthropology* 3, no. 4 (Fall 1980): 335–347.

Daniels, Les. *DC Comics: Sixty Years of the World's Favorite Comic Book Heroes.* Boston: Bullfinch Press, 1995.

DeMarco, Mario. "Superman—Everybody's Hero: Two Young Boys' Dream Finally Realized." *Good Old Days* 26, no. 7 (July 1989): 32–37.

———. "Superman: The Super Hero." *Antiques and Collecting* 93 (October 1988): 74–77.

Dorrell, Larry D., Dan B. Curtis, and Kuldip R. Rampal. "Book-Worms Without Books? Students Reading Comic Books in the School House." *Journal of Popular Culture* 29.2 (Fall 1995): 223–234.

Eco, Umberto. "The Myth of Superman." *In The Role of the Reader.* Bloomington: Indiana University Press, 1979.

Engle, Gary. "What Makes Superman So Darned American?" In *Popular Culture: An Introductory Text,* ed. Jack Nachbar and Kevin Lause, 331–343. Bowling Green, Ohio: Bowling Green State University Popular Press, 1992.

Feiffer, Jules. *The Great Comic Book Heroes.* New York: Dial Press, 1965.

Fleisher, Michael L. *The Great Superman Book.* New York: Warner Books, 1978.

Friedrich, Otto. "Up, Up, and Awaaay!!! America's Favorite Hero Turns 50, Ever Changing but Indestructible." *Time,* March 14, 1988, pp. 66–73.

Galloway, John T. *The Gospel According to Superman.* Philadelphia: A. J. Holman, 1973.

Gates, Henry Louis. "A Big Brother from Another Planet." *New York Times,* September 12, 1993, Section 2, pp. 51+.

Goodman, Ellen. "It's Tough Giving Up Your Cape and the Big S." *Kansas City Star,* July 28, 1981, p. 15A.

Harrington, Michael. "It's a Bird, It's a Plane, It's . . ." *The Spectator* 275, no. 8730 (November 4, 1995): 8–9.

Harris, Neil. "Who Owns Our Myths? Heroism and Copyright in an Age of Mass Culture." *Social Research* 52 (Summer 1985): 241–267.

Henderson, Jan Alan. "Still Super After All These Years." *American Cinematographer* 72 (October 1991): 42–48.

Hughes, Rob. "The Dawn of the Golden Age." *Collector's Showcase,* April–May, 1995, pp. 33–48.

Hugick, Larry. "Public to DC Comics: Resurrect Superman!" *Gallup Poll Monthly,* no. 326 (November 1992): 28–30.

Kauffman, Stanley. "Stanley Kauffman on Films." *The New Republic* 189, no. 3 (July 18 & 25, 1983): 22–23.

Keefer, Truman F. *Philip Wylie*. Boston: Twayne, 1977.

Kipniss, Marc. "The Death (and Rebirth) of Superman." *Discourse* 16, no. 3 (Spring 1994): 144–167.

Lang, Jeffrey S. and Patrick Trimble. "Whatever Happened to the Man of Tomorrow? An Examination of the American Monomyth and the Comic Book Superhero." *Journal of Popular Culture* 22, no. 3 (Winter 1988): 157–173.

Lederman, Marie Jean. "Superman, Oedipus, and the Myth of the Birth of the Hero." *Journal of Popular Film and Television* 7, no. 3 (1979): 235–245.

Leonard, Harris K. "The Classics—Alive and Well with Superman." *College English* 37, no. 4 (December 1975): 405–407.

Levin, Schneir. "Was Superman Jewish?" *Journal of Irreproducible Results* 41, no. 1 (January 1996): 5–6.

Ligorski, Mark. "The Masked Superhero." *Journal of the American Academy of Psychoanalysis* 22, no. 3 (Fall 1994): 449–464.

London, Herbert. "The Death of Superman." *First Things*, no. 31 (March 1993): 11–12.

Mandell, Paul. "It's a Bird, It's a Plane, It's." *American Cinematographer* 72 (November 1991): 66–72.

Marlowe, John W. "Some Thoughts on Nuns, Teachers, and Supermen." *Theory into Practice* 8, no. 2 (April 1969): 76–78.

McNair, Wesley. "The Secret Identity of Superman: Puritanism and the American Superhero." *American Baptist Quarterly* 2, no. 1 (1983): 4–15.

Minganti, Franco. "1939: Flying Eyes. Flight, Metropolis, and Icons of the Popular Imagination." *Storia Nordamericana* (Italy) 7, no. 1 (1990): 93–103.

Mitchell, Jane P. and Joseph D. George. "What Do Superman, Captain America, and Spiderman Have in Common? The Case for Comic Books." *Gifted Education International* 11, no. 2 (1996): 91–94.

Reynolds, Richard. *Super Heroes: A Modern Mythology*. Jackson, Miss.: University Press of Mississippi, 1992.

Rothfield, Lawrence. "At a Single Bound: Illiberal Reflections on 'Truth, Contingency, and Modernity.'" *Modern Philology* 90 (May 1993): Supplement: S134–S141.

Shusterman, Richard. "Popular Art." In *A Companion to Aesthetics*, ed. David Cooper, 336–340. Oxford: Blackwell, 1992.

———. "Popular Art and Education." In *The New Scholarship on Dewey*, ed. Jim Garrison, 35–44. Dordrecht, The Netherlands: Kluwer Academic, 1995.

Simons, Martin. "Montessori, Superman, and Catwoman." *Educational Theory* 38, no. 3 (Summer 1988): 341–349.

Snyder, John. "King of the Comic Book Premium." *Collector's Showcase* 14, no. 7 (October 1994): 35.

Wachtel, Paul L. "The Preoccupation with Economic Growth: An Analysis Informed by Horneyan Theory." *American Journal of Psychoanalysis* 51, no. 2 (June 1991): 89–103.

Waitman, Michael D. "Superman: Invulnerable to All but Kryptonite, Compassion, and Concupiscence." *Journal of Mental Imagery* 8, no. 3 (Fall 1984): 87–98.

Wilcox, Rhonda V. "Dominant Female, Superior Male." *Journal of Popular Film and Television* 24, no. 1 (Spring 1996): 26–33.

Williams, J. P. "All's Fair in Love and Journalism: Female Rivalry in Superman." *Journal of Popular Culture* 24 (Fall 1990): 103–112.

Zinn, Laura. "It's a Bird, It's a Plane—It's a Resurrection." *Business Week,* no. 3314 (April 12, 1993): 40.

Chapter 4
Juvenile Delinquency in Films During the Era of *Film Noir:* 1940–1959

Laurence Miller,
Western Washington University

I

A few years after the end of World War II, there was a sharp increase in juvenile arrest rates and cases heard in court (Lunden, 1964). This increase was paralleled by increased public attention and scrutiny. A vigilant, aroused, fearful, worried, and concerned public composed of the various media, parents, educators, social service agencies, and government and law enforcement officials intently discussed and argued the issues.

Interestingly, the motion picture industry did not markedly exploit this awareness and concern over juvenile delinquency. Given the number of films released during and after the war, extremely few dealt with the subject. A number of possible explanations can be posited. Perhaps the film industry believed that the public would not be receptive to such films, given the fear and anxiety that juvenile delinquency seemed to elicit in people. Afraid of running afoul of the Motion Picture Producers and Distributors of America (MPPDA) Film Code, the industry promised to commit itself to wholesome entertainment and not to demean correct standards of living. Transgressions in accepted morality in areas of crime, sex, and vulgarity—which juvenile delinquency could be expected to touch on—were to be avoided. In his 1933 book, *Our Movie Children,* Henry James Forman concluded:

The road to delinquency is heavily dotted with movie addicts, and obviously, it needs no crusaders or preachers or reformers to come to this conclusion.

And what could promote delinquency more than films about delinquency?

So, those films that were made were, for the most part, wholly removed from any realistic consideration of the subject. The best known films were those of the Bowery Boys series. The Dead End Kids were introduced in the 1937 film *Dead End,* where they were portrayed as fun-loving, lovable juvenile delinquents. In 1940, they became the East Side Kids and made a series of low-budget films at Monogram Studios. In 1946, they became the Bowery Boys and appeared in another series of low-budget films, which stressed action, low-brow comedy, silly jokes, and sight gags. The films were geared to a juvenile audience and proved to be very popular. However, their portrayal of juvenile delinquency was utterly removed from reality in its depiction of the behavior of juvenile delinquents, in the etiology of such behavior, and in conveying the perceived seriousness of the problems it posed.

It was only through film noir that any kind of realistic portrayal of juvenile delinquency and its vagaries was presented during the '40s. But, even though juvenile delinquency is a natural subject matter for film noir, very few films that can be called film noir dealt with it. In the two decades of film noir, from 1940 through 1959, which encompassed more than five hundred films, only four dealt with juvenile delinquency, and the first films did not appear until 1949. For those unfamiliar with film noir, a few words about it are in order.

II

Film noir is one of the most extensively studied and influential film genres. Film noir ("dark" or "black") is a French term which identifies a body of American films perceived by European film scholars as having cohesive and consistent themes. Film noir contrasts markedly with other film genres produced at the same time. Film noir viewed the world as an implacable, harsh, and dangerous place devoid of hope. Fate rules one's life. Film noir had a "black" mood as it presented a sinister netherworld of immorality, evil, violence, corruption, betrayal, vengeance, doom, criminal behavior, obsession, psychopathology, alienation, and human frailty. Film noir provided an uncompromising and unsentimental portrayal of human behavior and the environment. These noir themes were complemented by flashbacks, voice-overs, and, especially, by a unique visual style which stressed black and white photography, location shooting (often at night), odd camera angles and shadows, and rain-slicked streets. As Appel (1974) noted: "What unites the seemingly disparate kinds of films noirs is their dark visual style and their bleak vision of despair, loneliness and dread. In the best films noirs, the visual style and narrative structure work hand-in-hand in consistent, unified ensemble". Prominent examples of film noir are *The Maltese Falcon* (1941), *Double Indemnity* (1944), *The Postman Always Rings Twice* (1946), *The Big Sleep* (1946), *Out of the Past* (1947), and *Kiss Me Deadly* (1955). Although film noir officially ceased to exist after 1959, post-modern films noirs continue to be made, and some are among the most important American films (e.g., *Point Blank,* 1967; *Chinatown,* 1974; *L. A. Confidential,* 1997).

III

On first consideration, juvenile delinquency would seem to be a natural subject matter for film noir. Miller (1994) identified thirteen themes that recur in film noir and define its subject matter and philosophy. At least nine of these seem suitable for treatment within the context of juvenile delinquency: revenge, vengeance; framed, false accusation; policier (police procedural drama); menaced, blackmailed, held hostage; psychopathology, mental instability; pursued, on the run; prison life; double-crossed, betrayed. Additionally, the urban settings in which juvenile delinquents lived formed a natural noir environment, and the emphasis on environmental determinism by film noir is consistent with early explanations of juvenile delinquency. Also, juveniles (non-delinquent) had been successfully incorporated into a few films noirs (e.g., *The Accused,* 1948).

Yet, given the receptive subject matter juvenile delinquency provided, it was largely ignored or avoided by film noir. I believe that there are at least four reasons for so few juvenile delinquency films noirs: (1) The state of the motion picture industry in the '40s, which was discussed previously (public receptivity, conformity to the MPPDA Code). (2) The influence of the Bowery Boys series. These films may have co-opted the way juvenile delinquents were to be treated in films, and, of course, this depiction was anti-thetical to film noir. (3) Many of the films noirs were created by immi-grants. They may well have perceived American juvenile delinquency as an alien phenomenon with which they were unfamiliar, had no feelings for, or did not care about. The four juvenile delinquency films noirs were all directed by native-born Americans. Two of these films were directed by Nicholas Ray, who had a longstanding interest in youth and their problems. (4) Most important, I believe, is that the themes and philosophy of film noir could best be presented and represented through the behaviors of adults. The best films noirs feature scintillating and sophisticated dialogue, femmes fatales and an underlying, smoldering sexuality, and an air of world-weariness and cynicism. Juveniles, lacking the level of development, sophistication, maturity, and life experiences of adults, could not effectively convey these themes and philosophy. In the developmental theory of psy-chologist Erik Eriksen, an individual passes through eight stages of life. Juveniles are in the fifth stage of development (adolescence), but film noir deals mainly with the life experiences encountered in the sixth and seventh stages (early and middle adulthood). Thus, the concerns and life experi-ences of adolescents are markedly different than those of adults, and it is these adult experiences that form the crux of film noir.

Nevertheless, four juvenile delinquency films noirs were made. All four are realistic and powerful portrayals of juvenile delinquency in America during the '40s that accurately reflect the prevailing sociological theories of the time. And all four are totally removed from the slapstick silliness of the Bowery Boys films. Three of the four films were released during the middle of the film noir cycle in 1949. The fourth was released at the very end of the noir cycle in 1959.

IV

Two of the four films were directed by Nicholas Ray: *They Live by Night* and *Knock on Any Door*. Both were released in 1949. *They Live by Night* was based on the novel *Thieves Like Us* by Edward Anderson. In an early draft in 1946 Ray set the tone of the film when he wrote that it was a tender and tragic love story rather than a brutal crime movie. It was a morality story about two ill-starred, lost kids, much in the vein of *Romeo and Juliet*. This observation tellingly and clearly reveals Ray's emphasis on emotionality and intimacy in his storytelling and his sympathy for his juvenile protagonists, tragically enmeshed in a cruel and unforgiving world. This theme was revisited by Ray in his two other films dealing with juvenile delinquency, *Knock on Any Door*, and, especially, in his seminal (but non–film noir) film of the '50s, *Rebel Without a Cause*.

They Live by Night opens with a warm and affectionate shot of the two lovers, Farley Granger as Bowie and Cathy O'Donnell as Keechie. This happiness is frozen in subtitles written across the screen warning that Bowie and Keechie were never adequately prepared for life in this world. The lovers look up, startled, the credits appear, and we know they are doomed. Two hardened criminals, Chickimaw and T-Dub, engineer a prison break and take Bowie with them. Bowie, now 23, has been serving a life sentence for murder since age 16. The film tells the story of Bowie and his girlfriend Keechie and their doomed struggle to break away from the past and a life of crime and lead a normal existence. However, Bowie is sucked back into crime, ultimately betrayed, and killed by the police.

Ray's film of fugitive lovers is solidly in the film noir tradition. The film's power derives from the contrasting scenes of romantic tenderness and violence. Ultimately, this violence makes it impossible for Bowie and Keechie to escape the circumstances into which Fate has, through misfortune, cast them. The sense of noir environmental determinism is particularly evident. A basically decent but naïve adolescent, Bowie, out of curiosity, accompanies a gang that kills someone during the course of a robbery. As a youngster, Bowie saw his father killed and his mother run off with the man who killed his father. Near the end of the film a policeman observes of Bowie that it was inevitable he would lead this kind of life. It was probably society's fault that eventually Bowie would commit robbery and murder. Fate had sealed his eventual doom. What gives *They Live by Night* its particular poignancy is the appealing youthfulness, gentleness, vulnerability, and warmth of its youthful protagonists. Ray's sympathies clearly lay with Bowie and Keechie, albeit, in the eyes of society and the police, Bowie is a criminal who deserves what he gets.

The publicity campaign for the film stressed the theme of juvenile violence. However, the film, which cost $775,000, failed to find its audience and returned only $445,000 in receipts. Today, it is recognized as a masterpiece and a major film noir.

V

Knock on Any Door was Ray's second film, although it was released nine months prior to *They Live by Night,* which was completed in 1947. The film was adapted from Willard Motley's novel. Ray was invited to direct the film by Humphrey Bogart for Bogart's independent production company, Santana Productions. Ray's main contribution, other than his directing, was the casting. He had not chosen the subject, although it was very consistent with his sense of social consciousness, and he was consulted very little concerning the script. Consequently, the film is very different from *They Live by Night.* It is simple and straightforward and lacks the lyricism and subtlety of Ray's first film. Much of the film plays like a didactic sociological tract, espousing older prewar theories of delinquency that were now being supplemented by newer and different theories. The film is consistent with the theories of Clifford Shaw and Henry McKay. In the late '20s and '30s, they stated that delinquency reflected a geographical pattern. It proliferated in areas of high crime, social and urban disorganization, and a large immigrant population. Also, delinquency was not differentiated from other types of criminal behavior but was one stage in the developmental cycle of a criminal progressing toward increasingly serious crimes. The film conjures up juvenile delinquency films of the '30s (e.g., *Dead End*). Nevertheless, *Knock on Any Door* is film noir in its use of flashbacks, its emphasis on environmental determinism, the stark urban sets of city streets and tenements, and in the fatalism of its immortal line about living rapidly, dying early and still looking good in death.

Knock on Any Door tells the story of Nick Romano (John Derek), a juvenile delinquent with a record of petty crime, who is tried for the murder of a policeman killed during a robbery. Via flashbacks, the causes for Romano's criminal behavior are explored: poverty, no father, the oppression and vicissitudes of slum life. Nick's attempts to reform fail; his desperate and pregnant wife commits suicide; and, blinded with grief and rage, Nick commits robbery and murder. His lawyer makes a passionate speech to the jury, emphasizing how Nick's environment, immigrant background, reform school, and an indifferent society shaped Nick from a potentially good person into the criminal he became. Nevertheless, Nick is found guilty and sentenced to die. With an air of resignation, the lawyer observes that we all share Nick's guilt, that he could have risen rather than fallen, and that we can find him behind any door.

VI

City Across the River was also released in 1949. It was adapted by Irving Shulman from his novel *The Amboy Dukes.* (Shulman also wrote the novel on which *Cry Tough* was based as well as one of the initial screenplays for *Rebel Without a Cause.*) Maxwell Shane wrote the screenplay and directed the film. The film covers some of the same territory as *Knock on Any Door* but also anticipates some of the themes of the juvenile delinquency films of the '50s. The film opens with an introductory statement by newspaper columnist Drew Pearson:

> The city where juvenile crime flourishes always seems to be the City Across the River [Brooklyn, which is across the East River from Manhattan]. But don't kid yourself—it could be your city, your state, your house. It could just as well happen in any other large city where slum conditions undermine personal security and take their toll in juvenile delinquency.

The film tells the story of Frankie Cusack, who, according to Pearson, is "going down a confused road toward gangsterdom, toward murder." Frankie lives in a Brooklyn tenement. Both of his parents work, and Frankie spends his unsupervised free time with a gang of juvenile delinquents, the Dukes. At first reluctant to involve himself in the gang's criminal activities, he eventually becomes incorporated into the gang as a result of peer pressure and rebellion against his poor living conditions. His parents, concerned at Frankie's drift, try to buy a house in a suburb well away from Brooklyn, but his mother becomes sick, and the house money has to be used to pay medical bills. Frankie eventually becomes involved in the accidental shooting of a teacher and a friend and is apprehended by the police.

City Across the River is similar to *Knock on Any Door* in terms of its reflecting older theories which viewed juvenile delinquency as a product of urban slum life (witness the parents' attempt to move to the safety of the suburbs, away from the zone of social disorganization) and a stage in the progression to more serious crimes (hooliganism to murder). *City Across the River* is a film noir: a strong sense of environmental determinism permeates the film and there is some nice noir photography (city scenes, rain-slickened streets, flashing neon signs). However, in important respects, it is a much more complex and forward-looking film than *Knock on Any Door* in its reflection of the emerging post–World War II treatment of juvenile delinquency. It was the first juvenile delinquency film to deal with organized gangs, which emerged fully into public consciousness and became staple fare for films in the '50s. Drew Pearson's allusion to juvenile delinquency as occurring anywhere also anticipated '50s themes, which took delinquency into middle-class suburbs (although, in the same sentence, Pearson harks back to delinquency as being a product of the urban slums). The film reflected newer theories that viewed juvenile delinquency as a product of family disorganization. Both of Frankie's parents worked and so were not available much of the time to provide guidance and act as role models. The film also alludes to Robert Merton's theory that juvenile delinquency was a plausible, if maladaptive, response to the disparity between youthful aspirations and reality. For those denied access to the American dream, juvenile delinquency filled the gap. Early in the film, Frankie takes his younger sister to Manhattan. They stare in amazement, awe, and envy at the splendors that are unfolded before them. It is after this that Frankie develops a chip on his shoulder and becomes fully enmeshed in gang life, realizing that those good things are beyond his grasp.

VII

The '50s marked an important transition in the treatment of juvenile delinquency, by society, sociological theory, and films. In a sense, the '50s marked what can be called a Golden Age of juvenile delinquency, in terms of significant increases in its frequency, emergence of new types, and the concern and attention paid to it by the public and the various media. Beginning in 1948, the incidence of juvenile delinquency rose significantly faster than the increase of juveniles in the population. The number of cases more than doubled, while the number of juveniles increased by only about 20 percent. Articles in the media and comments by various officials gave the impression of rampant juvenile delinquency throughout America. (Later researchers suggested that the extent of this juvenile crime wave was greatly exaggerated.) The number of articles on juvenile delinquency referenced in *Readers Guide to Periodical Literature* increased five-fold between 1951 and 1957. There was a similar explosion in literature.

The '50s also ushered in a "new" juvenile delinquency. This new delinquency was a product of the rapid and profound changes in all levels of society which occurred during World War II and the postwar years: technological and cultural changes; demographic shifts in population; pressure on the family; urbanization and suburbanization; changing populations in schools; increased affluence; the rise of mass media, especially television; increased mobility; and relaxation of older moral standards. In society, these changes were correlated with new forms of delinquency, and old forms became much more common and vicious: auto theft, gang rumbles, drugs and alcoholism, matricide and patricide, sexual offenses, vandalism, etc. Additionally, delinquency moved visibly beyond the borders of urban slums into suburbia and the middle classes. All of these changes occurred in the context of an emerging youth culture which viewed itself as separate and distinct from—and often hostile and opposed to—adult society. With its own music, dress, interests, outlook on life, and code of conduct, a populous and influential constituency had emerged. Juvenile delinquency was viewed as a subculture within the larger youth culture.

The motion picture industry was certainly aware of these changing trends in delinquency and of the public's concern. A potentially vast audience of concerned adults and youths existed for these films. The era and social climate were right for the release of films which dealt with this new delinquency. There were three films which best captured the themes of the new delinquency during the '50s: *The Wild One* (1953), *The Blackboard Jungle* (1955), and *Rebel Without a Cause* (1955).

The interest in juvenile delinquency by film noir, which was slight during the '40s, was nearly nonexistent in the '50s. Only one film was produced, *Cry Tough,* which was released during the last year of film noir's existence, 1959. The '50s marked the beginning of the decline of film noir. Increasingly fewer films were produced. Many continued to deal with the same themes addressed during the '40s. Others were more topical, like *Kiss Me, Deadly* (1955), the most significant film noir of the '50s, which reflected changes in America in the '50s by dealing with the cold war and its attendant paranoia. However, by the end of the decade, only a handful of films noirs were produced. Like any art form, it was the victim of a natural demise over time, as society and the tastes of the public changed.

Influences of film noir can be seen in the juvenile delinquency films of the '50s. However, these may well have been unintentional and even coincidental. The three key juvenile delinquency films of the '50s are clearly not films noirs. I expect that a number of the same factors that led to delinquency being largely ignored by film noir in the '40s were operative during the '50s. Also, since many fewer films noirs were produced, there was much less opportunity for juvenile delinquency films noirs to be made. But, primarily, the themes that characterized expression of the new delinquency were largely incompatible with film noir and required expression via a new sensibility.

In producing juvenile delinquency films the motion picture industry faced a dilemma. Movies needed to be palatable for their opposing audiences of adults and juveniles. The films also had to remain within the moral guidelines dictated by the Motion Picture Production Code, even though many juvenile behaviors were outside that code (Gilbert, 1986).

VIII

The first of the key films, *The Wild One,* was released in 1953. It was produced by Stanley Kramer, directed by Laslo Benedek, and written by John Paxton. The film deals with the effects and repercussions of the invasion and occupation of a small California town by two motorcycle gangs. The film was based on an actual incident in which a biker gang took over Hollister, California, in 1947 and destroyed it.

The gangs are led by Johnny (Marlon Brando) and Chino (Lee Marvin). Like the characters in *They Live by Night,* the individuals in *The Wild One* are not teenagers but young adults in their twenties and thirties. However, the film is included in this essay because it dealt with a form of the new delinquency, biker gangs, and, most importantly, because the film introduced themes that were central to later juvenile delinquency films of the '50s. The primary theme of *The Wild One* is the conflict and antagonism between the bikers and society, as represented by the decent townspeople and police. The contempt each has for the others' values is apparent from the bikers' willful disruption of the town, their utter disrespect for its citizens, and the disparaging observations each makes about the other. When a biker with the initials BRMC on the back of his leather jacket is asked what it means, he replies Black Rebels Motorcycle Club. When Brando is then asked what he is rebelling against, he asks what they have. The filmmakers trod the fine line of appealing to its disparate audiences of youths and adults and adhering to the Moral Code. At the beginning of the film a printed statement warns that the shocking events about to unfold are a challenge to the public to ensure that they never happen again. At the end of the film, the police restore law and order and run the bikers out of town, but not before sternly lecturing Brando that they don't understand him at all and think he is both stupid and lacking any insight or character.

(Ironically, though, the statement serves only to emphasize the gulf between the youth and adult cultures and the lack of understanding between the two.)

Yet, it is apparent that, consciously or unconsciously, the sympathies of the film lay with the bikers. This is most obvious in casting Marlon Brando in the lead role. Brando's brilliant, compelling, and charismatic performance provided a model of the alienated hero of the '50s. (The famous poster of Brando sitting on his bike hung on the walls of many a youth, this author included.) On the one hand, he is "bad"—but bad in a seductive and alluring way: a born leader; tough and sullen, but also sensitive and vulnerable; an accomplished street fighter; irresistible to women; a young man who goes his own way and defies an uncomprehending and stuffy society. Brando's portrayal became an icon of the alienated and disaffected youth culture and paved the way for the other two key films of the '50s, *The Blackboard Jungle* and *Rebel Without a Cause*.

The Wild One reflects some influences of film noir (Brando's voice-over at the film's beginning, the black and white photography, a sense of menace, and Brando's alienation); however, it is most definitely not a film noir. *The Wild One* marked the turn of the juvenile delinquency film away from any direct connection with the philosophy of film noir and steered it in a direction toward social melodrama. The more personal themes of individual anxiety, anguish, and the strong sense of environmental determinism that appeared at least enough in the juvenile delinquency films of the '40s to qualify them as film noir were now replaced with broader themes of the clash between two cultures.

IX

The Blackboard Jungle was released in 1955. It was written and directed by Richard Brooks and based on the novel by Evan Hunter. In a few respects, the film harks back to the juvenile delinquency films of the earlier era. It takes place in a lower-class urban technical-trade all-male high school. It reflected older sociological theories that focused on the breakdown of the home caused by the war. A policeman intones that they were children during World War II. Their fathers were in the army and their mothers worked. They had no life at home or in the church or any place they could go. So they formed gangs, and gang leaders became their parents.

However, the film is right on the mark in expressing, like *The Wild One*, the clash between the emerging youth culture and adults, as seen in the ongoing conflict between the teachers and administration and the students who do not want to be there. The film accomplishes this more pointedly and convincingly than does *The Wild One*. By taking place in an urban environment, the characters and situations can be more easily identified with. The music reflects the youth culture's music. The credits unfold to Bill Haley and the Comets' *Rock Around the Clock*, a rock and roll anthem. The song's call to "rock around the clock tonight" obviously promotes an ethic of pleasure counter to the Puritan work ethic of adult society. In a key scene, a teacher brings his prized collection of jazz records to play for the students. The students loathe him, his music, and his values. They cruelly destroy his irreplaceable collection, and he is left to mutter, "I don't understand, I just don't understand." The students have their own music and their own values and culture.

The film, like *The Wild One*, has the obligatory warning at the beginning on public concern about the causes and effects of juvenile delinquency, especially as it affects schools, and the need for public awareness as the preamble to solving the problem. And an upbeat ending: The two hard case and incorrigible delinquents are subjugated and expelled and the other students are won over and become productive and hardworking students.

However, the lure and seductiveness of the defiance and opposition to the adult culture by the delinquents was unmistakable and irresistible (a situation not at all unlike that of white culture's attraction to the ominous themes of violence and misogyny of rap music). Youths in the audience repeatedly danced in the aisles and cheered the defiance, violence, and terror inflicted by the students on the administration and teachers. The film was a box office success and aroused significant and widespread opposition and alarm among adults.

Of the three key juvenile delinquent films of the '50s, *The Blackboard Jungle* comes closest to evoking film noir. It features a bleak urban setting, black and white photography, odd camera angles, wet streets, and film noir icon Glenn Ford in the title role. However, for the same reasons as *The Wild One*, *The Blackboard Jungle* is not film noir, but, rather, serves to emphasize the divergence between film noir of the '50s and the treatment of juvenile delinquency in films.

X

The most famous and influential juvenile delinquency film of the '50s, *Rebel Without a Cause,* was released shortly after *The Blackboard Jungle.* The title came from a book written by Robert Lindner in 1944, a study of imprisoned psychopaths. Nicholas Ray, who identified powerfully with the problems of youth, sold Warner Brothers a treatment about middle-class juvenile delinquency called *Blind Run.* Warner's took Lindner's title and set about to develop a screenplay. The first two attempts, by novelists Leon Uris and Irving Shulman, were unsuccessful, although Shulman used his screenplay as the basis for his 1956 book, *Children of the Dark.* The third writer, Stewart Stern, successfully completed the screenplay in twelve weeks. [I had the distinct pleasure of interviewing Stewart Stern at his home in Seattle, Washington, in September 1997. Several of his recollections about the film and his screenplay are incorporated into the following discussion.]

Rebel Without a Cause broke new ground in the treatment of juvenile delinquency. It was the first study of delinquency in middle-class suburbs rather than urban slums. This reflects the emergence of middle-class delinquency in the '50s, as a manifestation of the "new" delinquency. It is emphasized in the film by the conflicts between the middle-class youths, dressed in sport coat and tie or dresses, and the more traditional hoodlum types from the other side of the tracks, who dress in jeans, T-shirts, and black leather jackets.

The sympathies of the film lay wholly with its three protagonists, played by James Dean, Sal Mineo, and Natalie Wood. The sources of their problems and delinquent behavior reside in the dysfunctional family relationship each has and in their search for an emotionally fulfilling, warm, and secure family life. Dean's meek father is dominated by his mother, who is also highly critical of Dean. Wood seeks the love of her father and has to contend with a jealous mother. Mineo lives with his divorced mother and is ignored by her and by his absent father. In a touching scene in an abandoned house, the three attempt to form a family, an attempt that is short-lived and ends in tragedy. It is the despair and unhappiness with their family life that leads the three youths to search for fulfillment outside their families and in delinquency. This alienation is reinforced by two key scenes in the Griffith Park planetarium. A lecture on the universe concludes with the statement that humans existing by themselves are but a passing episode of little import. At the end of the film, Dean and Mineo discuss the end of the world, and, shortly after, Mineo is killed by the police.

The film does emphasize the toll extracted by delinquent behavior, primarily the tragic deaths of Mineo and of another youth in a car during a "chickie run". However, the blame for such behavior is placed squarely on uncomprehending, unfeeling, and unsympathetic adults and society. Audience sympathy for the youths was also no doubt immeasurably enhanced by the appealing and brilliant performances of the three leads, especially the charismatic James Dean.

Rebel Without a Cause is also unusual among juvenile delinquency films for its exploration of intimacy and affection among male youths. The affection and feeling between Mineo and Dean aroused concern among Code authorities about homosexual overtones, and, even today, homosexual allusions are mistakenly drawn (see, for example, the 1995 film *The Celluloid Closet*). I asked Stewart Stern about this, and he replied:

> The film came out at a time where the relationships between men were highly charged and sentimentalized by the war. For example, the act of putting up a pup tent, which was only wide enough to accommodate two bodies sleeping very close. Buddies in war time trained together, fought together, were loyal to each other, were brave for each other. The army encouraged a type of loyalty that slopped into love. But I cannot even imagine it [Mineo's and Dean's relationship] becoming a sexual incident. It was an intensely possessive and romantic relationship.

Rebel Without a Cause also emphasizes how far the treatment of juvenile delinquency in films had diverged from the sensibilities of film noir. The film does seem to have some noir aspects. It was shot on location in Los Angeles, the noir icon of urban settings. It was originally shot in black and white. (According to Stewart Stern, ten days of black-and-white shooting had been completed before it was discovered that the terms of renting the Cinemascope equipment required that the film be shot in color. Apparently, the new technology was not to be associated with an old form.) The alienation of the characters is apparent, and the film does have tragedy. However, the expression of this alienation and tragedy is quite different from its treatment by film noir. Like the other juvenile delinquency films of the

'50s, *Rebel Without a Cause* is more appropriately a social drama than film noir. When I asked Stewart Stern if his screenplay was at all influenced by film noir, he emphatically replied that it was not. At the time, he said, he did not know what film noir was. Rather, the film was influenced by his wartime experiences and other writers and directors whom he especially admired (Tennessee Williams, Paddy Chayefsky, William Inge, Horton Foote, Tad Mosel, Vittorio De Sica and Fred Zinneman).

XI

Cry Tough, the last of the juvenile delinquency films noirs, is a curious film. It was released in 1959, the last year of film noir. Although released nearly five years after *Rebel Without a Cause,* the film more appropriately belongs with the juvenile delinquency films noirs of a decade earlier. The film was adapted from Irving Shulman's book, written in 1949. Like *City Across the River* and *Knock on Any Door, Cry Tough* deals with the frustrations of tenement life and turning to crime as a way of coping and finding one's way out. Miguel Estrada (John Saxon) vows to go straight just after being released from prison. He meets Sarita, an ambitious illegal Cuban immigrant. She is arrested by immigration authorities. Miguel procures Sarita's bail through the intervention of the crooked Carlos, in exchange for a promise to commit a crime. The combination of Miguel's desire to escape the barrio, his frustration and anger at his lot in life, his reinvolvement in crime, and Sarita's goading him to take her away from the barrio prove lethal. Miguel plans a bold robbery, which is botched. In attempting to escape, Miguel is killed.

    Cry Tough is a film noir because of its urban slum environment, its strong sense of environmental determinism, and Miguel's involvement with the femme fatale, Sarita. Although similar to *Knock on Any Door* and *City Across the River, Cry Tough* explored new issues. The film was the only film noir to deal with Latino society in America. The film takes place in the Puerto Rican barrio in Spanish Harlem, Little Spain, and has a rich ethnic flavor. Older theories of juvenile delinquency had attributed its occurrence in immigrant communities to their lack of self-supporting elements of community order and the disorganization of urban life. Later theories of the mid-'50s (e.g., Albert Cohen's) viewed juvenile delinquency and gang behavior in immigrant communities not as an absence of social order (racial bias on the part of white sociologists?), but the wrong kind of order. In *Cry Tough* Puerto Rican society is accurately portrayed as highly organized, with a strong work ethic and desire to succeed. As in white society, juvenile delinquents existed as a subculture responding to the limited opportunities and frustrations of living in that culture.

Looking retrospectively at the treatment of juvenile delinquency by film noir, it is regrettable that more such films were not made during the '40s, when sociological theory and the philosophy of film noir were so consistent. The films noirs that were made were interesting, compelling, and revealing of what it was like to be a juvenile delinquent in the delinquent environment and subculture, and the whole issue of juvenile delinquency could have been enriched by more such films. By the '50s, sociological theory and film's treatment of juvenile delinquency had diverged from a dying film noir's world view, and so film noir really had little more to contribute.

Bibliography

Appel, Alfred. Nabokov's Dark Cinema. New York: Oxford University Press, 1974.

Eisenschitz, Bernard. Nicholas Ray: An American Journey. Boston: Faber & Faber, 1993.

Gilbert, James. A Cycle of Outrage. New York: Oxford University Press, 1986.

Lunden, Walter A. Statistics on Juvenile Delinquency. Springfield, Ill.: Charles C. Thomas, 1964.

Miller, Laurence. "Evidence for a British Film Noir Cycle." In Dixon, Wheeler and Winston, Eds. Re-Viewing British Cinema, 1900–1992. New York: State University Press, 1994.

———. Interview with Stewart Stern. Conducted by Laurence Miller, Seattle, Wash., September, 1997.

Filmography

They Live by Night Released by RKO, 1949. Produced by John Houseman. Directed by Nicholas Ray. Cinematography by George E. Diskant. Screenplay by Charles Schnee, from the novel *Thieves Like Us* by Edward Anderson. Cast: Cathy O'Donnell (Keechie), Farley Granger (Bowie), Howard da Silva (Chickamaw), Jay C. Flippen (T-Dub), Will Wright (Mobley), Marie Bryant (Singer).

Knock on Any Door Released by Santana Productions, 1949. Produced by Robert Lord. Directed by Nicholas Ray. Cinematography by Burnett Guffey. Screenplay by Daniel Taradash and John Monks, Jr., from the novel by Willard Motley. Cast: Humphrey Bogart (Andrew Morton), John Derek (Nick Romano), George Macready (District Attorney Kerman), Allene Roberts (Emma), Susan Perry (Adele), Mickey Knox (Vito), Barry Kelley (Judge Drake).

City Across the River Released by Universal, 1949. Produced by Maxwell Shane. Directed by Maxwell Shane. Cinematography by Maury Gertsman. Screenplay by Maxwell Shane, Dennis Cooper and Irving Shulman, from the novel *The Amboy Dukes* by Shulman. Cast: Stephen McNally (Stan Albert), Thelma Ritter (Mrs. Cusack), Luis Van Rooten (Joe Cusack), Jeff Corey (Lt. Macon), Sharon McManus (Alice Cusack), Sue England (Betty), Barbara Whiting (Annie Kane), Richard Benedict (Gaggsy Steens), Peter Fernandez (Frank Cusack), Richard Jaeckel (Bull), Anthony (Tony) Curtis (Mitch).

The Wild One Released by Columbia, 1953. Produced by Stanley Kramer. Directed by Laslo Benedek. Cinematography by Hal Mohr. Screenplay by John Paxton, based on a story by Frank Rooney. Cast: Marlon Brando (Johnny), Mary Murphy (Kathie), Robert Keith (Harry Bleeker), Lee Marvin (Chino), Jay C. Flippen (Sheriff Singer).

The Blackboard Jungle Released by Metro-Goldwyn-Mayer, 1955. Produced by Pandro S. Berman. Directed by Richard Brooks. Cinematography by Russell Harlan. Screenplay by Richard Brooks, from the novel by Evan Hunter. Cast: Glenn Ford (Richard Dadier), Anne Francis (Anne Dadier), Louis Calhern (Jim Murdock), Margaret Hayes (Lois Hammond), John Hoyt (Mr. Warneke), Richard Kiley (Joshua Edwards), Emile Meyer (Mr. Halloran), Horace McMahon (Detective), Sidney Poitier (Gregory Miller), Vic Morrow (Artie West), Rafael Campos (Pete Morales).

Rebel Without a Cause Released by Warner Brothers, 1955. Produced by David Weisbart. Directed by Nicholas Ray. Cinematography by Ernest Haller (cinemascope, Warner Color). Screenplay by Stewart Stern. Cast: James Dean (Jim), Natalie Wood (Judy), Sal Mineo (Plato), Jim Backus (Jim's Father), Ann Doran (Jim's Mother), Corey Allan (Buzz), William Hopper (Judy's Father), Rochelle Hudson (Judy's Mother), Nick Adams (Moose), Dennis Hopper (Goon), Edward Platt (Policeman).

Cry Tough Released by United Artists, 1959. Produced by Harry Kleiner. Directed by Paul Stanley. Cinematography by Philip Lathrop. Screenplay by Harry Kleiner, from the novel by Irving Shulman. Cast: John Saxon (Miguel Estrada), Linda Cristal (Sarita), Joseph Calleia (Senor Estrada), Joe De Santis (Cortez), Harry Townes (Carlos).

Chapter 5
Formal Education as a Lyrical Target: Images of Schooling in Popular Music, 1955–1980

B. Lee Cooper,
Reinhardt College

I. Introduction

Formal education constitutes a key foe for angry rap chanters and aggressive heavy metal headbangers. Their words depicting school experiences are invariably harsh. But '90s lyrical indictments of teachers, principals, and curricula as unresponsive, unintelligible, and irrelevant can be traced to the earliest rock performers. In fact, throughout the first quarter century of the post–Big Band Era (1955–1980), audio portrayals of junior and senior high school experiences ranged from mockery to rage. With ancestral roots as deep as Chuck Berry and images as vitriolic as those vocalized by Pink Floyd, it is little wonder that present-day singers and songwriters continue to deride public schooling. The following commentary provides a detailed analysis of recordings from the early Rock Era that illustrate adolescent disenchantment with institutionalized learning.

Despite the cacophony of criticisms from many reform-minded pressure groups, observations from one key group—students, the subject of the whole educational enterprise—are generally ignored. But youth has not remained mute. Scholars simply have not applied their critical skills to a wide enough variety of resources on this issue. Popular music, a principal artifact of youth culture, gives voice to a broad range of concerns, values, and priorities of young people. A thorough analysis of scores of popular songs demonstrates that lyrics consistently depict formal schooling as dehumanizing, irrelevant, alienating, laughable, isolating, and totally unworthy of any link with the Socratic tradition (Butchart and Cooper, 1987; Cooper, 1984). Some might argue, of course, that popular music does not actually reflect the perceptions of the audience per se. Most hit tunes, after all, are not written by students. Pop recordings are simply products of market devices. But lyricists and singers are clearly the troubadours of contemporary young people. To claim that they do not represent student perceptions because they are no longer students themselves is equivalent to arguing that balladeers of medieval Europe did not reflect the culture of courtly society because they were not part of the aristocracy. Troubadours in any age are honored precisely *because* their musical messages resound with the values and imagination of their audience. Indeed, modern troubadours are probably better mirrors of the culture in whose name they sing than their feudal predecessors. Unlike minstrels of old, modern rock musicians, although no longer students when they write or perform their music, have actually been in the classroom. Their medieval counterparts were never aristocrats.

Popular music has not always portrayed schooling in a negative way. Education appeared less frequently as a theme in the pre–Rock Era, but, when it did, lyrics were usually nostalgic, as in "School Days" or "In the Little Red School House." In addition, earlier education themes were generally oriented toward college students, even though only a small proportion of young people attended universities prior to 1950. From the 1906 recording of "College Life," through "Collegiate," "The Varsity Drag," "Betty Co-Ed," "The Sweetheart of Sigma Chi," to "The Whiffenpoof Song" in 1936, early popular music dealing with education emphasized the carefree joys of campus social life. Ironically, in an age when university attendance has become the norm, very few rock songs deal with college life. Most focus exclusively on public school experiences, particularly on secondary schooling (Butchart and Cooper, 1987). And, with very few exceptions—the Arbors' "Graduation Day" and the Beach Boys' "Be True to Your School"—the sentiments communicated are anything but nostalgic.

II. Images of Schools

"School days, school days,
Dear old golden rule days,
Readin' and writin' and 'rithmatic,
Taught to the tune of a hickory stick."

Sentiments of good times, firm discipline, and inculcation of basic communication and computation skills featured in the traditional tune "School Days" represent learning perceptions from another era. Whether accurate or inaccurate, realistic or idealistic, this song came to symbolize formal education during the early twentieth century. But, as Bob Dylan noted during the '60s, "the times they are a-changin.'" In 1954, the U.S. Supreme Court ordered American education to cease the practice of utilizing racially segregated, "separate but equal" learning arenas. But the integration of public schools wasn't the only revolution occurring in mid-'50s America. Currents of popular music were also beginning to flow more swiftly. The rock 'n' roll floodtide emerged when country music tunes and rhythm and blues songs found synthesizing spokesmen in Bill Haley, Otis Williams, Elvis Presley, Chuck Berry, Carl Perkins, and Jerry Lee Lewis. This popular music rampage, aided by influential disc jockeys, several technological recording inventions, motion picture hype (Blackboard Jungle), and improved record company promotional techniques, launched a fundamental change in America's musical tastes as well as in lyrical imagery (Friedlander, 1996; Hibbard and Kaleialoha, 1983).

As the Rock Era evolved, it enlisted more and more singers and songwriters who were drawn from and remained committed to youthful values (Goodall, 1991). Observations, ideals, and images contained in their songs were uncompromisingly student-oriented. This meant that public schools, the physical setting for so much teenage activity, were scrutinized, analyzed, and depicted in numerous song lyrics. The impact of this audio examination of American schooling is eminently clear—and staggering. Internal verification of current educational practices replaced external expectations and historic ideals concerning the nature of the learning enterprise. Neither truth nor reality could be guaranteed by this change in perspective and commentators. However, viewpoints drawn from actual student experience were undeniably sharper in assessing the behavior of principals, teachers, PTAs, student groups, and individual learners than the more theoretical observations offered by educational philosophers or other public school analysts (Cooper, 1983–84; Cooper, 1991).

No systematic, comprehensive statement of public school criticism can be found in the grooves of popular recordings (Butchart and Cooper, 1987). Nevertheless, several key ideas are present. Between 1955 and 1980, previously dominant preachment and pretense images of schooling were directly challenged. Lyrical idealism was not totally absent, of course. Admiration for teachers who were bright, deeply committed to learning, concerned about pupils, and engaged in a constant battle to overcome ignorance was eulogized in tunes like "To Sir With Love" and "Welcome Back." But a much more critical tone dominates the majority of lyrical commentaries about schooling. Teachers are generally condemned for being ignorant of student feelings ("Bird Dog"), for pursuing irrelevant classroom topics ("Wonderful World"), for corrupting student idealism ("The Logical Song"), and for intentionally stifling the development of pupils' social and political awareness ("Another Brick in the Wall"). It is difficult to imagine a more blatant denunciation of the entire educational system than Paul Simon's introductory phrases in "Kodachrome," where he dismisses his high school learning as "crap," marvels that he can still think, and ends with an ungrammatical claim that his ignorance doesn't prevent him from seeing "writing on the wall."

III. Definitions about Schooling

In order to illustrate the image of American public education present in popular music lyrics during the first quarter century of the Rock Era, it is necessary to isolate and define several key elements directly related to the formal schooling process. The following definitions govern the use of terminology in this study:

> *School:* the physical building (classrooms, hallways, cafeteria, restrooms, library, administrative offices, and teacher lounges) and the total potential learning environment available to students (special meetings and annual ceremonies, organization of school personnel, and institutional heritage).

Students: a group of young people ranging from 14 to 18 years old, both male and female, predominantly American, in all physical shapes, sizes, and psychological dimensions, from different ethnic, religious, and socio-economic groups.

Teachers: a group of adults ranging in ages from 22 to 65 years, both male and female, predominantly American, in all physical shapes, sizes, and psychological dimensions; primarily middle class, mostly white and Protestant, possessing at least four years of college education.

Principals: the chief administrative officers in the schools possessing at least five years of college education and several years of classroom teaching experience; a group of adults ranging in age from 30 to 65 years, predominately white, male, middle-class, Protestant, and American; in all physical shapes, sizes, and psychological dimensions.

Parents: adult men and women, mostly married, ranging in age from 32 to 55, of different ethnic backgrounds, religions, and social and economic conditions, political persuasions, and personal interests.

Community: the geographic area which constitutes the primary dwelling place for parents and students and for the vast majority of teachers and principals; it is also the site of the school.

Education: the primary goals of public education are transmitting factual knowledge, fostering socialization, and preparing students for democratic citizenship; teachers conduct a variety of learning activities under the administrative supervision of principals, with community involvement by individual parents and parent-teacher organizations.

Beyond defining these seven elements of American public education, it is also necessary to identify three perceptual perspectives in order to assess activities within the formal schooling environment:

Preachment: the ideals or highest goals of a social organization or of any person associated with that organization.

Pretense: justifications of specific actions within a social organization which are not functionally appropriate to furthering the ideals of that organization; a shadowy dimension of shifting personal attitudes and physical behaviors located between the zones of idealized preachment and actual practice.

Practice: activities which constitute the hour-by-hour, day-to-day operations of a social organization.

All seven elements within the formal schooling process—schools, students, teachers, principals, parents, the community, and education—are frequently depicted in early Rock Era songs. As might be predicted, most lyrical comments are directly related to personal involvement in real (practice) rather than ideal (preachment) school situations. Although practice may be more visible and more individually identifiable, many songs do contain lyrical segments which allude to all three dimensions. Based upon an impressionistic lyrical review, Table A illustrates the broad perspectives of formal education which exist in the analyzed popular recordings (Cooper, 1984). The radical divergence between preachment/pretense and practice was so sharp, according to most 1955–1980 lyrical commentaries, that one wonders if the American public school system might be malfunctioning.

Table A: Terms Illustrating Preachment, Pretense and Practice Imagery
about American Public Education in the Lyrics of Popular Songs, 1955–1980

Area of Lyrical Commentary	Preachment Images	Pretense Images	Practice Images
1. School	Human development	Alma mater	Separation from life
	Cultural repository	School loyalty	Isolation from peers
	Knowledge resource	Commencement	Irrelevance
	Civic center	Honor code	Social interaction
2. Students	Inquiry	Questioning	Friends, dancers
	Reflection	Participation	Clowns, romancers
	Rationality	Investigating	Victims, gangs
3. Teachers	Mentors	Friends	Baby-sitters
	Models	Counselors	Fools
4. Principals	Learning leader	Chief administrator	Authoritarian
	Experienced educator	Responsibility	Irresponsible
5. Parents	Loving concern	Guiding hands	Misunderstanding
	Family stability	Mature guides	Interference
6. Community	Democracy	Due process	Conformity
	Participation	Socialization	Hypocrisy

(Continued on next page)

Table A (*Continued*): Terms Illustrating Preachment, Pretense and Practice Imagery about American Public Education in the Lyrics of Popular Songs, 1955–1980,

Area of Lyrical Commentary	Preachment Images	Pretense Images	Practice Images
7. *Education*	Wisdom	Information	Regimentation
	Knowledge	Citizenship	Indoctrination
	Understanding	Decision-making	Illiteracy
	Freedom	Communication	Cynicism
	Creativity	Stability	Fear
	Diversity	Cooperation	Hostility

Lyrical images of American public education are lively, colorful, direct, and generally critical. A brief review of recorded commentaries on each of the seven elements of the formal schooling process follows.

IV. More Images of Schools

"School" is dually depicted as a state of mind as well as a physical entity. A few songs beckon students to recall "(Remember the Days of the) Old School Yard." Cat Stevens' nostalgic reverie is echoed by 18 spirited versions of "High School U.S.A." (created by grafting names of various metropolitan-area high schools into the lyrics) and recorded by Tommy Faceda, as well as by the Beach Boys' loyalty hymn "Be True to Your School," and by the Arbors' nostalgic "Graduation Day." But these tunes are atypical of the genre (Cooper, 1986). The majority of lyrics portraying school life portray the buildings and grounds as a series of sinister, segregated compartments which dictate varying kinds of student behavior.

The classroom is generally depicted as the dictatorial domain of a teaching tyrant who doesn't realize how mean her looks are, as Chuck Berry snorts in "School Day." Activities which occur in classrooms are conducted in lock-step, intimidating, teacher-directed fashion. A student like the Coasters' "Charlie Brown" may walk into the classroom cool and slow, but then he'd better become quiet, orderly, and without guile. By contrast, the hallways are always alive with noise. Rigidly enforced classroom silence and cerebral irrelevance give way to cacophonous peer chatter and delirious social interaction. Discussions of cars, sex, smokes, food, films, and immediate wants and needs occur in the jostling, locker-slamming hallway atmosphere. School corridors also lead to freedom (". . . down the hall and into the street" ["School Day"]); to a secret cigarette break in the restroom ("Smokin' in the Boys Room"); to a luncheon record hop ("High School Dance"); to more private activities in outdoor recreation areas ("Me and Julio Down in the Schoolyard"); and to the parking lot filled with decorated cars and vans. The key word to describe most lyrical observations about the school building is—escape. Even those songs which laud memories of bygone secondary school experiences, such as Adrian Kimberly's "Pomp and Circumstance, " praise commencement as the eternal relief felt by all alumni. This escapist theme is also clearly delineated in songs that depict the annual freedom period from June through August: Gary U.S. Bonds' "School Is Out," the Jamies' "Summertime, Summertime," and Alice Cooper's "School's Out."

V. Images of Students

Lyrical images of students vary greatly. Clear recognition of peer pressures and special interest groups within each school is illustrated in the Beach Boys' "I Get Around," Dobie Gray's "In Crowd," and Connie Frances' "Where the Boys Are." The isolation of nonconforming individuals and out-groups is depicted in The Crystals' "He's a Rebel," The Shangri-Las' "Leader of the Pack," Carol Jarvis' "Rebel," and Janis Ian's "At Seventeen" and "Society's Child." Although they comprise the most heterogeneous group within the public educational system, students are lyrically characterized as the least franchised ("Summertime Blues"), most harassed ("Yackety Yak"), most regimented ("Another Brick in the Wall"), least trusted ("Smokin' in the Boy's Room"), most humorous ("Charlie Brown" and "My Boy Flat Top"), most victimized ("My Generation" and "Society's Child"), and least understood ("It Hurts to Be Sixteen" and "You and Me Against the World").

Students are usually described as physically active and singularly non-contemplative. In fact, as Sam Cooke declared in his 1960 hit "Wonderful World," the typical romantic high school youth boasts (in parallel double negatives) about his ignorance of history, biology, a science book, and French. Nearly two decades later, Art Garfunkel, Paul Simon, and James Taylor revived Cooke's "(What a) Wonderful World" with yet another anti-intellectual refrain, adding the Middle Ages, the Rise and Fall, and "nothin' at all" to the areas of ignorance.

This sense of educational futility is a dominant element in popular lyrics. Paul Simon's 1973 song "Kodachrome," which begins with a stunning indictment of academic irrelevance, was followed three years later by an even more negative analysis of post–high school life in "Still Crazy After All These Years." This self-assessment was shared with a former high school girlfriend. Several other songs also capture poignant vignettes of post–high school reflections. Tunes like Bob Seger's "2 + 2 = ?" explore the meaning of a school friend's senseless death in Vietnam; Alice Cooper's "Eighteen" examines the "I'm a boy, but I'm a man" predicament of a recent high school graduate; and Bob Dylan's "Subterranean Homesick Blues" presents an image of an illogical, mean-spirited society which awaits formally educated, but non-streetwise youngsters.

VI. Images of Teachers and Principals

Adults who control the environment within public schools are neither admired nor respected. Even those few songs which praise individual teachers—"Mr Lee" by The Bobbettes, "To Sir With Love" by Lulu, and "Abigail Beecher" by Freddy Cannon—offer sharp, derogatory contrasts between the caring behavior and independent actions of their favored instructors and the general demeanor of the majority of teachers who are boobs, bumpkins, and boors. Chuck Berry, the Coasters, The Who, Janis Ian, Paul Simon, and dozens of other singers reinforce the simple message chanted by Pink Floyd in his ungrammatical warning to teachers to "leave them kids alone!"

If teachers are fools, antiquarians, babysitters, arbitrary actors, and persons generally out of touch with reality, principals are outright villains with malevolent motives and totalitarian instincts. Although very few lyrical commentaries are addressed directly to the chief administrative officers in schools, the implications of managerial rule-making authority and the harsh methods of discipline enforcement abound. The jangling bell system, a lock-step, class-to-class routine, depersonalized hall passes, regimented class changes, overly brief lunch periods ("School Days"), and dozens of other system-defining annoyances are passively attributed to the principal, though they are actively enforced by teachers.

Most distressing is the fact that teachers are universally defined antithetically to their students. They are without common sense ("Bird Dog"), cynical ("The Logical Song"), humorless ("School Days" and "Charlie Brown"), out of touch with personal problems, and representative of a system of thought and action that hides from, rather than confronts, genuine social problems ("Another Brick in the Wall"). Even John Sebastian's laudatory "Welcome Back"—a tribute to a single teacher's devotion and responsibility—carefully notes the exception to the norm.

VII. Images of Parents and the Community

Students generally regard the school system as an extension of the policy-making power and educational goals of parents and other members of the local community. Lyrics in many recordings depict the parental/principal/community nexus as the primary source of conformity, authoritarianism, hypocrisy, and frustration. At best, students dwell in a world where they are "Almost Grown." But parents and community leaders seem unwilling to accept occasional mistakes that are normal aspects of personal maturation and social development. Schools do not function as experimental stages for reflective consideration of alternative social, political, economic, and personal ideas and behaviors; instead, they are cloisters, cells, and societal buffers. Deviant behavior is harshly labeled ("The Rebel" and "Leader of the Pack") by a unified adult population ("Town Without Pity," "Sticks and Stones," and "Society's Child"). Insensitivity to growing pains ("At Seventeen") is compounded by intense social pressure to conform in thought, word, and deed ("Fortunate Son" and "The Free Electric Band"). Despite occasional public lapses between preachment and practice among community members ("Harper Valley P.T.A.") and parents ("That's the Way I Always Heard It Should Be"), schools remain bastions of patriotic, local ("Be True to Your School"), and moral ("Me and Julio Down by the Schoolyard") direction. Such a strong parental/communal stance obviously renders democratic processes, instructional independence, intellectual objectivity, and open communication among students and teachers impossible. The smothering hand of community control is lyrically chided in the Simon and Garfunkel ballad "My Little Town."

VIII. Image of Education

"Please tell me who I am?" This question paraphrases the more positively stated dictum, "Know Thyself" inscribed on the Temple of Delphi. But the question is central to the lyrical criticism of formal education posed by

Supertramp in their 1979 hit "The Logical Song." Echoing Rousseau's naturalistic educational premise, the lyric depicts an untutored youngster who views life as wonderful, beautiful, and magical. Then, he is sent away to school where he learns to be clinical, logical, cynical, sensible, responsible, and practical. Pink Floyd's "Another Brick in the Wall" challenged the formal educational system with a more direct stinging, chanting attack on education itself, thought control, dark sarcasm in classes, and teacher interference with students. The Supertramp/Pink Floyd assertions seem far more deep-rooted and radical than the humorous, exasperated tales of Chuck Berry and the Coasters. Yet they are logical extensions of lyrical critiques presented by Janis Ian, Paul Simon, and others who are understandably appalled by the failure of American education to meet or even to approach in practice its oft-repeated ideals. The laudable goals of fostering human dignity, creativity, freedom, individualism, knowledge, diversity, and objectivity are submerged in public schools beneath a miasma of regimentation, indoctrination, cynicism, arbitrariness, authoritarianism, local morality, and cultural bias. The disembodied voice of American youth—popular recordings—chant a consistent, sad refrain.

It might be easy to argue, in defense of enlightened teaching, that few popular songs could appropriately detail the virtues of an inspired history lecture, the potential delight of analyzing Shakespeare's sonnets, or the feeling of confidence gained by conducting a successful chemistry experiment. However, the weight of contemporary lyrical evidence is conclusive. Good teaching is an exception; inept classroom performance is expected and received. Similarly, belittling ridicule rather than reinforcing praise is the norm for dealing with students—from principals, from parents, from instructors, and (not infrequently) from insensitive, conforming peers as well. The public school arena is a polity that Aristotle would probably label an "unjust society"—where the "just" person (logical, creative, sensitive, democratic) will either become or be perceived as alienated and rebellious. What is even more regrettable, though, is the apparent success of this system in sustaining itself.

IX. Where Do Students Learn?

If public schools are such ineffective sources of learning, then how do young people gain knowledge? Although tunesmiths provide a spectacular variety of options, they seem to concur on one point. Most valuable ideas, information, social contacts, feelings, beliefs, and personal values are secured through individual experience outside of the classroom. Recorded commentaries argue "I Gotta Be Me," "My Way," "Just the Way You Are," and "You May Be Right." The individualistic road through life is not necessarily solipsistic, nor alienating, nor narcissistic. Once again, lyrical images of community pressures ("Town Without Pity"), peer criticisms ("Sticks and Stones"), parental restraints ("Yackety Yak" and "Summertime Blues"), church irrelevance ("Only the Good Die Young"), political skullduggery ("Won't Get Fooled Again"), and wage labor meaninglessness ("Wake Me, Shake Me," "Get a Job," "Take This Job and Shove It," and "Workin' at the Carwash Blues") tend to hinder personal development through outside-of-school contacts.

This study does not intend to suggest that 1955–1980 recordings are devoid of paeans to the joy of intellectual growth and self discovery. Abundant examples illustrate constructive personal experiences. Some are humorous, such as "Spiders and Snakes," "Mr. Businessman," and "Dead End Street;" some are serious, such as "Question," "Who Will Answer," and "Eve of Destruction;" and some are poignant, such as "Color Him Father," "Son of Hickory Holler's Tramp," and "Patches." In each of these instances, of course, the learning is directly connected to individual perceptions of personally meaningful life events. No organized, administered, routinized system can replace authentic human experience. Rousseau may not be correct about a person's natural bent toward goodness; however, Thoreau's concept of simplifying in order to enrich each man's life might serve as a guiding principle to revise and reshape formal education. Real learning, if those messages communicated in popular songs are to be believed, is intrinsically personal. Therefore, the bureaucratic public educational system of the United States is antithetical to the process of individual growth (Johnson, 1993). Is it any wonder that school consolidation, classroom and curriculum regimentation, computerization, teacher unionization, and other facets of mass education have further alienated so many students? Images of schools as minimal security detention centers ("Smokin' in the Boy's Room," "School Day," and "Charlie Brown") are more depressing than comic. The hard work of good principals, creative and caring teachers, and concerned parents to improve community schools may be futile because their efforts fail to take into account several fundamental educational prerequisites. Learning is intrinsically personal. The needs and experiences of

American students defy the factory-like organizational patterns which may have worked well during the post–World War I period. The shifting technology of American society—a car culture, a television culture, a computer culture—is dramatically altering the lives of young and old alike. Similarly, events of the past forty years, ranging from the launching of Sputnik and the prolonged Vietnam conflict to the attempted assassination of Ronald Reagan and the rise of Japanese economic dominance, have altered the collective psyche of students. But the primary audio barometer of America's youth culture—popular music—continues to illustrate the expectations, observations, assumptions, and goals of school-age people (Desmond, 1987; Epstein, 1994; Grossberg, 1984; Kotarba, 1987; Ross and Rose, 1994; Weinstein, 1994).

X. Conclusion

The observations in this study are undeniably as impressionistic and subjective as the lyrical evidence compiled to support it. Formal education is clearly not respected in contemporary lyrics. Worse than that, it is openly ridiculed and condemned. Singers and songwriters openly attack the narrowness of hypocritical community norms and praise the survival of individuals beyond the classroom. Contemporary performers are, to no small extent, minstrels and balladeers for America's youth. This indicates that they offer sprightly, rhythmic entertainment as well as admittedly fictionalized, sometimes overdramatized ("Subterranean Homesick Blues") pictures of life in a complex, confusing, highly industrialized, urbanized nation. Their messages should be heeded. Current problems of student illiteracy and in-school violence are indicative of chronic mismatches of persons and place (Cooper, 1984).

Rock music expresses youthful disenchantment, at least with efforts to socialize young people to a world in contradiction and crisis. But, nowhere in the music can one find attempts to understand this disenchantment. No genuine analysis is ventured. Unlike the spate of politically oriented music that emerged during the late '60s, rock music is devoid of authentic, constructive ideological comment. Rock lyricists are content to demand, "Teachers, leave them kids alone!" Rock music, then, reflects contemporary youth's fatalistic, uncritical view of the future (Butchart and Cooper, 1987). That view, with its lack of perspective or sense of options, should give pause.

There is, ultimately, a beguiling nihilism in the observation contained in Sam Cooke's oft-recorded, "Don't know nothin' 'bout nothin' at all."

The conclusions reached in this study are not invigorating. What is particularly sad, though, is that changes are unlikely to occur in a system dedicated to socialization rather than education, to increasing patriotism rather than objectivity, to establishing order rather than fomenting creativity, and to molding passive citizens rather than enlivening renaissance thinkers. The antischool legacy of early rock lyrics continues to echo in the verbal hostilities of Twisted Sister, in the taunting cynicism of Billy Joel, and in the general anti-institutional indictments of many gangsta rappers. Adolescent views of formal education remain stridently negative. The startling revelation for contemporary adults is that the persistent problems being identified on recordings actually exist. Formal learning is too significant to be stifled by an unresponsive and ever-burgeoning educational bureaucracy. While lyrics may be imperfect reflections of reality, they constitute a legitimate cry for revision and renewal of the entire American schooling system. Is anyone listening?

XI. Selected Discography of Education-Related Recordings, 1955–1980

"Abigail Beecher" (Warner Brothers 5409) By Freddy Cannon (1964)
"After School" (Decca 29946) By Tommy Charles (1956)
"After School" (Dale 100) By Randy Staff (1957)
"Almost Grown" (Chess 1722) By Chuck Berry (1959)
"Another Brick in the Wall" (Columbia 11187) By Pink Floyd (1979)
"At Seventeen" (Columbia 10154) By Janis Ian (1975)
"Back to School" (Checker 1158) By Bo Diddley (1967)
"Back to School Again" (Cameo 116) By Timmie Rogers (1957)
"Be True to Your School" (Capitol 5069) By Beach Boys (1963)
"Bennie and the Jets" (MCA 40198) By Elton John
"Bird Dog" (Cadence 1350) By Everly Brothers (1958)
"Cat's in the Cradle" (Elektra 45203) By Harry Chapin (1974)
"Charlie Brown" (Atco 6132) By Coasters (1959)
"The Class" (Parkway 804) By Chubby Checker (1959)
"Class Cutter (Yeah Yeah)" (Checker 916) By Dale Hawkins (1959)
"Class of '57" (Mercury 73315) By Statler Brothers (1972)
"Class of '49" (Starday 779) By Red Sovine (1966)
"Color Him Father" (Metromedia 117) By The Winstons (1969)
"Dead End Street" (Capitol 5869) By Lou Rawls (1967)

"Department of Youth" (Atlantic 3280) By Alice Cooper (1975)

"Dialogue (Part I and II)" (Columbia 45717) By Chicago (1972)

"Don't Be a Drop-Out" (King 6056) By James Brown (1966)

"Don't Drop Out of School" (ABC 10944) By Trends (1967)

"Don't Stand So Close to Me" (A & M 2301) By Police (1980)

"Eighteen" (Warner Brothers 7449) By Alice Cooper (1971)

"Eve of Destruction" (Dunhill 4009) By Barry Mcguire (1965)

"Everybody's Talking" (RCA 0161) By Harry Nilsson (1969)

"Fortunate Son" (Fantasy 634) By Credence Clearwater Revival (1969)

"The Free Electric Band" (Mums 6018) By Albert Hammond (1973)

"From a School Ring to a Wedding Ring" (ABC-Paramount 9732) By Rover Boys (1956)

"From the Teacher to the Preacher" (Brunswick 55387) By Gene Chandler and Barbara Acklin (1968)

"Got a Job" (Ember 1029)[?] By The Silhouettes (1958)

"Graduation Day" (ABC—Paramount 9700) By Rover Boys (1956)

"Graduation Day" (Capitol 3410) By Four Freshmen (1956)

"Graduation Day" (Garpax 44175) By Bobby Pickett (1963)

"Graduation Day" (Date 1561) By Arbors (1967)

"Graduation's Here" (Dolton 3) By Fleetwoods (1959)

"Harper Valley P.T.A." (Plantation 3) By Jeannie C. Riley (1968)

"Harper Valley P.T.A. (Later That Same Day)" (MGM 13997) By Ben Colder (1968)

"He's a Rebel" (Philles 106) By Crystals (1962)

"Hey Little Girl" (Abner 1029) By Dee Clark (1959)

"Hey, School Girl" (Big 613) By Tom & Jerry (1958)

"High School Confidential" (Sun 296) By Jerry Lee Lewis (1958)

"High School Dance" (Capitol 4405) By Sylvers (1977)

"High School Dance" (Specialty 608) By Larry Williams (1957)

"High School Days" (Fairlane 21020) By Bill Erwin and The Four Jacks (1962)

"High School Hero" (Tower St 5127) By Jake Hohnes (1970)

"High School Romance" (ABC—Paramount 9838) By George Hamilton IV (1957)

"High School U.S.A." (Atlantic 51-78) By Tommy Facenda (1959)

"High School Yearbook" (Liberty 1389) By Nitty Gritty Dirt Band (1980)

"I Am a Rock" (Columbia 43617) By Simon and Garfunkel (1966)

"I Am, I Said" (Uni 55278) By Neil Diamond (1971)

"I Get Around" (Capitol 5174) By Beach Boys (1964)

"I Think We're Alone Now" (Roulette 4720) By Tommy James and The Shondells (1967)

"(I Wanna) Dance With the Teacher" (Demon 1512) By The Olympics (1959)

"I Wish" (Tamla 54274) By Stevie Wonder (1977)

"I'm Going Back to School" (Vee Jay 462) By Dee Clark (1962)

"The 'In' Crowd" (Charger 105) By Dobie Gray (1965)

"It Hurts to Be Sixteen" (Big Top 3156) By Andrea Carroll (1963)

"It's Your Thing" (T-Neck 901) By Isley Brothers (1969)

"I've Got a Name" (ABC 11389) (?) By Jim Croce (1973)

"I've Gotta Be Me" (Reprise 0779) By Sammy Davis, Jr. (1968)

"Just the Way You Are" (Columbia 10646) By Billy Joel (1977)

"Kodachrome" (Columbia 45859) By Paul Simon (1973)

"The Last Game of the Season (A Blind Man in the Bleachers)" (Big Tree 16052) By David Geddes (1975)

"The Leader of the Pack" (Red Bird 014) By The Shangri-Las (1964)

"The Logical Song" (A & M 2128) By Supertramp (1979)

"Lonely School Year" (Rocket 40464) By Hudson Brothers (1975)

"Mama Told Me (Not to Come)" (Dunhill 4239) By Three Dog Night (1970)

"Mammas Don't Let Your Babies Grow Up to Be Cowboys" (RCA 11198) By Willie Nelson (1978)

"Me and Julio Down by the Schoolyard" (Columbia 45585) By Paul Simon (1972)

"Mr. Businessman" (Monument 1083) By Ray Stevens (1968)

"Mr. Lee" (Atlantic 1144) By Bobbettes (1957)

"My Back Pages" (Columbia 44054) By Byrds (1967)

"My Boy—Flat Top" (King 1494) By Boyd Bennett and His Rockets (1955)

"My Generation" (Decca 31877) By The Who (1966)

"My Little Town" (Columbia 10230) By Simon & Garfunkel (1975)

"My Old School" (ABC 11396) By Steely Dan (1973)

"My Way" (Reprise 0817) By Frank Sinatra (1969)

"New Girl in School" (Liberty 55672) By Jan and Dean (1964)

"New Kid in Town" (Asylum 45373) By Eagles (1977)

"Night Moves" (Capitol 4369) By Bob Seger and The Silver Bullet Band (1977)

"Ohio" (Atlantic 2740) By Crosby, Stills, Nash, and Young (1970)

"Okie From Muskogee" (Capitol 2626) By Merle Haggard and The Strangers (1969)

"Only Sixteen" (Capitol 4171) By Dr. Hook (1976)

"Only Sixteen" (Keen 2022) By Sam Cooke (1959)

"Only the Good Die Young" (Columbia 10750) By Billy Joel (1978)

"Open Letter to My Teenage Son" (Liberty 55996) By Victor Lundberg (1967)

"Patches" (Atlantic 2748) By Clarence Carter (1970)

"A Place in the Sun" (A & M 1976) By Pablo Cruise (1977)

"Please Come to Boston" (Epic 11115) By Dave Loggins (1974)

"Pomp and Circumstance (The Graduation Song)" (Calliope 6501) By Adrian Kimberly (1961)

"Queen of the Senior Prom" (Decca 30299) By The Mills Brothers (1957)

"Question" (Threshold 67004) By Moody Blues (1970)

"Rebel" (Dot 15586) By Carol Jarvis (1957)

"(Remember the Days of the) Old Schoolyard" (A & M 1948) By Cat Stevens (1977)

"Respect Yourself" (Stax 0104) By Staple Singers (1971)

"The Right Thing to Do" (Elektra 45843) By Carly Simon (1973)

"Rock and Roll (I Gave You the Best Years of My Life)" (Columbia 10070) By Mac Davis (1975)

"A Rose and a Baby Ruth" (ABC—Paramount 9765) By George Hamilton IV (1956)

"Roses Are Red (My Love)" (Epic 9509) By Bobby Vinton (1962)

"School Bell Rock" (King 5247) By Roy Brown (1959)

"School Bells Are Ringing" (Dimension 1004) By Carole King (1962)

"School Boy Crush" (Atlantic 3304) By Average White Band (1975)

"School Boy Romance" (ABC—Paramount 9888) By Danny and The Juniors (1958)

"School Bus" (Leader 808) By Kris Jensen (1960)

"School Dance" (ABC—Paramount 9908) By Dwayne Hickman (1958)

"School Day" (Chess 1653) By Chuck Berry (1957)

"School Day Crush" (Gone 5039) By Nicky and The Nobels (1959)

"School Days Are Back Again" (Imperial 5478) By Smiley Lewis (1957)

"School Daze" (Magic 93000) By Funn (1981)

"School Fool" (Mam 12553) By Mark Dinning (1957)

"School Is In" (Legrand 1012) By Gary "U.S." Bonds (1961)

"School Is Out" (Legrand 1009) By Gary "U.S." Bonds (1961)

"School of Love" (Koko 2112) By Tommy Tate (1972)

"School Teacher" (Reprise 1069) By Kenny Rogers and The First Edition (1972)

"Schoolbells" (Gone 5039) By Nicky and The Nobels (1959)

"Schooldays, Oh Schooldays" (Parkway 804) By Chubby Checker (1959)

"School's All Over" (World 10) By Adorables (1964)

"School's Out" (Warner Brothers 7596) By Alice Cooper (1972)

"See You in September" (Climax 102) By Tempos (1959)

"See You in September" (B. T. Puppy 520) By Happenings (1966)

"Seventeen" (King 1470) By Boyd Bennett and His Rockets (1955)

"She Was Only Seventeen" (Columbia 41208) By Marty Robbins (1958)

"Short Fat Fannie" (Specialty 608) By Larry Williams (1957)

"Skip a Rope" (Monument 1041) By Henson Cargill (1968)

"Smokin' in the Boy's Room" (Big Tree 16011) By Brownsville Station (1974)

"So You Want to Be a Rock 'N' Roll Star" (Columbia 43987) By Byrds (1967)

"Society's Child (Baby I've Been Thinking)" (Verve 5027) By Janis Ian (1967)

"Someone Saved My Life Tonight" (MCA 40421) By Elton John (1975)

"Son-of-a-Preacher Man" (Atlantic 2580) By Dusty Springfield (1969)

"Son of Hickory Holler's Tramp" (Columbia 44425) By O. C. Smith (1968)

"Spiders and Snakes" (MGM 14648) By Jim Stafford (1974)

"Sticks and Stones" (ABC—Paramount 10118) By Ray Charles (1960)

"Still Crazy After All These Years" (Columbia 0332) By Paul Simon (1976)

"Stood Up" (Imperial 5483) By Ricky Nelson (1958)

"Subterranean Homesick Blues" (Columbia 43242) By Bob Dylan (1965)

"Summertime Blues" (Liberty 55144) By Eddie Cochran (1958)

"Summertime Blues" (Decca 32708) By Who (1970)

"Summertime, Summertime" (Epic 9281) By Jamies (1958)

"Sweet Little Sixteen" (Chess 1683) By Chuck Berry (1958)

"Swingin' on a Star" (Dimension 1010) By Big Dee Irwin (1963)

"Swingin' School" (Cameo 175) By Bobby Rydell (1960)

"Sylvia's Mother" (Columbia 45562) By Dr. Hook (1972)

"Take This Job and Shove It" (Epic 50469) By Johnny Paycheck (1977)

"Talk of the School" (Capitol 4178) By Sonny James (1959)

"Taxi" (Elektra 45770) By Harry Chapin (1972)

"Teach Me Tiger" (Imperial 5626) By April Stevens (1959)

"Teach Me Tonight" (Epic 9504) By George Maharis (1962)

"Teach Your Children" (Atlantic 2735) By Crosby, Stills, Nash, & Young (1970)

"Teacher" (Reprise 0899) By Jethro Tull (1970)

"The Teacher and the Pet" (AGP 110) By Johnny Christopher (1969)

"Teacher, Teacher" (Columbia 41152) By Johnny Mathis (1958)

"Teacher's Pet" (Columbia 41123) By Doris Day (1958)

"Teenage Lament '74" (Warner Brothers 7762) By Alice Cooper (1974)

"That's Life" (Reprise 0531) By Frank Sinatra (1966)

"That's the Way I've Always Heard It Should Be" (Electra 45724) By Carly Simon (1971)

"To Be Young, Gifted and Black" (RCA 0269) By Nina Simone (1969)

"To Sir With Love" (Epic 10187) By Lulu (1967)

"Town Without Pity" (Musicor 1009) By Gene Pitney (1962)

"2 + 2 = ?" (Capitol 2143) By Bob Seger System (1968)

"Venus in Blue Jeans" (Ace 8001) By Jimmy Clanton (1962)

"Waitin' in School" (Imperial 5483) By Ricky Nelson (1958)

"Wake Me, Shake Me" (Atco 6168) By Coasters (1960)

"Wake Up Little Susie" (Cadence 1337) By Everly Brothers (1957)

"We Just Disagree" (Columbia 10575) By Dave Mason (1977)

"We May Never Pass This Way (Again)" (Warner Brothers 7740) By Seals and Crofts (1973)

"Welcome Back" (Reprise 1349) By John Sebastian (1976)

"(What a) Wonderful World" (Columbia 10676) By Art Garfunkel, James Taylor, and Paul Simon (1978)

"What Did You Learn in School Today" (Mercury 72257) By Chad Mitchell Trio (1964)

"What Good Is Graduation" (Corsican 0058) By Graduates (1959)

"What Is a Teenage Boy?" (Coral 61773) By Tom Edwards (1957)

"What Is a Teenage Girl?" (Coral 61773) By Tom Edwards (1957)

"When the Boys Get Together" (Warner Brothers 5308) By Joanie Sommers (1962)

"When the Boys Talk About the Girls" (Roulette 4066) By Valerie Carr (1958)

"Whenever a Teenager Cries" (World Artists 1036) By Reparata & The Delrons (1965)

"Where the Boys Are" (MGM 12971) By Connie Francis (1961)

"White Sport Coat (and a Pink Carnation)" (Columbia 40864) By Marty Robbins (1957)

"Who Are You" (MCA 40948) By The Who (1978)

"Who Will Answer?" (RCA 9400) By Ed Ames (1968)

"Why Can't My Teacher Look Like Mr. Novak" (Capitol 5325) By Jackie and Gayle (1964)

"Why Do Kids Grow Up" (Rust 5073) By Tandy and The Rainbows (1963)

"Why Don't They Understand" (ABC—Paramount 9862) By George Hamilton IV (1958)

"Wonderful World" (Keen 2112) By Sam Cooke (1960)
"Wonderful World" (MGM 13354) By Herman's Hermits (1965)
"Won't Get Fooled Again" (Decca 32846) By Who (1971)
"Woodstock" (Atlantic 2723) By Crosby, Stills, Nash, and Young (1970)
"Workin' at the Carwash Blues" (ABC 11447) By Jim Croce (1974)
"Yakety Yak" (Atco 6116) By Coasters (1958)
"Yesterday When I Was Young" (Dot 17246) By Roy Clark (1969)
"You and Me Against the World" (Capitol 3897) By Helen Reddy (1974)
"You May Be Right" (Columbia 11231) By Billy Joel (1980)
"You Never Can Tell" (Chess 1906) By Chuck Berry (1964)
"Young School Girl" (Imperial 5537) By Fats Domino (1958)
"Your Mama Don't Dance" (Columbia 45719) By Loggins & Messina (1973)

Bibliography

Adams, Peter M. "Music and Youth: Sounds and Significance," *Social Education,* 38 (April 1974): 356–363.

Arnett, Jeffrey Jensen. *Metal Heads: Heavy Metal Music and Adolescent Alienation.* Boulder, Colo.: Westview Press, 1996.

Barr, Robert D. "Youth and Music," in *Values and Youth: Teaching Social Studies in an Age of Crisis—No. 2* (Washington, D.C.: National Council for The Social Studies, 1971): 88–103.

Bennett, Tony, Simon Frith, Lawrence Grossberg, John Sheperd, and Graeme Turner (eds.). *Rock and Popular Music: Politics/ Policies/Institutions.* London: Routledge, 1993.

Binda, Kenneth J. (ed.). *America's Musical Pulse: Popular Music in Twentieth-Century Society.* Westport, Conn.: Praeger Books. 1992.

Bloodworth, John D. "Communication in the Youth Counter Culture: Music as Expression," *Central States Speech Quarterly,* 26 (Winter 1975): 304–309.

Brown, Elizabeth and William Hendee. "Adolescents and Their Music," *Journal of the American Medical Association,* 262 (September 22–29, 1989): 1659–1663.

Butchart, Ronald E. and B. Lee Cooper. "Perceptions of Education in the Lyrics of American Popular Music, 1950–1980," *American Music,* 5 (Fall 1987): 271–281.

Carney, George O. (ed.). *Fast Food, Stock Cars, and Rock 'n' Roll: Place and Space in American Pop Culture.* Lanham, Md.: Rowman and Littlefield, 1995.

Cooper, B. Lee. "Awarding an 'A' Grade to Heavy Metal: A Review Essay," *Popular Music and Society,* 17 (Fall 1993): 99–102.

———. "Can Music Students Learn Anything of Value by Investigating Popular Recordings?," *International Journal of Instructional Media,* 10,3 (1993): 273–284.

———. "Education," in *A Resource Guide to Themes in Contemporary Song Lyrics, 1950–1985.* Westport, Conn.: Greenwood Press, 1986.

——— and William L. Schurk. "From 'I Saw Mommy Kissing Santa Claus' to 'Another Brick in the Wall': Popular Recordings Featuring Pre-Teen Performers, Traditional Childhood Stories, and Contemporary Pre-Adolescent Perspectives, 1945–1985," *International Journal of Instructional Media,* 16, 1 (1989): 83–90.

————. "The Image of the Outsider in Contemporary Lyrics," *Journal of Popular Culture*, 12 (Summer 1978): 168–178.

————. *Images of American Society in Popular Music: A Guide to Reflective Teaching*. Chicago: Nelson-Hall, 1982.

————. "'It's a Wonder I Can Think at All': Vinyl Images of American Public Education, 1950–1980," *Popular Music and Society*, 9 (Winter 1984): 47–65.

————. "Lyrical Commentaries: Learning From Popular Music," *Music Educators Journal*, 77 (April 1991): 56–59.

————. *Popular Music Perspectives: Ideas, Themes, and Patterns in Contemporary Lyrics*. Bowling Green, Ohio: Bowling Green State University Popular Press, 1991.

————. "A Resource Guide to Studies in the Theory and Practice of Popular Culture Librarianship," in *Popular Culture and Acquisitions*, edited by Allen Ellis. Binghamton, N.Y.: Haworth Press, 1992): 131–146.

————. *A Resource Guide to Themes in Contemporary American Songs Lyrics, 1950–1985*. Westport, Conn.: Greenwood Press, 1986.

————. "Rhythm 'N' Rhymes: Character and Theme Images from Children's Literature in Contemporary Recordings, 1950–1985," *Popular Music and Society*, 13 (Spring 1989): 53–71.

———— and Wayne S. Haney. *Rock Music in American Culture: Rock 'N' Roll Resources*. New York: Harrington Park Press, 1995.

———— and Wayne S. Haney. *Rock Music in American Culture II: More Rock 'N' Roll Resources*. New York: Harrington Park Press, 1997.

————. "Sounds of Schooling in Modern America: Recorded Images of Public Education, 1950–1980," *International Journal of Instructional Media*, 11,3 (1983–1984): 255–271.

Curtis, Jim. *Rock Eras: Interpretations of Music and Society, 1954–1984*. Bowling Green, Ohio: Bowling Green State University Popular Press. 1987.

Denisoff, R. Serge. *Inside MTV.* New Brunswick, N.J.: Transaction Books, 1991 (1988).

———— and William D. Romanowski. 1991. *Risky Business: Rock in Film*. New Brunswick, N.J.: Transaction Books, 1991.

Desmond, Roger Jon. " Adolescents and Music Lyrics: Implications of a Cognitive Perspective," *Communication Quarterly*, 35 (Summer, 1987): 276–284.

Dotter, Daniel. "Rock and Roll Is Here to Stray: Youth Subculture, Deviance, and Social Typing in Rock's Early Years," in *Adolescents and Their Music: If It's Too Loud, You're Too Old*, edited by Jonathan S. Epstein (New York: Garland Publishing, 1994): 87–114.

Dunne, Michael. *Metapop: Self-Referentiality in Contemporary American Popular Culture*. Jackson: University Press of Mississippi, 1992.

Epstein, Jonathan S. and David J. Pratto. "Heavy Metal Rock Music, Juvenile Delinquency, and Satanic Identification," *Popular Music and Society*, 14 (Winter, 1990): 67–76.

————. "Misplaced Childhood: An Introduction to the Sociology of Youth and Their Music," in *Adolescents and Their Music: If It's Too Loud, You're Too Old*, edited by Jonathan S. Epstein (New York: Garland Publishing, 1994): xiii–xxiv.

———— (ed.). *Adolescents and Their Music: If It's Too Loud, You're Too Old*. New York: Garland Publishing, 1994.

Farber, Paul, Eugene F. Provenzo, Jr., and Gunilla Holm (eds.). *Schooling in the Light of Popular Culture*. Albany, N.Y.: State University of New York Press, 1994.

Fornas, Johan, Ulf Lindber, and Ove Sernhede (trans. Jan Teeland). *In Garageland: Rock, Youth, and Modernity*. New York: Routledge, 1995.

Friedlander, Paul. *Rock and Roll: A Social History*. Boulder, Colo.: Westview Press, 1996.

Frith, Simon. *Sound Effects: Youth, Leisure, and the Politics of Rock 'N' Roll*. New York: Pantheon Books. 1981.

Frith, Simon and Andrew Goodwin (eds.). *On Record: Rock, Pop, and The Written Word*. New York: Pantheon Books, 1990.

Giroux, Henry A. and Roger I. Simon. *Popular Culture: Schooling and Everyday Life*. Westport, Conn.: Bergin and Garvey, 1989.

Goodall, H. L., Jr. *Living in the Rock 'N' Roll Mystery: Reading Context, Self, and Others as Clues*. Carbondale, Ill.: Southern Illinois University Press, 1991.

Gordon, Robert. *It Came From Memphis*. Boston: Faber and Faber, 1995.

Grossberg, Lawrence. "Another Boring Day in Paradise: Rock and Roll and the Empowerment of Everyday Life," in *Popular Music 4: Performers and Audiences*, edited by Richard Middleton and David Horn (Cambridge: Cambridge University Press, 1984): 225–258.

_____. "The Politics of Youth Culture: Some Observations on Rock and Roll in American Culture," *Social Text*, 8 (Winter 1983–1984): 104–126.

Hakanen, Ernest A. and Alan Wells. "Music Preference and Taste Cultures Among Adolescents," *Popular Music and Society*, 17 (Spring 1993): 55–69.

_____ and Alan Wells. "Adolescent Music Marginals: Who Likes Metal, Jazz, Country, and Classical," *Popular Music and Society*, 14 (Winter 1990): 57–66.

Harris, James F. *Philosophy at 33 1/3 R.P.M.: Themes of Classic Rock Music*. La Salle, Ill.: Open Court Publishing, 1993.

Hendler, Herb. *Year by Year in the Rock Era: Events and Conditions Shaping the Rock Generations that Reshaped America*. Westport, Conn.: Greenwood Press, 1983.

Hibbard, Don J. and Carol Kaleialoha. *The Role of Rock: A Guide to the Social and Political Consequences of Rock Music*. Englewood, N.J.: Prentice-Hall, 1983.

Hilsabeck, Steven A. "The Blackboard Bumble: Popular Culture and the Recent Challenges to the American High School," *Journal of Popular Culture*, 18 (Winter 1984): 25–30.

Jochem, Phil. "Some Popular Songs Into Teachers," *Instructor*, 85 (October 1975): 40–42.

Johnson, Michael L. *Education on the Wild Side: Learning for the Twenty-First Century*. Norman, Okla.: University of Oklahoma Press, 1993.

Kirschner, Tony. "The Lalalooziation of American Youth," *Popular Culture and Society*, 18 (Spring 1994): 69–90.

Kotarba, Joseph A. (ed.). "Adolescents and Rock "n" Roll," *Youth and Society*, 18,4 (June 1987): 323–432.

Lipsitz, George. *Time Passages: Collective Memory and American Popular Culture*. Minneapolis, Minn.: University of Minnesota Press, 1990.

Martin, Linda and Kerry Segrave. *Anti-Rock: The Opposition to Rock 'N' Roll*. Hamden, Conn.: Archon Books, 1988.

Mcclary, Susan. "Same as It Ever Was: Youth Culture and Music," in *Microphone Fiends: Youth Music and Youth Culture*, edited by Andrew Ross and Tricia Rose (New York: Routledge, 1994): 29–40.

McLaurin, Melton and Richard Peterson, eds. *You Wrote My Life: Lyrical Themes in Country Music.* New York: Gordon and Breach, 1992.

McRobbie, Angela. "Shut Up and Dance: Youth Culture and Changing Modes of Femininity," *Cultural Studies,* 8 (October 1993): 406–426.

Pichaske, David R. *A Generation in Motion: Popular Music and Culture in the Sixties.* Granite Falls, Minn.: Ellis Press, 1989.

Pielke, Robert G. *You Say You Want a Revolution: Rock Music in American Culture.* Chicago: Nelson-Hall, 1986.

Reidelbach, Maria. *Completely Mad: A History of the Comic Book and Magazine.* Boston: Little, Brown and Company, 1991.

Rogers, Jimmie N. *The Country Music Message: All About Lovin' and Livin'.* Englewood Cliffs, N.J.: Prentice-Hall, 1983.

————. *The Country Music Message: Revisited.* Fayetteville, Ark.: University of Arkansas Press, 1989.

Rose, Tricia. *Black Noise: Rap Music and Black Culture in Contemporary America.* Hanover, N.H.: University Press of New England, 1994.

Ross, Andrew and Tricia Rose, eds. *Microphone Fiends: Youth Music and Youth Culture.* New York: Routledge, 1994.

Roszak, Theodore. *The Making of Counter Culture: Reflections on the Technocratic Society and Its Youthful Opposition.* Garden City, N.Y.: Doubleday Anchor Books, 1969.

Rowe, David. *Popular Cultures: Rock Music, Sport, and the Politics of Pleasure.* Thousand Oaks, Calif.: Sage Publications, 1995.

Scheurer, Timothy E. *Born in the U.S.A.: The Myth of America in Popular Music From Colonial Times to the Present.* Jackson: University Press of Mississippi, 1991.

Schultze, Quentin J., Roy M. Anker, James D. Bratt, William D. Romanowski, John W. Worst, and Lambert Zuidervaart. *Dancing in the Dark: Youth, Popular Culture, and the Electronic Media.* Grand Rapids, Mich.: William B. Eerdmans Publishing, 1991.

Snow, Robert P. "Youth, Rock 'n' Roll, and Electronic Media," *Youth and Society,* 18 (June 1987): 326–343.

Spring, Joel. *Images of American Life: A History of Ideological Management in Schools, Movies, Radio, and Television.* Albany, N.Y.: State University of New York Press, 1992.

Stanley, Lawrence A., ed. *Rap: The Lyrics.* New York: Penguin Books, 1992.

Stern, Jane and Michael Stern. *Encyclopedia of Pop Culture: An A to Z of Who's Who and What's What, From Aerobics to Bubble Gum to Valley of the Dolls and Moon Unit Zappa.* New York: HarperCollins Publishers, 1992.

Stevenson, Gordon. "The Wayward Scholar: Resources and Research in Popular Culture," *Library Trends,* 25 (April 1977): 779–818.

Verden, Paul, Kathleen Dunleavy, and Charles H. Powers. "Heavy Metal Mania and Adolescent Delinquency," *Popular Culture and Society,* 13 (Spring 1989): 73–82.

Vullinamy, Graham and Ed Lee, eds. *Pop Music in School* (revised edition). Cambridge, England: Cambridge University Press, 1980.

Walser, Robert. *Running With the Devil: Power, Gender, and Madness in Heavy Metal Music.* Hanover, N.H.: University Press of New England, 1993.

Weinstein, Deena. *Heavy Metal: A Cultural Sociology.* New York: Lexington Books, 1991.

———. "Rock Is Youth/Youth Is Rock," in *America's Musical Pulse: Popular Music in Twentieth-Century Society,* edited by Kenneth J. Binda (Westport, Conn.: Praeger Books, 1992): 91–98.

———. "Rock: Youth and Its Music," in *Adolescents and Their Music: If It's Too Loud, You're Too Old,* edited by Jonathan S. Epstein (New York: Garland Publishing, 1994): 3–23.

Whitburn, Joel, comp. *Top Pop Album Tracks, 1955–1992.* Menomonee Falls, Wisc.: Record Research, Inc., 1993.

———, comp. *Top Pop Singles CD Guide, 1955–1979.* Menomonee Falls, Wisc.: Record Research, Inc., 1995

———, comp. *Top Pop Singles, 1955–1993.* Menomonee Falls, Wisc.: Record Research, Inc., 1994

———, comp. *Top Rhythm and Blues Singles, 1942–1988.* Menomonee Falls, Wisc.: Record Research, Inc., 1988.

Chapter 6
Teenage Monsters and Their Meaning

Don G. Smith,
Eastern Illinois University

G. Stanley Hall coined the term "adolescent" in 1904. The word "teenager" came into our vocabulary in 1941, followed quickly by the term "juvenile delinquent." The American cinema reflected the growing concern of adults for young people aged thirteen to nineteen. Early examples include *Where Are Your Children* (1944), *I Accuse My Parents* (1944), *Delinquent Daughters* (1944), and *City Across the River* (1949, based on Irving Schulman's novel *The Amboy Dukes*). With the 1955 release of *Blackboard Jungle* and *Rebel Without a Cause,* the screen's depiction of American youth grew even darker as our alienated children challenged authority figures and wielded switch blades against all that adults held dear. One year later, swivel-hipped Elvis Presley appeared in his first film, *Love Me Tender,* and Bill Haley and the Comets enticed hormone-driven youngsters to *Rock Around the Clock.*

The youth of America may have been forming a frightening counter-culture, but it was not until 1957, with the release of *I Was a Teenage Werewolf,* that a teenager literally became a monster on the movie screen. The popularity of *Teenage Werewolf* spawned subsequent teenage monster films in the late '50s. What that and subsequent teenage monster films of the '50s suggests deserves more critical attention than it has thus far received.

I. I Was a Teenage Werewolf

Let us begin with *I Was a Teenage Werewolf.* Tony (Michael Landon), an outstanding student at Rockdale High School, gets into fights at the slightest provocation. Moody, tempramental, and hypersensitive, Tony is a constant concern to his school principal (Louise Lewis), detective Sergeant Donovan (Barney Phillips), and girlfriend, Arlene (Yvonne Lime). After Tony beats up one of his best friends at a Halloween party, he agrees to accept medical assistance from Dr. Brandon (Whit Bissell). Unfortunately, Dr. Brandon uses Tony as a subject of an experiment in regression. Placing Tony under hypnosis, Dr. Brandon succeeds in taking the teenager back in time to a primitive, animal period in his evolution. Thereafter, Tony periodically turns into a werewolf and commits unpremeditated murders in Rockdale. When one of his friends identifies Tony as the werewolf, police hunt the confused killer to Dr. Brandon's laboratory. After the werewolf kills Dr. Brandon and his assistant, police bullets end Tony's confused reign of terror.

Tony is a sociopath who cannot adjust to parents, teachers, and other students. When Sergeant Donovan asks him why he can't control his temper, Tony replies, "People bug me." Arlene's parents berate Tony because he doesn't have a job. "You've got to bow to authority," Arlene's father tells him. Tony's father, a working man who has reared the boy since his mother's death, advises Tony that "Sometimes you have to do things the other fellow's way," to which Tony answers, "I don't like being pushed around." So, in the first teenage monster movie of the '50s we have a boy, raised by a single parent, who cannot conform to social expectations. But to what sort of society will Tony not conform? Historian David Halberstam writes:

> Three decades later, the fifties appear to be an orderly era, one with a minimum of social dissent. Photographs from the period tend to show people who dressed carefully: men in suits, ties, and—when outdoors—hats. The women with their hair in modified page-boys, pert and upbeat. Young people seemed, more than anything else, 'square' and largely accepting of the given social covenants. At the beginning of the decade their music was still slow and saccharine, mirroring the generally bland popular taste.[1]

The adults in *I Was a Teenage Werewolf* largely conform to Halberstam's description. The teenagers, however, are definitely end-of-the-decade models; their music is rock 'n' roll. It is probably no accident that Tony's Elvis-style, combed-back hair is just a little longer than that of his peers. Perhaps it was no accident that the first teenage monster sprouted the long hair of the werewolf. But against what is Tony rebelling? Halberstam continues:

In the years following the traumatic experiences of the Depression and World War II, the American Dream was to exercise personal freedom not in social and political terms, but rather in economic ones. Eager to be part of the burgeoning middle class, young men and women opted for material well-being. . . . security meant finding a good white-collar job with a large, benevolent company, getting married, having children, and buying a house in the suburbs.[2]

But Tony isn't interested in the American Dream. He isn't even interested in getting a job. The freedom he wants is personal and social, not economic. He couldn't care less about saving up enough money to buy Betty Furness' latest Westinghouse refrigerator. As Stephen King approvingly puts it,

Landon becomes the fascinating embodiment of everything you're not supposed to do if you want to be good . . . if you want to get along in school, join the National Honor Society, get your letter, and be accepted by a good college where you can join a frat and drink beer like your old man did.[3]

Tony wants to be left alone to live his own life on his own terms. This attitude, when pushed to its extreme under hypnosis, turns Tony into a murdering werewolf. As Aristotle said, the man who lives beyond society must either be a god or a monster. It is clear which Tony is! Of course, Tony would not have taken the extreme path of werewolfery had it not been for Dr. Brandon, a scientist and intellectual. In the '50s, just as in every other epoch of American history, "we, the people" distrusted intellectuals as amoral, naive, and atheistic. Intellectuals were different, not quite like us, susceptible to the cry of communism and other siren songs of corruption. We liked Ike because Ike was one of us. Stevenson was an egghead, one of those untrustworthy thinkers. The message of *I Was a Teenage Werewolf*, of course, is that individuality is commendable unless it turns into a sociopathic desire to murder the American Dream. Then, the police must enter and eliminate the threat. Tony's death, though regrettable, is finally necessary.

Stephen King, however is probably correct in his assessment of the movie's enthusiastic reception by teenagers:

Undoubtedly, part of the reason for the movie's meteoric takeoff at the box office had to do with the liberating, vicarious feelings the movie allowed these war babies who wanted to be good. When Landon attacks the pretty gymnast in the leotard, he is making a social statement on behalf of those watching. But those watching also react in horror, because on the psychological level, the picture is a series of object lessons on how to get along—everything from 'shave before you go to school' to 'never exercise in a deserted gym.'[4]

II. Teenage Monster

That same year, Howco International entered the teenage monster sweepstakes with a film appropriately titled *Teenage Monster*. In this film, the teenager becomes a monster through no fault of his own (teenagers didn't ask to be born) and afterward becomes demoralized by the cruel adult world. The setting is the West, where Ruth (Anne Gwynne) and Jim Cannon (Jim McCullough) and their nine-year-old son, Charles (Stephen Parker), live in a shack adjacent to an old gold mine. Jim barely makes a living working the mine, but the family is happy. Then, one morning, a ball of fire falls from the sky and explodes near the mine. Ruth runs from the house, finds her husband dead and her son transformed into a hairy, werewolf-like monster. As seven years pass, Ruth tries to keep her son hidden in the house, but he periodically emerges to kill the sheep and cattle of area farmers. At the age of sixteen, Charles (Gilbert Perkins) is a huge, hairy, and very dangerous imbecile with an urge to kill. Ruth discovers a rich vein at the mine, becomes wealthy, and buys a house in town. Of course, Ruth continues her attempt to hide Charles. Sheriff Bob Lehman (Stuart Wade), a family friend for many years, thinks Ruth has been a widow long enough and proceeds to woo her. One evening, while Bob and Ruth are out to dinner, Charles breaks loose, kills a man, frightens children with his appearance, and kidnaps pretty waitress, Kathy North (Gloria Castillo). When Ruth gets home, she finds Kathy locked in a closet by Charles. Kathy, who now knows of the monster's existence, blackmails Ruth. When Ruth pays her $500 in hush money, she flashes it in front of her pool-hustler boyfriend, Marv Howell (Charles Courtney). Marv takes her money, infuriating Ruth enough to send Charles to kill him. The teenage monster is, of course, putty in the hands of the wily waitress, the only girl he has ever known. Kathy then decides to appropriate Ruth's fortune by inciting Charles to kill both Ruth and Sheriff Bob. She tells Charles that Ruth and Bob are planning to turn him in to the law for his crimes. When Charles discovers that Kathy has been using him, he grabs her and carries her into the mountains where a pursuing posse shoots him on the edge of a precipice. He and Kathy fall to their deaths while Bob and a terrified Ruth look on.

Teenage Monster strongly implies that greedy adult Kathy North is the scenario's real monster. Charles, like teenagers everywhere, is what he is by no choice of his own. Just as American culture extended childhood, turning what used to be the initial stages of adulthood into adolescence, the fire ball from space turned Charles into a monster. Since teenagers and monsters were already associated in the minds of an increasingly concerned adult population, the theme must have resonated with troubled teens across America; and it must have made wheels turn in the minds of teens who had not yet experienced the generation gap full force. At least, Ruth stands by Charles, but she must do so covertly, hiding him from public view for his own protection. How many parents in the '50s cringed to see their sideburn sporting, leather jacket-wearing sons "escape" from the house, unable to prevent the inevitable embarrassment?

III. I Was a Teenage Frankenstein

When their *I Was a Teenage Werewolf* took in over $2 million in less than a year, American International Pictures quickly produced a follow-up double feature comprised of *I Was a Teenage Frankenstein* and *Blood of Dracula* (1958). Both films would continue *Teenage Monster's* theme of the teenager as innocent victim. In *Teenage Frankenstein,* Professor Frankenstein (Whit Bissell), a guest lecturer from England, talks Dr. Karlton (Robert Burton) into becoming an unwilling accomplice in his secret plan to assemble a human being from the parts of dead bodies. When a football team is involved in a horrible highway accident, Frankenstein recovers a muscular corpse with a horribly mutilated face and secrets it back to his laboratory. There, he activates the teenage monster (Gary Conway) with electricity and teaches it to talk. The monster soon escapes from the laboratory, enters the home of a beautiful girl, and clumsily kills her when she becomes hysterical and starts screaming. When the monster returns to the lab, and Frankenstein's secretary (Phyllis Coates) threatens to bring the police, Frankenstein orders the monster to kill her. Frankenstein also realizes he must find a new face for the creature. Taking the monster to lover's lane, Frankenstein has the monster kill a handsome young man and carry the body back to the laboratory. The face graft successful, Frankenstein plans to dismantle his monster and transport it to England. Understandably fearful of being dismembered, the monster kills Frankenstein and feeds his remains to alligators. Distressed at this turn of events, Dr. Karlton runs for help. When Dr. Karlton returns with the police, the monster, who is maddened with fright, backs into the electrical dial board and is destroyed.

In *Teenage Frankenstein,* unlike in *Teenage Werewolf* (where the theory of classical tragedy is at work), the adolescent monster has no character flaw that leads to his doom. He is simply the victim, first, of an accident, and, second, of an amoral, adult intellectual. His hormones run wild when he kills a screaming girl (teenage boys take rejection hard), and when he commits murders at lover's lane, but other than those two indiscretions, he is just a big, confused kid—the victim of an unscrupulous adult. Teenage audiences in the late '50s must have loved the implications. As Robert Brustein wrote in *Partisan Review,* "What these films seem to be saying, in their underground manner, is that . . . the adolescent feels victimized by society—turned into a monster by society."[5] This is the second entry in a film series designed to exonerate criminal deviants from responsibility and to legitimize a culture of victimization. *Blood of Dracula,* billed second under *Teenage Frankenstein,* continued the trend.

IV. Blood of Dracula

Filmed under the working title *I Was a Teenage Dracula, Blood of Dracula* tells the story of Nancy Perkins (Sandra Harrison), a teenager who hates her stepfather for marrying too soon after her mother's death. When Nancy becomes impossible to control, her father and stepmother enroll her against her wishes at a school for girls. Once enrolled in the school, Nancy hates her enforced surroundings. Myra (Gail Ganley), one of the students, tells Nancy that, without her sponsorship, Nancy will not be accepted by the other girls. Myra also impresses on Nancy that she is assistant to the chemistry teacher, Miss Branding (Louise Lewis), and that Myra can use this position to make Nancy's life miserable and affect her grades. Nancy's violent, rebellious nature immediately convinces Myra that Nancy is the perfect girl for Miss Branding's experiments. Together, Myra and Miss Branding arrange an accident whereby Miss Branding will gain Nancy's confidence. When the plan works, Miss Branding promises Nancy that, if the unhappy teenager will trust and obey her implicitly, Miss Branding, using an amulet from the Carpathian Mountains, will release in her a force which will give her control over her own emotional stresses. Secretly, Miss Branding hopes to prove her thesis, which has been rejected by all her male colleagues. Her thesis is that mankind can be saved from its own follies only by unleashing a power latent in human beings that will dwarf the power of the atomic bomb. Soon Nancy becomes a vampire, a teenage Dracula, murdering her fellow students. When Nancy seeks relief from the "bad dreams" she is having, Miss Branding refuses to help. Nancy turns into a vampire, kills Miss Branding, and is simultaneously pierced through the heart. Police arrive to find both the teacher and Nancy dead.

Blood of Dracula's Nancy Perkins is a female version of *Teenage Werewolf*'s Tony, only not nearly as high-strung and dangerous. It is clear that Nancy's parents don't understand her, and, because she is misunderstood, she acts out. She obviously does not fit in with the snobbish students at the girl's prep school where she is sent against her will. Nancy falls under the power of Miss Branding, an early film feminist who explains her lack of acceptance by the scientific community as follows:

> Learn something from this. We live in a world ruled by men, for men. They won't even consider my thesis. They mock me, and worse. They're convinced they're on the right track. But before they're proven wrong—and I can do that—they'll destroy the world through their reckless experiments. . . . I'm not against progress, but the search for power in the wrong place. If they continue, do you realize what the people of the future will be like? Monsters—grotesque, misshapen, frightened fiends. Isotopes and fall-out in our lungs and in our glands, distorting natural shape and proportion. No one can calculate the hazards of radiation. There is a power strong enough to destroy the world buried within each of us if only we can unleash it. I can release a destructive power in a human being that would make the split atom seem like a blessing. After I've demonstrated clearly that there is a more terrible power in us than man can create, scientists will give up their destructive experiments. They'll stop testing nuclear bombs. Nations will stop looking for new artifical weapons because the natural ones—we, the human race—will be too terrible to arouse. War will no longer be a calculated risk because it can only end in total destruction.

It is interesting that Miss Branding's ravings are quite in sync with the anti-scientific ravings of contemporary feminist science. Those closed-minded, power-hungry male scientists mock her because she hypothesizes that an ancient Transylvanian amulet can unlock vampiric tendencies in human beings and save the human race. Those males certainly are bigoted and nar-row! More to our concern, however, is that Miss Branding, like *Teenage Werewolf*'s Dr. Brandon (note the similarity in their names) and *Teenage Frankenstein*'s Professor Frankenstein, turns a teenager into a monster in order to prove a pet scientific hypothesis. The teenage monster is again more sinned against than sinning. The sinner is the adult, the scientist so preoccupied with his or her own pet theories and so enthralled in the prob-lems created by adult society, that the life of a poor misunderstood teenager is expendable. The teenager is the victim. The teenager did not cause the problems; adults did! Yet the teenager must pay the ultimate price. What a town without pity can do!

When *I Was a Teenage Frankenstein* and *Blood of Dracula* were originally released as a double bill in 1957, ads proclaimed the pairing "Fiendish, Frenzied, Blood-Chilling! Nothing Like This In All The History Of Hor-ror!" From the standpoint of what these counter-culture panderings implied about adults, the ads were probably right!

V. How to Make a Monster

Next in the series is American International's *How to Make a Monster* (1958). Set at American International Studios, the plot concerns Pete Drum-mond (Robert H. Harris), chief makeup artist for twenty-five years, who is pink-slipped by the new management from the East, Jeffrey Clayton (Paul Maxwell) and John Nixon (Eddie Marr), who plan to make musicals and comedies instead of the horror films for which Pete has created his remark-able monster makeups and made the studio famous. Pete, who is doing makeup for the studio's last horror film, *Frankenstein Meets Werewolf*, vows to use the very monsters the studio is abandoning to kill Clayton and Nixon. By mixing a mind-numbing ingredient into his foundation cream and persuading the young actors that their careers are through unless they place themselves in his power, he hypnotizes his teenage werewolf and teenage Frankenstein, Larry Drake (Gary Clarke) and Tony Mantell (Gary Conway), and sends them on missions resulting in the deaths of Clayton and Nixon. Studio guard Monahan, a self-styled detective, shows Pete and Rivero—Pete's reluctant assistant and accomplice—his little black book in which he has jotted down many facts related to the murders. Apprehensive, Pete makes himself up as a primitive monster and kills Monahan in the studio commissary. Pete and Rivero later invite young Larry and Tony to a farewell party at Pete's house, which is a virtual museum of all the monsters Pete has created. Pete stabs Rivero to death in the kitchen and hides his body. Unaware that they have been the instruments of Pete's revenge, the young actors become suspicious and try to escape. Pete attacks them with a knife, but Larry knocks over a candelabra, setting the house afire. Pete burns to death while trying to rescue the lifelike heads of his monster "children," and police arrive in time to save Larry and Tony.

It was an interesting idea to revive the teenage werewolf and teenage Frankenstein in a film in which the teenage actors playing the monsters are, while in makeup, actually hypnotized into killing people. As was the case in *Teenage Werewolf* and *Blood of Dracula,* the youngsters do not know they are committing crimes. Again, youth is the unwitting victim of unscrupulous adults.

VI. Teenage Caveman

How to Make a Monster played the top half of a double bill that included *Teenage Caveman.* In that film, a primitive superstitious people dwell in a barren, rocky land. The people are bound by The Law, a semi-religious code that forbids them to go across the river to the lush lands. Though these lands promise a better life, the tribe fears a monster said to dwell there. When his father is hurt, the boy (Robert Vaughn) leads a group of other boys across the river. After several harrowing adventures, the boy's father, who has recovered from his injuries, comes after him. The father takes the boy home, and the tribe demands the boy's death for breaking the law. The father persuades the tribe to pardon the boy, and the boy agrees to remain silent about the land beyond the river. When the boy becomes a man, he marries and takes his young wife across the river. The tribe follows him with intent to kill, learns that the monster it fears is really only a man in disguise, and decides to cross the river for a better life. At the end we discover that the story actually takes place in the future after the earth has been devastated by an atomic war.

Teenage Caveman, though it does not feature a teenage monster, deserves comment here because of its depiction of a teenager whose courage and vision lead him to disobey his backward elders, even at the risk of death. The film depicts adults as hopeless slaves to tradition, and youth as the vanguards of a better future. Ads for the film promise "Prehistoric Rebels Against Prehistoric Beasts." The rebels, of course, are the teenagers, but these rebels have a cause. If society is to progress, someone has to take the lead, and it isn't going to be an adult! In fact, the film implies that the primitive world of the future will be caused by the foolishness of adults whose blindness ushers in atomic war.

VII. Teenage Zombies

As the decade of the '50s neared its end, Governor Films produced *Teenage Zombies* (1959). The film concerns Regg (Don Sullivan), Julie (Mitzie Albertson), Skip (Paul Pepper), Pam (Bri Murphy), Morrie (Jay Hawk), and Dot (Nan Green), six energetic teenagers who plan to go water skiing in Regg's speedboat. Morrie and Dot decide not to go along, and Regg says he will pick them up when the kids return from skiing. Regg, Julie, Skip and Pam go water skiing and decide to have a picnic on an island. On the island they spot a number of zombies and a woman (Katherine Victor) identifying herself as Dr. Myra. The zombies, led by Ivan (Chuck Niles), lock the teenagers in cages, and Dr. Myra informs them that they will be used in experiments she is conducting in her laboratory. The doctor, it seems, is experimenting with a nerve gas that puts human beings into a zombie-like state. She and foreign agents plan to use the gas to turn a sizable percentage of the world's population into zombies. When their friends do not return, Morrie and Dot get the sheriff (Mike Concannon), who, unknown to the teenagers, is really working with Dr. Myra. Though two of the teenage girls are briefly turned into zombies, the teenagers overpower the forces of evil and save the day (and presumably the world).

Teenage Zombies returns to a theme prevalent in the '50s: the paranoid fear that someone or something is trying to change us, to make us over, to control us. Though the theme appears often in horror/science fiction films of the '50s, the most enduring treatments of the theme are William Cameron Menzies' *Invaders from Mars* (1953) and Don Siegel's classic *The Invasion of the Body Snatchers* (1956). The theme has two obvious sources: America's fear of communism (a threat from without), and America's fear of an enforced or mindless conformity (a threat from within). As Andrew Dowdy writes:

If we only had the movies by which to measure cultural change, those of the fifties would give us an image of an America darkly disturbed by its own cynical loss of innocence, an America prey to fears more pervasive and intense than anything admitted to during the war years.[6]

Consider Katherine Victor's musings from *Teenage Zombies*: "Ivan, the perfect slave: desires to work; perfect health; and obeys every command. With half the people on earth in his condition, we could have the epitome of civilization." Undoubtedly, many teenagers thought that adults harbored similar thoughts toward the younger generation and the future.

While '50s teenage monster films exploit America's general paranoia, they also exploit America's anti-intellectual tendencies. According to Richard Hofstadter's Pulitzer Prize-winning *Anti-Intellectualism in American Life*, Americans have always distrusted the intellect. Without a doubt, the teenage monster films of the '50s reinforce this anti-intellectualism. In four of the six films we have examined, scientists use teenagers as guinea pigs for their experiments, illustrating Hofstadter's contention that Americans view intellectuals as amoral. This is nothing new, of course. Intellectuals in '30s and '40s horror/science fiction films were also suspect. But after scientists led us to victory in World War II with the creation of the atomic bomb, '50s America viewed scientists as potential saviors, the purveyors of progress, the behind-the-scenes personnel who would invent our next timesaving device, our next modern product. But the teen exploitation horror/science fiction films of the '50s did not hold out such promise. In those films, paranoia held sway. The youth of America did not trust the adult generation that had weathered the depression and won World War II. American youth wanted freedom from that debt and license to be themselves. These wants required a rebellion against the concept of life as an endless search for greater physical comfort and against success defined as a house in Levittown with a new Westinghouse refrigerator. In essence, they required a rebellion against the American Dream.

VIII. Teenagers from Outer Space

Though, for the average viewer, it is one of the least interesting films of the '50s teenage monster films, the last film we will consider is, without doubt, a summary of all that came before, as well as a portent of what was to come in the '60s. The film is Warner Brothers' *Teenagers from Outer Space* (1959).

In the film, a group of teenagers arrives on earth in a spaceship, bringing with them a lobster-like beast called a Gargon that quickly grows to gigantic proportions when fed. It is the mission of the extraterrestrial teenagers to carry out the wishes of their elders by scouting Earth as a possible feeding ground for Gargons, which have a taste for flesh. Derek (David Love), one of the invaders, escapes from the group in order to explore the new planet for himself. Thor (Bryan Grant), however, pursues him with a deadly ray gun. Once in the city, Derek meets Betty Morgan (Dawn Anderson) and her amiable grandfather (Harvey B. Dunn). Derek falls in love with Betty and decides to defend earthlings against his teenage peers, his elders, and the Gargon. Meanwhile, Thor disintegrates a number of people as he closes in on Derek's whereabouts. Derek finally overcomes Thor, only to find that the Gargon has gotten food, grown to gigantic proportions, and gone off to devour the town. Derek manages to destroy the Gargon, but then is faced with the horrible news that his elders, including his father, are on their way to Earth on a mission of destruction. Torn by love for his father and love for Betty and other earthlings, Derek misdirects the fleet, causes it to crash to Earth, and saves the world from destruction.

Teenagers from Outer Space was written, produced, and directed by Tom Graef. Appearing in the credits as actor David Love, Graef stars as Derek, the teenager troubled by the deadly imperialism of his father and those of his father's generation. Faced with doing his duty as a good little soldier or betraying his elders to save the girl and civilization he has grown to love, Derek sides with love and destroys his own father and others of his father's generation who seek only power and planetary self-interest. The message is clear. America has become too imperialistic, too absorbed in her own growth at the expense of the rest of humanity. It is the older generation, the one that weathered the Depression and won World War II, that is to blame. The young idealist must oppose such a mentality, fight off members of his own generation imbued with the elders' destructive philosophy, and act out of love (note the actor's pseudonym) for the benefit of humanity.

IX. Analysis

Let us review the ground we have covered. *I Was a Teenage Werewolf* was a film made by adults for teenagers. While acknowledging that the lives of some teenagers are hard, it made the point that, though some adults may prey upon teenagers for their own ends, the teenager who becomes mons-terous becomes so as a result of his own character flaws. The seven teenage monster films that followed, all made by adults, laid the blame at the feet of the adult generation. Adults, in effect, assumed the guilt of turning inno-cent teenagers into monsters. *Teenagers from Outer Space* laid the founda-tion for the '60s counterculture, suggesting that teenagers must make a choice. Should they follow in the footsteps of their elders and seek eco-nomic expansion through imperialism, or should they be guided by love, a positive emotion that dictates rebellion against elders, even in modes most extreme? *Teenagers from Outer Space* made clear that teenagers should opt for love—the quintessential message of the '60s youth counterculture.

Now let's be clear about a few things. We have been examining movies here, products designed for mass consumption, products designed to make money. We are examining so-called ephemera, films made for an evening's entertainment, and nothing more. I would suggest, however, that films carry a greater impact than just an evening's entertainment. Entertainment designed for the masses can reflect changes in world view of the masses. Therefore, entertainment is important for the world view of a nation. The casual viewer or reader might assume that entertainment does not alter or shape public perceptions, but I would argue that it can. I would only point to Leni Riefenstahl, Hitler's brilliant propagandist filmmaker, as a counter to those who claim that films cannot shape attitudes and opinions.

In 1944, Helen Valentine launched *Seventeen* magazine, which encour-aged retailers and manufacturers for the first time to target a teenage audi-ence, particularly teenage girls. The magazine stressed the teenagers' desire for personal freedom coupled with a pitch for personal responsibility. By the mid-'50s, businessmen were replacing the emphasis on personal respon-sibility with a wholesale pandering to teenage counterculture–rock 'n' roll music being the most visible example.

In the late '50s, studio executives searched for ways to exploit the grow-ing teenage market. Teenage monster movies were among a wave of pro-ductions that included such exploitation titles as *Hot Rod Girl* (1956), *Hot Rod Gang* (1958), *High School Hellcats* (1958), and *The Cool and the Crazy* (1958). Though these films highlighted adolescent "Sturm und Drang," they were not as bleakly antiadult as the teenage monster films. In the lat-ter, adults are predators who create the objects of their own fear. With the possible exception of Tony in *Teenage Werewolf,* the adolescent monsters themselves are blameless. Note also how the image of the scientist changes in horror/science fiction films from the early to late '50s. In the first half of the decade, scientists and science itself are ambiguous. While scientific progress is responsible for creating many horrors, science is usually also humankind's savior. In the teenage monster films of the late '50s, scientists are uniformly evil. This is an example of how those films portray an adolescent vision in which hope is replaced with despair, and trust in authority is replaced with distrust and fear. If the paranoid style was prominent in the American vision, it was nowhere more prominent than in the teenage monster films.

In a review of Grace Palladino's book *Teenagers: An American History*, Diana West writes:

> . . . where Palladino examines the record, she sees only the rise of the teenger; equally important, however, is the death of the grownup. One is not possible without the other. The fact is, as consumerism became the American pastime, and as consumption, particularly consumption of entertainment, became driven by the infantile yearnings of adolescents, the influence of the adult on taste and behavior rapidly diminished. . . . [By 1965] the grown-up was dead, and a brave new age of infantilism was upon us. Since then, we have seen the rise of adolescents—and adolescently influenced adults—who have scarcely any links to their predecessors, cut adrift as they are from the moral strictures and social conventions of the past. The results—the teenage epidemics of premarital sex and illegitimacy, suicide, and violence, drug abuse and alcohol abuse—are not pretty.[7]

It is arguable that the rise of adolescent popular culture and the adults' abdication of their role as transmitters of culture have helped bring us to the point where we find ourselves today. In her review of Disney's *The Hunchback of Notre Dame*, Marian Kester Coombs writes that the process of cultural deterioration is already well underway:

> The principal subversion [in the film] is not the happy ending, but the stylized hatred of straight, mainstream, adult society. Back when actual adults were in charge, this vision of kids in control, of the inmates taking over the asylum, was a harmless distraction. But now look who's president. And look at the ugly chaos spreading throughout the school system and wherever else youth congregates; nihilism is no longer just a cartoon.[8]

It is one of the great dangers in a capitalist democracy that adults are free to mock themselves before the inexperienced and unformed if such mocking leads to financial profit. Unfortunately, the young are only too eager to see films praising the wisdom and virtue of the immature and the greed, heartlessness, and stupidity of the mature. When the doctors abdicate, the inmates are only too eager to run the asylum. The trouble is that the doctors don't get to leave. Instead, they must stay and suffer the consequences of their abdication. The young naturally seek guidance from adults, and in all cultures predating mid-'50s America, adults had risen to discharge their duty. Since the mid-'50s, however, adults have lost faith in the basic goodness of Western culture in general and in American culture in particular. Postmodern America is a country devoid of any sincere religious faith and devoid of any real faith in traditional American values. Nietzsche describes nihilism as a psychological state in three stages. First, "becoming has no goal." Second, "there is no grand unity in which the individual could immerse himself completely as in an element of supreme value." Third, the individual will

> pass sentence on this whole world of becoming as a deception and [he will] invent a world beyond it, a true world. But as soon as man finds out how that world is fabricated solely from psychological needs, and how he has absolutely no right to it, the last form of nihilism comes into being: it includes disbelief in any metaphysical world and forbids itself any belief in a true world. . . . the world looks valueless.[9]

There is little difference between nihilism and postmodernism. In a world without value or truth, the young seek only entertainment and creature comforts. Adults who have no answers to the questions of the young abdicate all responsibility for leadership and become as children. The seeds of American nihilism were planted before the advent of cinematic teenage monsters, but cinematic teenage monsters were among the first sprouts to break the soil.

Endnotes

1   David Halberstam, *The Fifties* (New York: Villard Books, 1993), p. x.
2   *Ibid.*, p. x.
3   Stephen King, *Dance Macabre* (New York: Everest House, 1981), p. 34.
4   *Ibid.*, p. 34.
5   Robert Brustein, "Reflections on Horror Movies," *Partisan Review* 25 (Spring, 1958): 288–296.
6   Andrew Dowdy, *The Films of the Fifties: The American State of Mind* (New York: William Morrow and Company, 1975 [1973]), pp. 66–67.

7   Diana West, "Review of *Teenagers: An American History* by Grace Palladino," *New Criterion* 15,1 (1996): 140.

8   Marian Kester Coombs, "Mondo Quasimodo," *Chronicles* 20,11 (1996): 47.

9   Friedrich Nietzsche, *The Will to Power,* ed. with commentary by Walter Kaufman (New York: Vintage, 1967), pp. 12–13.

Bibliography

Brustein, Robert. "Reflections on Horror Movies." *Partisan Review* 25 (Spring 1958): 288–296.

Coombs, Marian Kester. "Mondo Quasimodo." *Chronicles* 20, no. 11 (1996): 47.

Dowdy, Andrew. *The Films of the Fifties: The American State of Mind.* New York: William Morrow and Company, 1975 (1973).

Halberstam, David. *The Fifties.* New York: Villard Books, 1993.

King, Stephen. *Dance Macabre.* New York: Everest House, 1981.

Nietzsche, Friedrich. *The Will to Power.* Edited with commentary by Walter Kaufman. New York: Vintage, 1967.

West, Diana. Review of *Teenagers: An American History,* by Grace Palladino. In *New Criterion* 15, no. 1 (1996): 140.

Chapter 7
Mayfield After Midnight: Images of Youth and Parenting in *Leave It to Beaver*

Michael B. Kassel,
University of Michigan, Flint

I. Introduction

June Cleaver is not alone. Over the past forty years she has been joined by a chorus of academics who are equally "worried about the Beaver." Much of the discourse surrounding *Leave It to Beaver* has focused on its sins of omission and its preoccupation with middle class suburbia. In Comic Visions, David Marc characterized *Leave It to Beaver* and other family sitcoms as "benevolent Aryan melodramas" devised to promote middle class values.[1] In *The Way We Never Were,* Stephanie Coontz posited *Leave It to Beaver* as the snare which caught Americans in a "nostalgia trap" founded in a past that never was.[2] While both authors have helped uncover the serious limitations of the series, they have also made it difficult to explore *Leave It to Beaver* as anything more than a sorry blot on our cultural landscape.

However, *Leave It to Beaver* is much more than the result of media economics, societal intolerance, or the idiosyncratic world vision of its creators Joe Connelly and Bob Mosher; for beneath the surface of *Leave It to Beaver*'s modern kitchen and lily-white environment lay the more universal story of children and parents surviving the postmodern age. Placed in greater historical perspective, *Leave It to Beaver* reveals surprisingly relevant insights into its contemporary society's commitment to suburbia, scientific child-rearing, and consensus. At bottom, *Leave It to Beaver* offers a highly relevant commentary on America's long-standing commitment to the perfectibility of the family, particularly in regard to the complex relationship existing between parent and child.

II. Why Suburbia?

Relevance in popular culture artifacts rarely arises out of a contented society; it is endemic of a crisis that is either grossly apparent or, as in the case of *Leave It to Beaver,* masked by a shaky consensus. According to Todd Gitlin, relevance in popular culture emerges out of the media's particular reading of public sentiment:

> What comes across the small screen amounts to an entertaining version of the world (to ideology, in a word) but whatever conspiracy theorists may think, this is not because the networks are trying to indoctrinate the helpless masses. No, the networks generate ideology, most indirectly and unintentionally, by trying to read the popular sentiment and tailoring their schedules toward what they think the cardboard people they've conjured up want to see and hear.[3]

The ideology that television executives may have been reading into the '50s and early '60s audience was based on a growing postwar suburban ideal that was grounded, in part, in the ethnic and racial discrimination that preceded its portrayal on television. Indeed, at the time of *Leave It to Beaver*'s 1957 debut, approximately one-fifth to one-fourth of all Americans lived in predominately white suburbs,[4] the product of the Federal Housing Authority and real estate developers' efforts to red-line blacks out of the suburban landscape.[5] Such discrimination was not new to the twentieth century; it was rooted in the nineteenth-century suburbs forged by the middle class elite. According to Robert Fishman's *Bourgeois Utopias,* these early suburbs were not only important for what they included, but for what they excluded as well.[6] Consequently, the nineteenth-century middle-class move to suburbia was based, in part, on its growing fear of the urban environment, which came to house the growing number of poor working class and minorities who toiled in the factories and shops that helped the middle-class elite earn its entry into greener ground.[7] Although suburbia changed drastically in the postwar period, the modern suburbanite maintained the prewar suburban legacy of prejudice. As the GI Bill, a booming economy, and cheap available housing encouraged the postwar rush to suburbia, new residents entered within the context of a long-standing suburban ideal.[8]

Television networks were quick to latch on to the suburban phenomenon. Indeed, *Leave It to Beaver* was not the first suburban sitcom, but a late
arrival to the trend launched by such series as *Ozzie and Harriet* (1952) and
Father Knows Best (1954). One of the earliest programs to move to the suburbs was *The Goldbergs,* a popular radio sitcom transplanted to television in
1949. Five years later, *The Goldbergs* moved from New York row houses to
the fictional suburb of "Haverville," which, according to Marc, connotes
"The Village of the Haves."[9] To Marc, this move was predicated by television's desire to whiten the ethnic images that had been part of television's
golden age. In *Prime Time Families,* Ella Taylor argues that such moves were
grounded in the network's obsession with "least objectionable programming"—the process of providing images least likely to upset the mainstream American status quo.[10] Both arguments are certainly valid and help
explain why no Jewish families replaced *The Goldbergs* after their 1954 can-
cellation. While such sins of omission were not inevitable, they certainly
provided indifferent networks with an easy way out.

While it is imperative that scholars continue to explore the uncomfortable history of race and ethnicity in television, there are other factors that
contributed to the family sitcom's adoption of suburbia. One frequently
overlooked aspect involves the history of television production itself, which,
in the early '50s, moved from its urban New York setting (the capital of
network radio) to Hollywood. As New York's cosmopolitan influence was
gradually replaced by Southern California's marked decentralization—California is the epitome of single-dwelling tract development[11]—the writers
and producers' views of the world no doubt changed as well. Indeed, it
appears that, as writers lost their connection to New York, they became less
inclined to locate their programs in urban settings. This change is perhaps
best evidenced by the suburban values of two of the period's most powerful
producers, Desi Arnaz and Danny Thomas, who both sought an escape
from the hectic pace of life on the road. Desi Arnaz and Lucille Ball
believed that their suburban California ranch would help them better survive their tumultuous marriage.[12] Danny Thomas sought more time with
his family; the title of his successful series *Make Room for Daddy* was based
on the line his children would say when their "occasional" show business
father would return from road trips that often kept Thomas away for
months at a time.[13] The feeling of security that Arnaz and Thomas thought
they had found in suburbia was echoed by others who flocked to Holly-

wood to work in the relatively stable brand of episodic network entertainment. To pose an analogy, if working on the road was urban, the daily grind of weekly sitcoms was suburban. Thus, long before Hollywood began selling suburbia to America, its pivotal players had already sold it to themselves.

The most compelling explanation of the family sitcom's adoption of suburbia, however, is found in the strong ideological connection between suburbia and child-rearing. While the GI Bill and affordable housing helped transform suburbia from a middle class utopia to a mass setting that included the white working class, many of its prewar ideological underpinnings (particularly those regarding children) remained. Indeed, the American suburb's pristine image was built on the back of the city. Long before '50s intellectuals began attacking the vacuous life of the suburbs, a vast nineteenth and early-twentieth-century literature posited the city as the enemy of family and child welfare. "On balance," wrote Kenneth Jackson in *Crabgrass Frontiers*, ". . . the American metropolis was more a symbol of problems and of evil than of hope, love or generosity."[14] Catherine Beecher, in her *Treatise on Domestic Economy* (1841) convinced her privileged contemporaries that suburbia held the key to a moral Christian home.[15] This ideology did not wither in the postwar suburban transformation. According to Scott Donaldson, the postwar suburban disillusionment of the '50s and '60s was due, in part, to the suburbs' failure to live up to the utopian promises its ideologues had so long espoused.[16] Connelly and Mosher were not isolated from this American family ideology, which no doubt contributed to their conscious decision to place a series dedicated to youth and parenting in the heart of suburbia. Nevertheless, just as the real suburbia revealed its flaws, so too did the Cleaver's Mayfield.

Contrary to popular myth, Mayfield was not perfect. Gerald Jones in *Honey, I'm Home* notes that the Cleavers' happy home was surrounded by a large number of troubled youth hailing from highly dysfunctional families (the most significant being America's favorite wise guy, Eddie Haskell). According to Jones,

> Eddie wasn't just a bad kid, a symbol of self-indulgence or of the big world waiting to seduce the innocent (although he was often both). He was trying to prove a point about natural conflicts, irreconcilable differences, clashing ideologies. Like the Kingfish [a character Connelly and Mosher created during their tenure with *Amos and Andy*], he was a retrograde figure, resisting forward movement of the group and pursuing happiness in willfully contrary directions.[17]

The appearance of Eddie Haskell raises an interesting question in regard to
the academic discourse surrounding the series: If the goal of *Leave It to
Beaver* was to venerate the white middle class, why would the series allow
for that environment to produce not only Eddie Haskell, but other problem children including Clarence "Lumpy" Rutherford, Larry Mondello,
and Gilbert Bates? Apparently, a happy home required more than a nuclear
family residing along tree-lined curvilinear streets.

   Leave It to Beaver was the product of more than long-standing intolerance and "least objectionable programming." At bottom, *Leave It to Beaver*'s
suburban setting provided a convenient vehicle for the universal ideal of the
perfectibility of the family. Indeed, according to at least one episode, the
suburban environment was not even requisite to healthy child development. In "The Grass Is Always Greener," Beaver befriends the neighborhood trash man, who feels that Beaver would make a wonderful playmate
for his two little boys, Chris and Pete. The trash man invites Beaver to his
urban home near the city dump. June, a captive of her middle class sensibilities, is worried about the impact this visit may have on the Beaver, but
Ward convinces June to let their son go and enjoy the day. When Beaver
returns, he is full of wonderful stories of the urban dump and looks forward
to visiting again. June, worried about the Beaver's new fascination with life
across the tracks, suggests he invite his new friends to the Cleaver home.
Chris and Pete are awed by the fresh air and green, wide open spaces. Yet,
in the midst of what appears to be (and, in many respects, is) a mere ven-
eration of middle class suburbia, Chris and Pete challenge June's preconceived notions and prejudices by appearing more well mannered and better
behaved than any of Mayfield's own privileged suburban youth.[18] Behind
this dramatic turn, embedded within this episode's highly complex set of
messages, emerges *Leave It to Beaver*'s central thesis: environment is second
to upbringing.

III. Building a Better Beaver Through Science

   Leave It to Beaver was first and foremost a show about parenting and
childhood. Therefore, it dealt with the issues of youth and parenting as no
show had done before. Unlike Jim Anderson of *Father Knows Best*, who
worried about whether he would be voted father of the year, or Ozzie Nelson, who was preoccupied with getting back the quarter he had loaned to

his neighbor, Ward and June Cleaver had no problems independent of their children. If Ward and June were perfect in solving their children's problems, it was only because social science had told them it was possible.

The application of psychology and sociology to parenting is rooted in the late nineteenth century, when children began taking center stage in American family life. A brief overview of this complex history would begin with the rise of social instruction publications that proliferated in the late nineteenth century. In the early twentieth century, John Watson's work in behaviorism made psychology a fixture of American child-rearing.[19] During the progressive era, child-rearing, particularly in regard to infants, became a major focus of the middle class women who began their tenure at Hull House and went on to help forge federal child welfare policy.[20] Robert and Helen Lynd, in their classic study of mid-'20s Muncie, Indiana, found that the application of innovative social techniques was most frequently applied to children, who were much more susceptible to change than adults.[21] The postwar baby boom revived popular interest in innovative child rearing, and Dr. Spock became a fixture of American homes. Thus, by the time Ward and June Cleaver arrived on the scene, parenting was a science backed by a wealth of professional and popular literature. While Ward may have professed that he would not be made to feel guilty by popular psychology books,[22] they often seemed to do just that. Consequently, the Cleavers, following the vast parenting literature of their day, not only discussed the right way to raise their sons but made critical assessments of how they handled— and mishandled—various situations.

For all the generalizations regarding Ward and June's effective parenting skills, the Cleavers—particularly Ward—were more often than not prone to mishandle their kids' troublesome situations. In "The Haircut," Ward's plan to reestablish Beaver's responsibility with money backfires when Beaver loses his haircut money en route to the barber shop. Afraid to face his father, Beaver turns to Wally, who grudgingly agrees to give Beaver a haircut. When the amateur cut leaves Beaver nearly bald, the brothers use a wool cap to hide the hairdo. Later at dinner, the cap comes off; the truth comes out; and both Wally and Beaver are sent to their room while Ward and June discuss the appropriate punishment. While Ward is hurt because his boys have deceived him, June places the situation in psychological perspective using dialogue straight out of the pages of contemporary parenting and child development literature.[23] If Ward and June were unrealistically successful parents, it was not in their freedom from making mistakes but in their willingness to realize their errors—at least until the next episode, when the cycle of problem, misunderstanding, and resolution was repeated.

If the Cleavers' great perceptive skills painted too perfect a picture of parenting, other Mayfield parents quickly brought the viewer back to reality. Snatches of conversation uttered across dozens of episodes by Wally and Beaver's pals reveal homes either dominated by screaming parents who resorted to corporal punishment or lenient parents who had neither the courage nor stamina to say "no." Eddie Haskell, the most rebellious youth in sitcom history, was the product of an overprotective mother and harried father whose interest in domestic tranquility led them to overindulge Eddie. Beaver's apple-chomping pal, Larry Mondello, was the product of an anxious mother and conspicuously absent father whose frequent business trips left Mrs. Mondello alone to deal with oafish Larry and his depression-ridden sister. Clarence "Lumpy" Rutherford's problems were the result of the impossible expectations held out by his overbearing father, Fred, who was too proud to admit that his son was below average. Unable to control his own neurosis, it is not surprising that Fred often replaced sound psychological parenting with an old-fashioned slap across the mouth.[24]

Unlike many of their Mayfield cohorts, Ward and June never resorted to physical abuse. Even Marc is quick to paraphrase Robert S. Alley's argument that "the classic domesticoms . . . actually contain many highly relevant (and in some cases, quite liberal) political and social messages, especially in the area of parent-child relations."[25] Ward and June were not superparents endowed with mystical powers. They simply used the tools available through the popular parenting literature of their time.

IV. The Organization Dad

In 1956, William Whyte Jr. published his classic, *The Organization Man,* an indictment of the group mentality that had taken hold of postwar middle class American life. One year later, Connelly and Mosher provided America with Ward Cleaver, television's greatest example of the organization type. Just like Whyte's organization man, Ward saw getting along as not simply a matter of unknowing conformity, but as a moral imperative.[26] Ward's specific job remains a mystery, but, unlike Ozzie Nelson, Ward was often seen behind a desk. True to the organization type, Ward's time was not spent on tangible production but on supervising the work of others. A cog in the corporate machine, Ward (depending on the episode one watches) was either involved in marketing or management. Like Whyte's organization man, Ward's specific role was not as important as the fact that he held a comfortable position within a secure firm—a man in the middle of middle management.[27] What mattered most to the organization man was tolerance in the context of serving the needs of the group.

The growing importance of group tolerance is explored quite well in "Larry's Club," in which Beaver becomes involved in the Bloody Five, a childhood version of the exclusive clubs that were quite common to prewar suburbia. Beaver seems willing to go along with the exclusionary practices of the club until they decide to blackball his pal, Larry Mondello. When Ward learns of the actions of the Bloody Five, it upsets his organization sensibilities. Toward the end of the episode, Ward turns to Beaver and delivers a parable designed to inculcate the organization man's sense of tolerance and fair play. Ward's message: while it is fine to band together to help one another, it is wrong to do so at the exclusion of others.[28] As a good organization kid, Beaver grasps this positive lesson quite quickly and ends forever his association with secret societies.

For all his connections to the organization ideal, Ward did not conform completely to Whyte's ideal type. According to Whyte, the organization man accepted and embraced modernity, finding his roots not in some nostalgic vision of the past, but in the professional and suburban communities he had forged.[29] Ward, however, frequently drew on the Protestant ethic of his past, and his *gemeinschaft* roots were often drawn into conflict with the *gesellschaft* world he had inherited. Rather than embrace modernity, Ward often pined for the good old days, in which the living was easy and the children had more respect.

Ward's nostalgic feelings are best explored in "The Happy Weekend," in which Ward attempts to give his boys a taste of the simpler life he once enjoyed at rustic Shadow Lake. Trouble starts before the trip begins, however, when Wally and Beaver tell Ward they have already made plans with Eddie to see the latest B-movie, *Jungle Fever*. Ward will have none of that; the family is bound for a weekend of some good old-fashioned fun whether they like it or not. Upon their arrival, Ward soon finds that picturesque Shadow Lake has been corrupted by modernity. The first assault on Ward's pristine past occurs when June and the boys find a small strip mall that offers comic books for the kids and a hairdresser for June. Later, Ward and his boys learn that the lake has been artificially stocked to accommodate people's growing desire for a maximum catch with minimum effort. The ultimate insult comes when Wally and Beaver find Shadow Lake's most impressive feature (a cliff overlooking the town's drive-in theater that is showing *Jungle Fever*). Wally and Beaver spend their last night at Shadow Lake taking turns watching the film through binoculars.[30]

Ironically, while "The Happy Weekend" has Ward depart from Whyte's ideal type, the departure is based in Ward's discomfort with the same sort of mass, "organized" fun that disturbed Whyte himself. Of course, the problem of mass culture and its effects on children were not unique to the '50s; the Lynds explored it in their '20s investigation of Middletown. Nevertheless, "The Happy Weekend," with its strip malls, stocked ponds, and drive-in theaters, clearly shows how pervasive consumer culture had become in the postwar era. On the eve of the '60s, not even nature was free from modernity.

V. Mayfield Meets the Real World

In *Comic Visions*, David Marc wrote that the "sitcom romanticized the suburb as an idyllic small town that was located not merely miles from the modern city but the better part of a century away as well."[31] However, as "The Happy Weekend" reveals, many of the problems facing the Cleavers did not surface out of a static, vacuous environment, but were endemic of a dynamic, changing culture that managed to make its presence felt deep in the heart of Mayfield and its environs. Consequently, such relevant issues surfaced in *Leave It to Beaver.*

Perhaps the most compelling of the issue-oriented *Leave It to Beaver* episodes is "Beaver's House Guest," in which Beaver's summer camp friend, Chopper Cooper, comes for a visit. As Beaver soon discovers, Chopper, the product of divorced parents, is a very mature child. Gregarious and optimistic, Chopper appears quite indifferent to his situation, buoyed by the superficial perks of divorce—an unending stream of gifts showered upon him by two bickering parents competing for his affection.

This sort of attention appeals to Beaver's less-thoughtful materialism, and he spends the better part of the episode in a selfish quest for a Cleaver divorce. Beaver finally realizes the downside of divorce when Chopper gets a call from his mother. Sad and depressed after another scathing verbal exchange with her ex-husband (off-screen, of course), Mrs. Cooper asks

Chopper to return home and console her. Familiar with the devastating effects of his parents' arguments, Chopper is not surprised that he must end his happy weekend.

On the surface, "Beaver's House Guest" appears to be little more than an indictment of divorce, but, as with most episodes, the message is not that simple. Indeed, earlier in the episode, when Beaver asks his dad to define divorce, Ward does not denounce it but describes it as an option couples take when they are "hopelessly incompatible." What truly troubles Ward is the way Chopper's parents are confusing and hurting the young boy by playing him against the middle. In the last scene, when Ward returns from Chopper's home, he tells June of his discussion with Mrs. Cooper, who, thanks to Ward's meddling, is beginning to realize the damaging effects she and her ex-husband are having on their son. Ultimately, "Beaver's House Guest" appears to argue that, even in divorce, proper parenting skills can work wonders.[32]

Leave It to Beaver's exploration of divorce is not surprising; Joe Connelly's parents divorced when he was quite young, and Bob Mosher was raised by his aunt.[33] One could certainly probe the psychological impact Connelly and Mosher's childhoods had on the series as a whole, but the sensitivity and pathos of this episode indicate that the two producers were speaking from experience. While divorce was statistically more significant in Connelly and Mosher's day than it was in the late '50s, the episode allowed them to express another common *Leave It to Beaver* theme: Parents should not shield their children from serious or uncomfortable issues.

Perhaps no episode explores this theme better than "Beaver and Andy," in which Beaver unwittingly gives a shot of brandy to an alcoholic handyman working in the Cleaver home. Beaver's unfortunate mistake is the direct result of Ward and June's refusal to openly acknowledge Andy's drinking problem. When Beaver admits that he gave Andy a drink, Ward becomes furious. Wally quickly rises to Beaver's defense, reminding his parents that they never discussed the true nature of Andy's problem. Realizing his error, Ward announces the moral of the story (a moral that is quite the opposite of the popular impression of the series): that parents must avoid shielding children from life's problems.[34] Placed in the context of similar story lines, another common *Leave It to Beaver* theme emerges: Parents must equip their children with the proper skills necessary to navigate a troubled world.

This theme is brought home in two other episodes. In "One of the Boys," Wally considers joining the Barons, another exclusive Mayfield boys club. As good organization people, Ward and June are upset. However, rather than lecture Wally, as did Ward with Beaver in "Larry's Club," Ward stakes his hope on the consensus-laden guidance that he and June have provided Wally over the years. When Wally finds the Barons to be little more than spoiled brats who hang around in a big house, play pool, and "knock" other kids, Wally does his parents proud and walks away. Wally faces a similar situation in "Box-Office Attraction," in which a sophisticated young adult woman, Marlene, takes a liking to him. When Wally discovers that Marlene drinks, smokes, and hangs around in a pool hall, he puts his hormones in check and just says "no."[35] While Gerald Jones suggests that this episode may indicate Wally's own sexual dysfunction,[36] he fails to acknowledge that there were teenagers who did make such decisions. Grace Palladino, in *Teenagers,* notes that a minority of privileged teens made the sort of choices that took them along a career path as opposed to a lifestyle of excess and reckless abandon.[37]

Each of these episodes paints a portrait of a quiet suburbia and its children being rocked by outside forces. Whether the problem was divorce, drinking, or quasi–juvenile delinquency, the only real control parents had lay in the example they set for their children—which is exactly what social scientists had been arguing all along. While many of the issues in these episodes were not specific to the '50s, *Leave It to Beaver* was certainly far removed from the idyllic nineteenth-century setting suggested by Marc. By bringing these problems to Mayfield—and the viewing audience—Connelly and Mosher showed that suburbia was no panacea for the temptations that existed in an increasingly complex twentieth century.

The greatest assault on Mayfield's bliss came from its own children, the product of the same suburbia as Wally and Beaver. At the bottom of these problems lay peer pressure and the need for acceptance. For example, when Wally's male friends boast of their beard growth in "The Shave," Wally is compelled to borrow Ward's razor and begin shaving. In "Wally's Haircomb," Wally shocks his mother and father by sporting a rock-and-roll inspired "jelly-roll" haircut imported to Mayfield by Eddie Haskell. When Beaver commits the mortal sin of liking his teacher in "Beaver's Crush," he must prove himself among his peers by sneaking a coiled snake into her desk. When Whitey Whitney calls Beaver a "chicken" in the classic episode

"In the Soup," Beaver climbs into the giant steaming cup on the Zesty Soup billboard to prove his emerging manhood (not to mention his gullibility).[38]

The unending search for peer acceptance among children and adolescents was the most relevant issue addressed by *Leave It to Beaver.* "In the years immediately following the end of the Second World War, an active social life became the measure of success for more teenagers than ever before," writes Palladino. "The quest for popularity—for dates, invitations, and a sought-after group of friends—assumed new importance in the postwar world."[39] The lengths to which some Mayfield youths would go to obtain friendship were, indeed, astounding. When Gilbert Bates first arrives in Mayfield, he makes up tall tales of his father in order to win the other kids' attention. The most disturbing example of the need for acceptance is found in "Beaver and Kenneth," in which a shy, new kid at school steals from his classmates and then passes the loot off as gifts to Beaver in order to win Beaver's friendship and earn a ticket of entry into the popular crowd.[40]

As was the case with teens and preteens in most American cities, suburbs, and towns, Mayfield's could not afford to be seen as odd or "square," and popularity was most often defined in terms of appearance. Ward, the organization man, was well aware of the psychological importance of conformity and often supported Wally and Beaver's desire to fit in. In "Wally's Haircomb," Ward accepts Wally's wild new hairstyle as harmless rebellion, reminding June that they cannot force Wally to be different. In "Beaver's Jacket," Beaver has little trouble convincing Ward to buy him a $23.76 jacket which has become the latest school fad. In "Beaver's Football Award," Ward allows Beaver to go along with the crowd and dress casually for an awards banquet; when Beaver winds up being the only kid to follow through on the informal dress, he ends up feeling like "a creep." In "Wally and Dudley," the whole Cleaver family gets into the peer pressure act when they help transform a square teen into a regular "Big Man On Campus."[41] While stories of haircuts and snazzy jackets appear quite trivial in comparison to the sort of problems TV kids encounter today, these stories accurately reflect the '50s youth culture which was coming to define itself along superficial lines. At bottom was that everpresent consensus mentality. It was not simple conformity; as with adults, the need to fit in had become a moral imperative.

VI. Beaver Versus the Establishment

Long before it became fashionable to distrust anyone over thirty, Wally and Beaver were wise to the hypocrisies of the adult world. Indeed, *Leave It to Beaver* was permeated by an "us and them" mentality in which Mayfield youth struggled to make sense of the authoritarian, arbitrary nature of adult behavior. Produced in part from a child's-eye view, *Leave It to Beaver* was often obliged to portray adults as deplorable beings who would stop at nothing to achieve their goals—even if it meant taking advantage of a little kid. In "Perfume Salesmen," Wally and Beaver get taken by a New York firm that fails to adequately reward their efforts to sell the company's foul-smelling perfume. In "Beaver Finds a Wallet," Beaver's good deed of return-ing a lost wallet results in great disappointment when the callous owner fails to deliver a promised reward. When Beaver opens his house to a tramp in "Beaver's Good Deed," the indigent man responds by stealing one of Ward's suits. In "Beaver, The Caddy," a wealthy country-club member poses a moral crisis for Beaver when he asks the young lad to help him cheat on his golf score.[42]

Perhaps the clearest indictment of adulthood occurs in "Beaver Takes a Drive," in which Beaver and Gilbert accidentally slip the parking brake on Ward's car and roll it into the street. Unable to move the car, Beaver causes a minor traffic jam along Pine Street. The frustrated adults begin screaming and honking their horns in anger. Wally fares no better with the adults when he arrives on the scene; only one man displays any form of kindness by asking Wally if he needs help. Wally nods politely, finds a spare key, and moves the car into the driveway, only to be met by another adult—a cop who gives him a ticket for driving without a license. Appearing later in front of the juvenile traffic court judge, Wally tries to explain the impossi-bility of the situation, indicating how the yelling adults had made him reluctant to ask for the help he needed to legally move the car into the driveway.[43]

Yet, for all the problems caused by anonymous adults, the most fre-quent friction occurred between parent and child, particularly among May-field's less settled families. To Eddie Haskell, kids were engaged in a cold war with their parents. Eddie viewed mothers and fathers as wardens and likened freedom to "going over the wall."[44] To Eddie, summer camp and boarding school were little more than convenient places for parents to "dump" their kids, and any parent who ever said "no" was merely engaging in the expression of capricious power. Although Wally was too wise to be swayed by Eddie, Beaver often took the troublemaker quite seriously. For example, when Ward refused to allow Beaver to order an accordion, Eddie posited the blame on Ward's insecurity that Beaver would become famous.[45] Although Eddie was merely "giving Beaver the business," as Wally would say, one has to question the type of home life that fostered such thoughts. In the meantime, Beaver was forced to learn his lesson the hard way.

The generation gap worked both ways, and Mayfield parents—including the Cleavers—frequently viewed children with suspicion as well. While Ward often displayed keen insight into the child's mind—expressed across dozens of episodes in his folksy, "immutable laws of childhood"—he also believed that parents had the right to resort to benign forms of subterfuge in order to stay one step ahead of their children. Emerging from this atmosphere of mistrust was the clear understanding that parents and children inhabited separate spheres which could only be breached through reason, listening, and mutual respect. While it took a TV family to have the time, patience—and script—to attempt to bridge the gap, viewers were not the only ones surprised by Ward and June's success—Mayfield's other parents and children stood just as stunned.

VII. Conclusion

If Americans have a single collective belief, it is in the ubiquity of the media. Consequently, we take seriously those images that saturate the American psyche in first run and rerun, season after season. When we look back on the '50s and see a nation of plenty standing proudly alongside another America of poverty and despair, we become indignant toward those shows that appear to venerate the callous mainstream. However, media images, like the problems they perpetuate, are never as one-dimensional as they first appear. While *Leave It to Beaver* certainly suffered from the intolerant excess of the '50s, it was also keenly aware of the problems that lurked below its fragile mask of consensus. In thinking about the shortcomings of *Leave It to Beaver,* we must never feel that our interpretation of the artifact is complete, for its problematic images coexist with the sitcom's own discomfort with its time.

While *Leave It to Beaver* has provided fodder for a number of arguments regarding the series' social impact, one simple fact remains: Even if *Leave It to Beaver* had been designed simply to venerate the conservative white middle class, it certainly failed to do so. In 1963, when the last *Leave It to Beaver* episode aired, America witnessed such harbingers of change as the publication of Betty Friedan's *The Feminine Mystique,* the continuing rise of the civil rights movement, and the assassination of John F. Kennedy. While *Leave It to Beaver* certainly contributed to America's nostalgic and mythical view of the family, its most conservative messages, in their time, were lost in a massive wave of social and cultural change. Given the surprising insights into the relevant issues of its day, *Leave It to Beaver* is, indeed, much more interesting for its social commentary than for its mainstream predictability.

Leave It to Beaver's greatest social commentary involves its exploration of the complex relationship existing between parent and child. Inspired by America's obsession with the perfectibility of the family, the Cleavers used the scientific tools of their day to survive within the highly organized structure imposed upon the postwar family. Yet beneath *Leave It to Beaver*'s image of perfection and innocence lay the imperfect reality of Mayfield after midnight—a world of problems both imported and indigenous to its beloved suburbia. A world in which the dark age of consensus was giving way to an emerging youth culture which would attack the very conventions in which it was raised. A world that, within just a few short years, would never be the same again. In *The Way We Never Were,* Stephanie Coontz spends a fair amount of time arguing that *Leave It to Beaver* is not a documentary. Yet, in a very peculiar way, that is exactly what it is.

Endnotes

1 Marc, David, *Comic Visions* (Boston: Unwin Hyman, 1989), p. 52.
2 Coontz, Stephanie, *The Way We Never Were* (New York: Basic Books, 1992), p. 29.
3 Gitlin, Todd, *Inside Prime Time* (New York: Pantheon Books, 1985), p. 203.
4 Jones, Gerald, *Honey, I'm Home* (New York: St. Martin's Press, 1992), p. 88. Jones estimates that "By 1953, one out of five Americans lived in the suburbs . . ." Scott Donaldson, *The Suburban Myth* (New York: Columbia University Press, 1969), p. 4. Donaldson estimates that 50 million people lived in the suburbs by 1960.
5 A thorough discussion of "red-lining" is found in Jackson, Kenneth, *Crabgrass Frontiers* (New York: Oxford University Press, 1985), pp. 197–218.
6 Fishman, Robert, *Bourgeois Utopias* (New York: Basic Books, 1987), p. 6.
7 *Ibid.* See pages 77–91.

8   Donaldson, p. 22.

9   Marc, p. 51.

10 Taylor, Ella, *Prime Time Families* (Berkeley: University of California Press, 1989), p. 40.

11 Fishman, pp. 155–156.

12 Arnaz, Desi, *A Book* (New York: Warner Books, 1976), p. 238.

13 Thomas, Danny, *Make Room for Danny* (New York: Putnam, 1991), p. 12.

14 Jackson, p. 69.

15 Fishman, p. 122.

16 Donaldson, p. 216.

17 Jones, Gerald, *Honey, I'm Home* (New York: St. Martin's Press, 1992), p. 126.

18 Connelly, Joe; Mosher, Bob, producers, "The Grass Is Always Greener," *Leave It to Beaver*, Gomalco Productions, 1958.

19 Leahey, Thomas Hardy, *A History of Psychology* (Englewood Cliffs, New Jersey: Prentice Hall, 1987). For a full discussion of Watson and parenting, see pp. 350–354.

20 A complete discussion of the role middle-class women played in forging United States children's welfare policy can be found in Muncy, Robyn, *Creating a Female Dominion* (New York: Oxford University Press, 1991).

21 Lynd, Robert S. and Helen M., *Middletown* (New York: Harcourt-Brace & Company, 1929), p. 500.

22 Connelly & Mosher, "Borrowed Boat," 1959

23 Connelly & Mosher, "The Haircut," 1957.

24 Applebaum, Irwyn, *The World According to Beaver* (New York: Bantam Books, 1984), p. 85.

25 Marc, p. 108.

26 Whyte, William, Jr., *The Organization Man* (New York: Simon and Schuster, 1956), p. 394.

27 Ibid., p. 27.

28 Connelly & Mosher, "Larry's Club," 1960.

29 While the organization man's pragmatic acceptance of modernity is echoed throughout Whyte's work, a detailed discussion is found in Whyte, Chapter 21, "The Transients," pp. 267–280, and Chapter 22, "The New Roots," pp. 280–298.

30 Connelly & Mosher, "The Happy Weekend," 1958.

31 Marc, p. 53.

32 Connelly & Mosher, "Beaver's House Guest," 1960.

33 Applebaum, p. 16.

34 Connelly & Mosher, "Beaver and Andy," 1960.

35 Connelly & Mosher, "One of the Boys," 1961; "Box-Office Attraction," 1962.

36 Jones, p. 159.

37 Palladino, Grace, *Teenagers* (New York: Basic Books, 1996), p. 163.

38 Connelly & Mosher, "The Shave," 1958; "Wally's Haircomb," 1959; "Beaver's Crush," 1957; "In the Soup," 1961.

39 Palladino, p. 98.

40 Connelly & Mosher; "Beaver and Gilbert," 1959; "Beaver and Kenneth," 1959.

41   Connelly & Mosher, "Beaver's Jacket," 1962; "Beaver's Football Award," 1962; "Wally and Dudley," 1959.
42   Connelly & Mosher, "The Perfume Salesmen," 1957; "Beaver Finds a Wallet," 1959; "Beaver's Good Deed," 1962; "Beaver, The Caddy," 1963.
43   Connelly & Mosher, "Beaver Takes a Drive," 1961.
44   Jones, p. 126
45   Connelly & Mosher, "Beaver's Accordion," 1959

Bibliography

Applebaum, Irwyn. *The World According to Beaver.* New York: Bantam Books, 1984.

Arnaz, Desi. *A Book.* New York: Warner Books, 1976.

Coontz, Stephanie. *The Way We Never Were.* New York: Basic Books, 1992.

Donaldson, Scott. *The Suburban Myth.* New York: Columbia University Press, 1969.

Fishman, Robert. *Bourgeois Utopias.* New York: Basic Books, 1987.

Gitlin, Todd. *Inside Prime Time.* New York: Pantheon Books, 1985.

Jackson, Kenneth. *Crabgrass Frontiers.* New York: Oxford University Press, 1985.

Jones, Gerald, *Honey, I'm Home.* New York: St. Martin's Press, 1992.

Leahey, Thomas Hardy. *A History of Psychology.* Englewood Cliffs, N.J.: Prentice Hall, 1987.

Lynd, Robert S. and Helen M. Lynd. *Middletown.* New York: Harcourt-Brace & Company, 1929.

Marc, David. *Comic Visions.* Boston: Unwin Hyman, 1989.

Muncy, Robyn. *Creating a Female Dominion.* New York: Oxford University Press, 1991.

Palladino, Grace. *Teenagers.* New York: Basic Books, 1996.

Taylor, Ella. *Prime Time Families.* Berkeley: University of California Press, 1989.

Thomas, Danny. *Make Room for Danny.* New York: Putnam, 1991.

Whyte, William, Jr. *The Organization Man.* New York: Simon and Schuster, 1956.

Leave It to Beaver Episodes

Connelly, Joe, and Bob Mosher, producers. "Beaver's Accordion," *Leave It to Beaver,* Gomalco Productions, 1959.

———. "Beaver and Andy," *Leave It to Beaver,* Gomalco Productions, 1960.

———. "Beaver, The Caddy," *Leave It to Beaver,* Gomalco Productions, 1963.

———. "Beaver's Crush," *Leave It to Beaver,* Gomalco Productions, 1957.

———. "Beaver Finds a Wallet," *Leave It to Beaver,* Gomalco Productions, 1959.

———. "Beaver's Football Award," *Leave It to Beaver,* Gomalco Productions, 1962.

———. "Beaver Gets 'Spelled," *Leave It to Beaver,* Gomalco Productions, 1957.

———. "Beaver and Gilbert," *Leave It to Beaver,* Gomalco Productions, 1959.

———. "Beaver's Good Deed," *Leave It to Beaver,* Gomalco Productions, 1962.

———. "Beaver's House Guest," *Leave It to Beaver,* Gomalco Productions, 1960.

———. "Beaver and Kenneth," *Leave It to Beaver,* Gomalco Productions, 1959.

———. "Beaver's Jacket," *Leave It to Beaver,* Gomalco Productions, 1962.

————. "Beaver Takes a Drive," *Leave It to Beaver,* Gomalco Productions, 1961.

————. "Borrowed Boat," *Leave It to Beaver,* Gomalco Productions, 1959.

————. "Box-Office Attraction," *Leave It to Beaver,* Gomalco Productions, 1962.

————. "The Grass Is Always Greener," *Leave It to Beaver,* Gomalco Productions, 1958.

————. "The Haircut," *Leave It to Beaver,* Gomalco Productions, 1957.

————. "In the Soup," *Leave It to Beaver,* Gomalco Productions, 1961.

————. "Larry's Club," *Leave It to Beaver,* Gomalco Productions, 1960.

————. "One of the Boys," *Leave It to Beaver,* Gomalco Productions, 1961.

————. "The Perfume Salesmen," *Leave It to Beaver,* Gomalco Productions, 1957.

————. "The Shave," *Leave It to Beaver,* Gomalco Productions, 1958.

————. "Wally and Dudley," *Leave It to Beaver,* Gomalco Productions, 1959.

————. "Wally's Haircomb," *Leave It to Beaver,* Gomalco Productions, 1959.

Chapter 8
Shakin' All Over: Teenagers, Consumption, and Social Change in Postwar Britain

Bill Osgerby,
University of North London, England

> Today, the teenagers pay the piper—largely because they are the most numerous group with money to spare on this kind of thing—and the tunes they call have their elders in a whirl. With astonishment, dismay, curiosity or even fear, the adults find themselves on the outside, looking in at a vast industry with an annual turnover of many millions which is entirely devoted to the satisfaction of caprices and whims expressed by those who, only a few years ago, were expected to be seen and not heard. (Leslie, 15)

I. Twist and Shout: Beatlemania and the Iconography of Youth in Postwar Britain

Britain in the early '60s was a land possessed. There was no escape. The Beatles were everywhere. In 1962 the Fab Four were already enjoying moderate success but were still only one among a motley assortment of aspiring young popsters. In 1963 it all changed. Beatlemania tore through Britain like a mop-topped whirlwind, and the Beatles were transformed into a social phenomenon. By December, seven of their records presided over the Top Twenty; the band had headed a Royal Variety Performance; and their every appearance was besieged by hordes of screaming young fans. The press fell over themselves to chart the foursome's every exploit, while merchandisers jostled to cash in on the Beatles frenzy. British high-streets brimmed with all manner of Beatle-bounty—from collarless Beatle jackets to plastic figurines and bubble-gum cards. In London's Bethnal Green, meanwhile, a factory worked round the clock to keep up with demand for 'Beatle Wigs'—the firm boasting orders from such bastions of the British Establishment as Eton college and Buckingham Palace (the hairpiece commissioned by a member of the royal staff rather than the Queen herself).

John, Paul, George and Ringo even had political currency. On tour in America in 1964, the band had been wined and dined by the British Ambassador, and on return to Britain, they were acclaimed by Sir Alec Douglas Home, the Conservative Prime Minister, as "our best exports" and "a useful contribution to the balance of payments." At this, the Labour opposition were indignant, Harold Wilson (Liverpool M.P. and leader of the Labor Party) protesting that the Conservatives were "trying to make the Beatles their secret weapon" (Davies, 222). Yet Wilson himself was not above capitalizing on the Beatles' kudos. In 1964, the Labor leader jumped at the opportunity to present the band with Variety Club awards—the Beatles greeting Wilson with characteristic humour, addressing the Labor statesman as "Mr. Dobson." In 1965, meanwhile, Wilson played an even more illustrious gambit—the honors list of his recently elected government—investing the band as members of the Order of the British Empire. (The Queen later presented the giggling Beatles with their prestigious MBE medals.)

Wilson's honoring of the Beatles, however, was more than simply a good-natured gesture by an affable man of the people. It was a calculated political manoeuvre. In courting the Beatles, Wilson was co-opting the language of dynamic youth and swinging modernity that had come to the fore in '60s Britain. The Beatles personified an iconography of youth which encapsulated sentiments about the much broader state of postwar Britain. Changes in the lives and culture of British youngsters seemed to embody much wider patterns of social transformation, and during the '50s and '60s in Britain, debate around youth came to function as an ideological vehicle for the expression of a more general set of hopes and fears. The principal intentions of this paper, therefore, are twofold. First, it seeks to chart the major social and economic changes that combined to highlight the visibility of British youth as a distinct cultural group during the '50s and '60s. Second, it aims to analyse the capacity in which the "youth question" operated as an ideological vehicle during this period. Here, attention will focus on the way in which the youth debate functioned as a medium through which fundamental shifts in Britain's social boundaries and cultural relationships were explored, made sense of and interpreted.

II. A Distinctive Teenage World:
The Formalization of Youth in Postwar Britain

"Youth" was not a social category new to Britain after 1945. Many features of young peoples' lives after World War II had been anticipated by earlier social, economic, and cultural trends. Since the nineteenth century, spectacular subcultural groups had existed among sections of working class youth,[1] while the degree of disposable income possessed by many working youngsters sowed the seeds of a commercial youth market which steadily flourished between the wars.[2] Nevertheless, while points of continuity have to be acknowledged, there remain strong grounds for seeing World War II as a crucial turning point in the development of British youth culture. In the decades that followed 1945 a range of factors conjoined to accentuate young peoples' social and cultural profile—to the extent that many contemporary commentators became convinced that postwar youth was manifestly distinct from previous generations of British youngsters.

Demographic change played an important part in emphasizing the identifiability of postwar youth. A baby boom in the aftermath of the war was temporary but significant, seeing the British youth population during the '50s and '60s grow, both in absolute numbers and as a percentage of the national total.[3] Additionally, scientific evidence suggested that, with higher standards of living, children were maturing at an earlier age, which maturation further contributed to ideas of a qualitatively distinct younger generation.[4] Sufficient in themselves to enhance youth's postwar social profile, these factors were augmented by developments which worked to further formalize notions of young people as an identifiable social group. The school-leaving age was due to be raised to fifteen in 1939, but, with the outbreak of war, had been postponed. During wartime, however, the expansion of Britain's education system came to be viewed as a fundamental priority; youth increasingly were seen as a national resource whose potential had formerly been squandered through educational inadequacy. As a consequence, the 1944 Education Act established free secondary education for all children, while the school-leaving age was finally raised to fifteen in 1947. This formalization of age categories within the field of education was complemented by the simultaneous expansion of the youth service. During the war, the shortage of 'respectable' leisure provisions came to be regarded as a significant gap in the socialization of youth, and a National Youth Committee was established to administer grants to youth organizations that, it was felt, could be relied upon to marshal young people's leisure responsibly. Under the 1944 Education Act, moreover, it became the statutory responsibility of Local Education Authorities to provide adequate recreational facilities for young people in their areas. Taken together, therefore, the reorganization of the education system and the expansion of the youth service worked to formalize and institutionalize conceptualizations of youth as a discrete social entity associated with specific needs and problems.

The postwar institutionalization of youth as a distinct age category was further augmented by the introduction of National Service in 1948. Deferment was available to those completing apprenticeships or courses of education (and about 16 percent were exempted on medical grounds), but, on average, 160,000 young men were annually conscripted for two years' training in the armed forces. Conscription further fostered a sense of 'generational consciousness' in Britain—National Service detached young men from the ties of their domestic environment and gathered them together with thousands of others undergoing the same experience.[5] Furthermore, the posting of young National Servicemen to military bases in the heart of the British countryside brought the subcultural styles of urban youth to rural communities which otherwise would have been relatively untouched by rock 'n' roll, "winkle-picker" shoes, and the whole universe of postwar youth culture.

Demographic shifts, the expansion of secondary education and the youth service, and the introduction of conscription undoubtedly contributed to the greater social profile of British youth after 1945. More important than these factors, however, was the intensification of long-term trends in the British economy—the decline of heavy industries, the movement of capital into lighter forms of production (especially the manufacture of consumer durables), the expansion of production line technologies, trends towards "de-skilling," and the movement of labor out of direct production and into distribution. The impact of these trends registered on the workforce as a whole but held their greatest consequences for young workers.[6] De-skilling and production line technologies created a demand for flexible, though not especially skilled, workers. Cheaper to employ than adults, young people were an ideal source for this labor. Indeed, rather than undertaking a period of relatively poorly paid training or apprenticeship, many youngsters much preferred the relatively high immediate rewards offered by unskilled and semi-skilled work.

The increase in youth's economic muscle made a profound impression on social commentators. As early as 1947, a Ministry of Education report had drawn attention to the financial power accruing young workers, observing that

> ... when juvenile workers are scarce, as they are now, and are likely to continue to be, he [sic] quickly realises that he may not be so unimportant as he seemed at first; and after two or three years his income may be larger compared with his needs and with his contribution to his maintenance than at any other period of his life. (Ministry of Education, 47)

This equation of youth with affluence became a recurring theme of the postwar decades. Especially important in sedimenting images of a generation of young workers possessing unprecedented wealth was the research of Mark Abrams, conducted for the London Press Exchange during the late '50s. According to Abrams, youth, more than any other social group, had materially prospered in postwar Britain. Compared to prewar levels, Abrams calculated that young people's real earnings had risen by 50 percent (roughly double that of adults) while youths' discretionary spending had risen by as much as 100 percent, representing an annual expenditure of around £830 million (Abrams, 1959: 9). Further, Abrams contended that this spending was concentrated in particular consumer markets (for instance, representing 44 percent of total spending on records and record players and 39 percent on bicycles and motorcycles) which, he conjectured, represented the rise of "distinctive teenage spending for distinctive teenage ends in a distinctive teenage world" (Abrams, 1959: 10).

Recited almost verbatim in a multitude of contemporaneous books, newspapers and magazines, Abrams' statistics played an important role in crystallizing the idea of a newly affluent body of young people patronizing a youth market of unprecedented scale. Room exists, however, to qualify many of his points. First, Abrams' rather idiosyncratic definition of teenagers as "those young people who have reached the age of fifteen but are not yet twenty five years of age and are unmarried" (Abrams, 1961: 3) would have undoubtedly concealed differences of earnings and expenditure within the group. Second, his discussion of total expenditure and average earnings would, again, have disguised major differences and disparities. Third, Abrams took no account of marked regional variations—less widely publicized, locally based research suggesting levels of youth consumption much less than that of Abrams' "affluent teenagers."[7] Nevertheless, while Abrams' research may have distorted and exaggerated the scale of young people's economic power, the broad sweep of his claims was accurate. In the '50s and '60s, the wage packets of young workers may not have been bulging, yet, compared to those of their predecessors, they were certainly more replete. Notions of a more affluent younger generation, then, were subject to a degree of exaggeration but were not entirely mythological. Many young people did enjoy a degree of relative prosperity on entering the world of work, an affluence which underpinned a huge expansion of Britain's commercial youth market.

III. Please Please Me: The Growth of the Commerical Youth Market

Though the '50s and '60s witnessed growing levels of consumer spending within the working class as a whole, it was young workers unfettered by family responsibilities who were most able to enjoy the fruits of a higher disposable income. The range of products geared to the postwar youth market was literally boundless, consumer industries interacting with and reinforcing one another in their efforts to exploit youth spending. This expansion of the youth market had its greatest impact in the field of popular music. Symbolic of youth's growing importance to the music industry was the rise of the 7-inch, 45 r.p.m. single (introduced in 1952 and accounting for 80 percent of British record sales by 1963), as well as the introduction of sales-based singles' charts (the first British singles' chart appeared in *New Musical Express* in 1952, followed by *Record Mirror*'s 'Top Fifty' in 1954) and the emergence of the pop star as a cultural phenomenon, most strikingly manifested in 1956 with the arrival from America of rock 'n' roll. The initial wave of American stars such as Bill Haley, Little Richard, Chuck Berry, and Elvis Presley was soon supplemented by homegrown talent, such as Tommy Steele, Billy Fury, Adam Faith, and Marty Wilde, and, with the rise of British Beat and rhythm and blues in the early '60s, bands such as the Beatles and the Rolling Stones were soon dominating the world pop market.

As adult audiences declined, the film industry also began to focus more explicitly on the youth market. In America, producers such as Roger Corman and Sam Katzman pioneered the "teenpic"—low-budget, quickly released films geared to a young audience, especially the drive-in market.[8] The British film industry, too, attempted to exploit youth demand. Although Britain had nothing to match the scale and profligacy of the American teenpic industry, the '50s and '60s saw the release of a host of British films that courted a young audience by featuring pop idols such as Cliff Richard, Tommy Steele, and, later, the Beatles.[9]

In contrast to the cinema, British radio was much less willing to associate itself with postwar changes in popular music and youth culture. During the late '50s rock 'n' roll could be heard by tuning in to American Forces Network or Radio Luxembourg but was largely ignored by the BBC as a consequence of restrictions on "needle time"[10] and antipathy toward a music that officialdom deemed an inferior and unduly commercial cultural form. It was not, therefore, until the appearance of unlicensed (so-called pirate) stations, such as Radio Caroline, in the early '60s and the subsequent launch of the BBC's Radio One in 1967 that Britain saw radio programmes specifically geared to the youth audience.[11] The younger medium, television, on the other hand, responded more swiftly to the postwar youth scene, and both the BBC and ITV (Britain's first commercial channel, launched in 1955) made many forays into the field during the '50s and '60s. Initially, programs such as Hit Parade (1952), Music Shop (1955) and Off the Record (1956) were rather muted in the directness of their appeal to youth. By the later '50s, however, a more fully formed youth-oriented genre had begun to emerge with shows such as Six-Five Special (1957), Oh Boy! (1958) and Juke Box Jury (1959).[12]

The explosion of British pop music in the mid-50s was a shot in the arm to many traditional entertainment venues whose adult patrons had begun to drift away. Instead, a younger generation of customers packed into dance halls, clubs, and variety theatres, with audiences flocking to see concert tours of pop stars, organized by impresarios such as Larry Parnes, and, later, appearances by headline bands, such as the Beatles and the Rolling Stones. Other businesses also thrived on youngsters' patronage. The brewing industry did not seriously attempt to penetrate younger sections of the market until the late '60s, and, as a consequence, pubs retained a dull, dingy, even rather boring image. Coffee bars, on the other hand, blossomed. The preeminent focal point to British teenage life, the coffee bar was a place where youngsters could gather and freely chat amongst themselves or dance to their favorite records on the jukebox (itself appearing in much greater numbers from the mid-'50s), all for the price of a cup of foamy espresso or a bottle of Coca-Cola. The most famous coffee bars were in London—the Gyre and Gymble in Charing Cross, the Breadbasket near Middlesex Hospital, and the Two I's (where, legend has it, Tommy Steele was discovered) in Old Compton Street—but most provincial towns also developed their own network of espresso bars and "dives."

Often furnished in a pseudoexotic style (with bullfight posters, bamboo fixtures, tropical plants, an occasional shell or Mexican mask) coffee bars generated an excitingly cosmopolitan aura and stand as one of the most enduring images of not only '50s youth style but British culture more generally during the period.

The eruption of Beatlemania in 1963, therefore, was constituent in a broader proliferation of the commercial youth market in Britain during the '50s and '60s. Increases in the disposable income of many young workers laid the basis for a burgeoning commercial sector—its scale considerably reinforcing notions of the postwar youth experience as qualitatively different from that of earlier generations. Beyond this, however, the period also saw the youth market take on symbolic significance: perceived changes in the lifestyles of young people increasingly treated as a benchmark of much wider and more fundamental changes in patterns of British cultural life.

IV. Signs of the Times: The Symbolic Dimension to Youth in Postwar Britain

It may be inevitable that conceptions of youth and chronological age will prominently figure in attempts to make sense of change in society. At instances of especially profound transformation, however, youths' metaphorical capacity becomes powerfully extended. In Britain, the two decades that followed 1945 marked just such a period—the "youth question" coming to function as a focal point in discussions of the broader social, economic and cultural state of the nation.[13]

It is impossible to understand the postwar saliency of youth as a cultural category in Britain without considering the wider societal context. During the war, German bombing, lack of investment, and the sheer weight of wartime demand had taken a heavy toll on British industry. By the beginning of the '50s, however, recovery was under way. Throughout the '50s and early '60s, full employment and demand for labour sustained rises

in real earnings and laid the basis for a steady growth in consumer spending. Moreover, three terms of Conservative government between 1951 and
1964 saw reductions in interest rates and taxes and the relaxation of hire
purchase controls—promoting higher street sales and prompting, in 1957,
Prime Minister Harold Macmillan's famous remark that the British people
had "never had it so good." It is difficult to measure precisely the degree to
which this new spending lay in the hands of the working class, though they
clearly benefited, with a growing number of working-class households
boasting televisions, motor cars, washing machines, and an ever spiralling
range of domestic appliances and consumer durables.

Though economic prosperity and a marked growth in living standards
were warmly greeted, commentators from across the political spectrum
viewed the cultural implications of these changes with greater anxiety.
Antipathy toward the forms and institutions of what was seen as a com-
mercialized mass culture was nothing new. Similar fears had existed in the
late nineteenth century, while the '30s saw notions of a cultural levelling
down increasingly center on the idea of "Americanization." America, the
home of monopoly capitalism and commercial culture, came to epitomize
the processes of debasement and deterioration which, many commentators
argued, were coming to characterize popular cultural forms and practices in
Britain. As Dick Hebdige shows, this use of America as a paradigm "for the
future, threatening every advanced industrial democracy in the western
world" (Hebdige, 52–53) intensified after 1945, the growth of working
class affluence prompting heightened anxieties that British culture was set
to become a degraded and desocialized mass. Developments in British
youth culture were treated as symbolic of this trajectory of cultural decline.
The work of writer and academic Richard Hoggart exemplified these concerns. In *The Uses of Literacy,* Hoggart decried the "candy floss world" with
its "canned entertainment and packeted provision" which, he claimed,
offered a culture that was shallow and insipid compared to that of his interwar boyhood. Moreover, it was typical of the period that Hoggart should
single out the younger generation as emblematic of the growing paucity of
contemporary cultural life. Modern youth was, for Hoggart, a "hedonistic
but passive barbarian," the writer deploring "the juke box boys" with their
"drape suits, picture ties and American slouch" who spent their evenings in
"harshly lighted milk bars" putting "copper after copper into the mechani-
cal record player" (Hoggart, 248–250).

A perceived rise in rates of juvenile crime was also taken as evidence of cultural degeneration. Within both popular opinion and academic enquiry, there arose the widely held belief that the destruction of the war, the absence of fathers, and the long working hours of mothers had all contributed to a breakdown in processes of socialization and a consequent rise in levels of delinquency. Among the leading exponents of this perspective, stood the journalist T.R. Fyvel who, through a number of articles and his study *The Insecure Offenders*, helped popularize the notion that postwar increases in juvenile crime were, at least partly, "the expression of a particularly disturbed generation, a delayed effect of the war" (Fyvel, 51). Fyvel's opinions found empirical support from research conducted for the Home Office by Leslie Wilkins and published as *Delinquent Generations* in 1960. Juggling with reams of statistics, Wilkins claimed that children born between 1935 and 1942 were more prone to delinquency than those born in any other seven-year period, and, he argued, the highest delinquency rates were to be found among those who had been four- and five-year-olds during the war.[14] Nevertheless, Wilkins judged that wartime conditions were not alone responsible for subsequent rises in levels of juvenile crime. In addition to the destabilizing effects of the war, Wilkins also cited the recent stylistic preferences of the young as an important contributory factor, arguing that "one of the most disturbing features of the pattern of postwar criminal statistics is the recent crime wave among young adult males between seventeen and twenty-one years of age. The crime wave among young males has been associated with certain forms of dress and other social phenomena" (Wilkins, 9).

Nor was Wilkins alone in his speculation. Throughout the postwar period, the new fashions of the young were a recurring theme in attempts to understand the apparent upsurge of juvenile crime. In the early '50s the association of particular styles of dress with what was perceived to be a new wave of vicious delinquency crystallized around two notorious murder cases. The first, in 1952, saw the controversial conviction and subsequent execution of nineteen-year-old Derek Bentley for the shooting of a police officer in Croydon. The second, in 1953, saw twenty-year-old Michael Davies convicted and sentenced to death (later commuted to life imprisonment) for the stabbing of a youth on Clapham Common.[15] In both cases, the dress of the young defendants became symbolically significant. The press drew attention to their "flashy," "American-style" clothes and demeanor, the two accused being presented as the embodiment of a dissipation of traditional culture and values, which was judged to be a growing feature of life in postwar Britain.

Throughout the postwar decades, it became commonplace to draw links between young people's sartorial preferences, growing levels of delinquency, and a general decline in cultural values. During the early '50s these anxieties found coherence around the figure of the "Teddy boy." First identified by the media in the working class neighbourhoods of South London in 1954, the Ted was soon presented as a shockingly new apparition haunting street corners and dance halls all over the country. The Teddy boys' negative image was compounded as the press cited them as central protagonists in both a spate of cinema "riots" that followed screenings of the film *Rock Around the Clock* in August 1956 and a wave of racist attacks in Nottingham and Notting Hill in 1958. By the end of the '50s the Ted's drape suit had been superseded by the "Italian" look of short, "bum freezer" jackets and "slim Jim" ties, though dominant reactions to the "mods" of the early '60s replicated many of those that had earlier attended the Teds.

Like the Teddy boys before them, the mods' style was often judged to represent not simply a mode of dress but a symbol of national decline and cultural degradation. Negative responses to the mods were exemplified, above all, in the anxieties that surrounded the "invasion" of several seaside towns in 1964. Working class youngsters had traditionally visited seaside resorts at holiday times, but Easter 1964 was cold and wet, and facilities for young people were poor, with the result that a few scuffles broke out between local youths and visiting Londoners. The violence was isolated and small-scale, yet the media response was melodramatic and overwrought, newspaper reporters regaling their readers with stories of a "day of terror" in which whole towns had been overrun by marauding mobs "hell-bent on destruction."[16] Social responses to youth, however, were never entirely negative. Throughout the postwar period, a recurring duality saw young people both vilified as the most deplorable evidence of cultural bankruptcy and, almost simultaneously, celebrated as the exciting precursor to a prosperous future. Alongside the sense of apprehension and uncertainty that surrounded representations of youth there was always a more positive set of responses and attitudes. Throughout the late '50s and early '60s, for example, there appeared a wealth of official research, both nationally and locally based, which presented youth as a category integral to wider social changes.

The tone of much of this work was reassuring. Certainly, studies, such as that produced by the Labor Party's Youth Commission (1959) and the British Medical Association (1961), voiced a few reservations about trends in the lifestyles of young people; yet, overall, their conclusions were favourable, indeed almost celebratory, presenting young people as a group whose vibrant energy was kept in check by their mature sense of responsibility.

The media could also present youth in radiant terms. Newspapers and magazines, especially, helped popularize notions of youth as an excitingly new social force—a vigorous and uplifting contrast to the tired and outmoded conventions of the traditional social order. The field was led by the *Daily Mirror,* where the theme of youth, along with an explicit appeal to a young readership, became a recurring feature as the paper sought to maintain its share of market sales while offering a meaningful response to the rapid pace of social change. The '50s saw the *Mirror* increasingly jump on the youth bandwagon, publishing several books on the quickly developing universe of pop music and, in 1957, sponsoring a "Rock 'n' Roll Express" to take American rock 'n' rollers Bill Haley and the Comets to London after they had arrived at the port of Southampton for their first British tour. Sharing this enthusiastic interest in youth culture was the magazine *Picture Post.* Despite its share of histrionic articles on "Boy Gangsters," the tone of *Picture Post*'s coverage was generally positive, culminating in 1957 with a four-part series, "The Truth About Teenagers," which revealed "what teenagers are, what they hate and what they hope for" (*Picture Post,* 18 March–8 April, 1957).

This positive stereotyping of British youth reached its apex in the milieu of "Swinging London" during the early '60s. Here, the throbbing dance floors of the capital's nightclubs and the fashionable boutiques of Carnaby Street came to embody notions of a Britain that was moving boldly into a new age of growth and optimism. In the world of fashion, especially, designers, such as Mary Quant, pioneered an image of youthful chic, their impact underlined in 1962 when the cover of the first edition of the *Sunday Times* Magazine featured a teenage Jean Shrimpton modelling a sleeveless Quant dress. (The same newspaper later praised Quant for "jolting England out of its conventional attitude towards clothes.") This enthusiastic embrace of the imagery of youth even extended to subcultural groups. While the mods were reviled as the bete noire of the affluent society, they were also lauded as stylish consumers par excellence. Superficially clean-cut and well-dressed, the mod's appearance was amenable to co-option within notions of postwar dynamism and modernity. The mods were treated as the trendsetters of '60s stylishness and mobility, and the press eagerly charted changes in the minutiae of mod dress and music. Even in 1964, at the height of concerns about mod violence, the *Sunday Times* Magazine featured a sumptuous nine-page photospread chronicling the finesse and intricacies of mod style (*Sunday Times* Magazine, 2 August 1964).

Overall, then, the late '50s and early '60s saw the imagery of youth increasingly deployed as a shorthand signifier for unbridled pleasure in what seemed to be a dawning age of hedonistic consumption. Young peo-ple seemed to embody all that the consumer dream stood for and, through-out the period, advertisers habitually used images of youth to associate their products with dynamic modernity and "swinging" enjoyment. This equa-tion of youth with consumption was exemplified, above all, by the addition of the term "teenager" to everyday vocabulary. First coined by American market researchers during the mid-40s, the term was formalized in the early '50s through the research of organizations such as the Student Mar-keting Institute, Teenage Survey Incorporated, and Eugene Gilbert and Company, which, in conjunction with an avalanche of books, magazine, and newspaper articles, revealed to the U.S. public what appeared to be a new social caste with its own culture and lifestyle.[17] By the late '40s, the word "teenager" had been imported into Britain and was rapidly integrated into popular discourse, the press making liberal use of the term by the early '50s.

In the image of the teenager, postwar notions of affluent prosperity found their purest manifestation. Taken as the quintessence of social trans-formation, teenagers were perceived as being at the sharp end of the new consumer culture, distinguished not simply by their youth but by a partic-ular style of conspicuous, leisure-oriented consumption. As Peter Laurie contended in his anatomy of *The Teenage Revolution,* published in 1965, "The distinctive fact about teenagers' behaviour is economic: they spend a lot of money on clothes, records, concerts, make up, magazines: all things that give immediate pleasure and little lasting use" (Laurie, 1965: 9). The teenager, then, was far more than a simple descriptive term. Rather, the teenager was an ideological terrain upon which a particular definition of postwar change was constructed. Central to notions of the teenager was the idea that traditional class boundaries were being eroded by the fashions and lifestyles of newly affluent gilded youth (*The Economist,* 11 January 1958).

Teenagers were presented as a class in themselves, what Laurie (11) termed a "solidly integrated social bloc," whose vibrant, hedonistic culture seemed to be a symbolic foretaste of good times waiting around the corner for everyone. Teenage consumption, therefore, became the defining emblem for the economic changes which, many commentators argued, were steadily ameliorating social divisions, neutralizing traditional class conflicts, and ushering in a new epoch of prosperous "post capitalism." This, therefore, was exactly the discourse that politicians, such as Alec Douglas Home and Harold Wilson, sought to appropriate through their fêting of the Beatles.

V. Conclusion: Where Did Our Love Go?

The contrasting representations of youth in Britain during the '50s and '60s were obviously stereotypes which often bore tenuous relation to social reality. Yet their symbolic power was potent, images of youth serving as a key motif around which dominant interpretations of social change were constructed. While social responses to youth were always marked out by a degree of ambiguity, the late '50s and early '60s saw a set of generally positive images come to the fore—personified in the cheery ebullience of the Beatles. Here, youth was taken as the epitome of a Britain in which the sheer pace of economic growth seemed set to engender a newly prosperous age of fun, freedom and social harmony. The teenage myth, however, was generated from an unstable set of social and economic conditions. In retrospect, the prosperity of the postwar decades can be seen as insecure and transient, the ephemeral trappings of a precarious "age of illusion" (Bogdanor and Skidelsky, 7). Much of the consumer boom was, for example, based on the vulnerable economic foundation of short term credit, Britain's higher purchase debt rising faster between 1956 and 1959 than at any other time either before or since. Moreover, postwar affluence depended on a level of growth that the British economic infrastructure was simply not in a position to maintain, and, by the late '60s, the scale of these problems had become apparent, and the period was punctuated by a series of economic crises and industrial unrest. By the end of the '60s, an atmosphere of discord and friction had come to characterize British society. The ideologies of affluence, prosperity, and consent, which had articulated social relations during the '50s and early '60s, thus became untenable, giving way to polit-ical programmes more visibly confrontational and coercive.[18]

Against this background, representations of young people also changed. Though responses to youth were never exclusively negative, the late '60s and early '70s saw a greater degree of hostility within political comment and media coverage. For example, the skinhead style, which first began to make its presence felt in British youth culture in the mid-'60s,[19] was unequivocally presented as a violent and menacing presence stalking British streets. Whereas the mods' flamboyant style of conspicuous consumption allowed them to be easily incorporated within a discourse of classless afflu-ence, no such co-option was possible with the skinheads, whose self-con-scious invocation of a traditional working class heritage (through their dis-tinctive uniform of steel-toe-capped work boots, rolled-up jeans, braces, and convict-style cropped hair) was irreconcilable with notions of disap-pearing social divisions in a prosperous Britain. However, whereas working class subcultures such as the skinheads were understood as socially delin-quent symptoms of deterioration, the emergence of a more middle class counterculture (especially its more overtly political elements) was cast as an active cause of cultural degeneration and social instability.[20] Amid the revo-lutionary ferment of 1968, therefore, media and political responses stigma-tized and vilified the counterculture, and a coercive backlash saw increas-ingly repressive measures directed against social elements deemed either permissive or subversive.[21]

Notions and representations of youth, therefore, have the capacity to play a metaphorical role in the ways sense is made of more general social developments, especially at times of dramatic social change. This was espe-cially true of Britain in the two decades that followed World War II, young people becoming an important (possibly the most important) ideological vehicle for the discussion of wider shifts in social relations and changes in British cultural life. During the late '50s and early '60s, the affluent teenager was promoted as the figurehead of Britain's march into a new era of prosperous consumerism. By end of the '60s, however, the confident rhetoric of growth and social cohesion had begun to crumble in the face of economic crisis and industrial decline—a shift which found its corollary in the rise of an increasingly negative set of responses to British youth culture.

Endnotes

1   The most authoritative account of working class youth subcultures in Victorian and Edwardian Britain is provided in Pearson (1983).

2   The work of David Fowler (1992; 1995) offers a meticulous survey of British young-sters' life and culture between the wars.

3   According to Department of Employment (206–207) statistics, numbers of young peo-ple in Britain grew from just over three million in 1951 (representing 8 percent of the national population) to just over four million in 1966 (10 percent of the national pop-ulation).

4   This perspective was exemplified in "Growing Up Faster," an article written by Alex Comfort and published in *The Listener* in 1960.

5   Strangely, the experience of National Service has been subject to relatively little scrutiny by British historians. The best existing accounts of National Service, its history and the experiences of National Servicemen are provided in Chambers and Landreth, Johnson (ed.) and Royale.

6   A concise overview of the impact of economic change on employment patterns among British youth is provided in Roberts.

7   Research such as Cyril Smith's study of youth in the town of Bury and Jephcott's sur-vey of Scottish youth produced figures for earnings and consumption much less than those arrived at by Abrams. The popular picture of affluent teenagers, Smith con-cluded, "grossly simplifies the very real differences in income among them."

8   The history of the American "teenpic" industry is documented in Doherty.

9   The rise and fall of the British pop film is meticulously charted in Medhurst.

10 Since the '30s, an agreement between the BBC and representatives of the record indus-try and the Musicians Union had placed time limits on the radio broadcast of com-mercially produced records. This had originally been intended as a measure to protect both the profits of British record companies (who blamed falling record sales on the broadcast of recorded music) and the interests of musicians (who were anxious that records should not be used as a cheap alternative to live performance).

11 Accounts of the development of pop radio during this period are provided in Hind and Mosco (7–18) and Barnard (32–49).

12 A history of British television's early forays into the field of pop music can be found in Hill.

13 For further exploration of this metaphorical facet of youth debates see Smith, Immirizi and Blackwell (242); Clarke, Hall, Jefferson and Roberts (9–74) and Davis.

14 Wilkins' calculations and conclusions were, in fact, seriously flawed. Not only were his statistical inferences invalid, but he failed to consider variations of delinquency rate between different types of offence and ignored nonindictable offences altogether. More-over, by the '60s, the generation of youngsters born in the years following the war had begun to register rates of delinquency even higher than their immediate predecessors.

15 In both cases, serious doubt exists as to the guilt of the accused. It is possible that the authorities sought to make salutary examples of both Bentley and Davies, demonstrat-

ing to the public that the juvenile "crime wave" was being firmly dealt with. For details of the Bentley and Davies cases see, respectively, Yallop and Parker.

16 In his now classic study, Stanley Cohen shows how the melodramatic press coverage of these events actually served to engender and amplify subsequent disturbances.

17 For overviews of the growth of the commercial youth industries in America during this period see Gilbert (196–211); Doherty (17–41) and Palladino (96–174).

18 According to authors associated with the Birmingham Centre for Contemporary Cultural Studies, Britain during the late '60s and early '70s saw the rise of a political order which was increasingly willing to rule through force and compulsion rather than consensus and consent. See Hall, Critcher, Jefferson, Clarke and Roberts.

19 Informed and well-documented histories of the development of skinhead style are provided in Knight and Marshall

20 These arguments were originally developed in Clarke, Hall, Jefferson and Roberts (72).

21 This more coercive shift was marked by a more determined enforcement of drug laws, followed by police raids on the offices of underground publications such as *It* and the closure of clubs like Middle Earth and UFO after police raids had prompted landlords to withdraw leases. In 1970, the authoritarian offensive against the underground press continued, with *Oz* Editors Richard Neville, Jim Anderson and Felix Dennis prosecuted, and subsequently imprisoned, for obscenity. A more coercive set of official responses also made itself felt in the sphere of public order. In 1968, demonstrations against the Vietnam war were subject to aggressive and often brutal policing, with the intimidatory use of mounted officers and police "snatch squads," while, in February 1970, punitive prison sentences were passed on six defendants after police had battled with protesters objecting to the presence of representatives of the Greek military junta at the Garden House Hotel in Cambridge.

Bibliography

Abrams, Mark. *The Teenage Consumer.* London: Press Exchange, 1959.

———. *Teenage Consumer Spending in 1959.* London: Press Exchange, 1961.

Barnard, Stephen. *On the Radio: Music Radio in Britain.* Milton Keynes: Open University Press, 1989.

Bogdanor, Vernon and Robert Skidelsky, eds. *The Age of Affluence, 1951–64.* London: Macmillan, 1970.

British Medical Association. *The Adolescent: Observations Arising From Discussion Among Members of the British Medical Association.* London: B.M.A., 1961.

Chambers, P. and A. Landreth. *Called Up: The Personal Experiences of Sixteen National Servicemen.* London: Allan Wingate, 1955.

Clarke, John, Stuart Hall, Tony Jefferson, and Brian Roberts. 'Subcultures, Cultures and Class: A Theoretical Overview.' In *Resistance Through Rituals: Youth Subcultures in Post-War Britain,* edited by Stuart Hall and Tony Jefferson, 9–74. London: Hutchinson, 1976.

Cohen, Stanley. *Folk Devils and Moral Panics: The Creation of the Mods and Rockers.* St. Albans: Paladin, 1973.

Comfort, Alex. 'Growing Up Faster,' *The Listener,* 14, No. 1632 (7 July, 1960).

Davies, Hunter. *The Beatles: The Authorized Biography.* London: Granada, 1978.

Davis, John. *Youth and the Condition of Britain: Images of Adolescent Conflict.* London: Athlone, 1990.

Department of Employment. *British Labour Statistics Historical Abstract 1886–1968.* London: HMSO, 1968.

Doherty, Thomas. *Teenagers and Teenpics: The Juvenilization of American Movies in the 1950s.* London: Unwin Hyman, 1988.

Fowler, David. 'Teenage Consumers? Young Wage-Earners and Leisure in Manchester, 1919–39.' In *Workers' Worlds: Cultures and Communities in Manchester and Salford, 1880–1939,* edited by Andrew Davies and Steven Fielding, 133–155. Manchester: Manchester University Press, 1992.

―――. *The First Teenagers: The Lifestyle of Young Wage-Earners in Interwar Britain.* London: Woburn, 1995.

Fyvel, T.R. *The Insecure Offenders: Rebellious Youth in the Welfare State.* Harmondsworth: Pelican, 1963.

Gilbert, James. *A Cycle of Outrage: America's Reaction to the Juvenile Delinquent in the 1950s.* Oxford: Oxford University Press, 1986.

Hall, Stuart, Chas Critcher, Tony Jefferson, John Clarke, and Brian Roberts. *Policing the Crisis: Mugging, the State and Law and Order.* London: Macmillan, 1978.

Hebdige, Dick. 'Towards a Cartography of Taste, 1935–1962.' In *Hiding in the Light: On Images and Things,* 45–76. London: Routledge, 1988.

Hill, John. 'Television and Pop: The Case of the 1950s.' In *Popular Television in Britain: Studies in Cultural History,* edited by John Corner, 90–107. London: BFI, 1991.

Hind, John and Stephen Mosco. *Rebel Radio: The Full Story of British Pirate Radio.* London: Pluto Press, 1985.

Hoggart, Richard. *The Uses of Literacy.* Harmondsworth: Penguin, 1958.

Jephcott, Pearl. *A Time of One's Own.* Edinburgh: Oliver and Boyd, 1967.

Johnson, B.S., ed. *All Bull: The National Servicemen.* London: Quartet, 1973.

Knight, Nick. *Skinhead.* London: Omnibus, 1982.

Labour Party Youth Commission. *The Younger Generation.* London: Labour Party, 1959.

Laurie, Peter. *The Teenage Revolution.* London: Anthony Blond, 1965.

Leslie, Peter. *Fab: The Anatomy of a Phenomenon.* London: Macgibbon and Kee, 1965.

Marshall, George. *Spirit of '69: A Skinhead Bible.* Dunoon: ST Publishing, 1991.

Medhurst, Andy. 'It Sort of Happened Here: The Strange, Brief Life of the British Pop Film.' In *Celluloid Jukebox: Popular Music and the Movies Since the 1950s,* edited by Jonathan Romney and Adrian Wootton, 60–71. London: BFI, 1995.

Ministry of Education. *School Life: A First Enquiry into the Transition From School to Independent Life (Clarke Report).* London: H.M.S.O., 1947.

Palladino, Grace. *Teenagers: An American History.* New York: Basic Books, 1996.

Parker, Tony. *The Ploughboy.* London: Hutchinson, 1965.

Pearson, Geoffrey. *Hooligan: A History of Respectable Fears.* London: Macmillan, 1983.

Roberts, Kenneth. *Youth and Employment in Modern Britain.* Oxford: Oxford University Press, 1995.

Royale, Trevor. *The Best Years of Their Lives: The National Service Experience 1943–63.* London: Cornet, 1988.

Smith, A.C.H., Elizabeth Immirizi, and Trevor Blackwell. *Paper Voices: The Popular Press and Social Change, 1935–65.* London: Chatto and Windus, 1975.

Smith, Cyril. *Young People: A Report on Bury.* Manchester: University of Manchester, 1966.

Wilkins, Leslie. *Delinquent Generations.* London: H.M.S.O., 1960.

Yallop, David. *To Encourage the Others.* London: Corgi, 1990.

II
Contemporary African-American Youth and Rap Music

Chapter 9
Rap, Race, and Representation

Francis N. Njubi,
San Diego State University

I. Introduction

This paper examines the lyrics, rituals, symbols, and objects that make hip hop a musical subculture with a distinct style that has developed over the last two decades. It analyses the conditions under which rap/hip hop emerged; how it developed from street corners and parks in the Bronx to the global multimedia phenomenon that it is today; and its relationship to the cultural industries and to the instruments of law and order and the state. I argue that, although rap music is articulated to the cultural industries, it still constitutes a refusal to conform and thus represents a breakdown of consensus in the society. Rap's glorification of violence, guns and drugs, and its challenge to copyright and obscenity laws can be seen as a magical resolution of the marginalization and poverty in the inner cities. Thus "gangsta" rappers play out their fantasies in both rap videos and in real life. Like punk rock, rap/hip hop is designed to shock. It reflects a breakdown of social norms and order and is viewed as a threat to the capitalist, white supremacist system. Yet, like punk rockers, rappers express their anger and hatred to a largely white teenage audience and are produced by corporations that control the cultural industries. To unravel this web of contradictions, one must take into account both the discursive aspects of the form and the material conditions of its existence. This paper is informed by a black cultural studies perspective in that it examines the meaning of hip hop in the broader cultural context. In other words, how is rap music represented in the media, who controls the images of black youth today, and how representative are these representations? For the purposes of this study the term "raps" will be used to refer to the music/lyrics, while "hip hops" will refer to the subculture (hairstyles, clothing, language, graffiti, dance styles, attitudes) that has developed around rap music and its stars.

The emergence of rap music and the style of hip hop onto the cultural scene raises several fundamental questions about the contemporary role of music in culture and about the notions of identity and difference that animate contemporary cultural theory. In the early 1970s, Clive Campbell (Kool DJ Herc), a Jamaican immigrant, introduced the sound system from the "dub" and dance hall reggae style that had developed in the ghettos of Kingston, Jamaica, to the Bronx in New York (Rose, Dyson 1995, Toop). "Sound System" block parties, where DJs and Dub poets perfected the style of rapping over repetitive beats, scratching and sampling, became an instant hit and developed quickly into the street culture called hip hops, which included the explosion of street/subway graffiti and break dancing. By combining the Sound System with toasts, boasts, the dozens, and other Afro-American linguistic games and strategies, rap has become a dazzling blend of Afro-Caribbean and Afro-American musical traditions. Two decades after its dubious origins in the streets of New York, rap is a multimedia phenomenon that pervades U.S. and global popular culture in films, television, music videos, and high profile court cases. The rap image has been used to sell everything from guns to underwear to black and white nationalism. Hip hop is clearly one of the most significant youth subcultures to emerge in the contemporary cultural landscape, and this is reflected both in the amount of attention it has received from scholars and in bizarre attacks from establishment figures like Robert Dole, Tipper Gore, Dan Quayle and Bill Clinton. It has been the subject of intense and heated debate in the media, courts of law and academe, as well as within the black community. The debates have ranged from questioning the artistic merit of the form to its relationship to the cultural industries and its authenticity as a black cultural practice. These debates have been reflected in rap's lyrics which have seen a resurgence of the discourse of black nationalism and authenticity. This can be seen in the coining of terms such as "crossover" and "represent," and the debates over who is, or is not, a member of the "old-school" or whose work qualifies as "message rap." Clearly, there are distinctions to be made between different kinds of rap music: the pop-rap phenomenon that is specifically made for crossover audiences and dance halls—M.C. Hammer, Fresh Prince, Heavy D; the "Message Rap" of the black nationalists like Public Enemy, Afrika Bambaata, Lakim Shabazz, Poor Righteous Teachers; and the nihilism of gangsta rappers like 2Pac Shakur, Ice T, Dr. Dre and Snoop Doggy Dogg. Given the diversity of forms and messages in the rap phenomenon, what makes gangsta rap the dominant form? How does the close relationship between gangstas and the cultural industry impact on the popularity of the form? These questions can only be answered by examining the phenomenon from a historical perspective.

The social anxieties and moral panics reflected in the debates over authenticity, the artistic merit, and the deviancy and legality of the form, repeat almost exactly the panics that broke out after the emergence of blues and jazz. It is, therefore, necessary to locate rap in the social history of black music, which I shall examine below.

II. The Roots of Black Music

Black American musical traditions have been a major element of focus for the African-American scholarship community for over 100 years. Within this tradition, the work of W.E.B. Du Bois clearly stands out as the most influential in the study of race, class, and representation. Indeed, Du Bois focused almost exclusively on issues that today are considered the preserve of cultural studies. Not only was he specifically concerned with the political economy of black cultural forms like music, literature, and religion, he was heavily influenced by Marxism and leftist politics in his mature writings. In an essay titled "The Sorrow Songs," published in *The Souls of Black Folk* (1903), Du Bois wrote:

> And so by fateful chance the Negro Folk Song—the rhythmic cry of the slave— stands today not simply as the sole American music but as the most beautiful expression of human experience born this side of the seas. It has been neglected, it has been and is half despised, and above all it has been persistently mistaken and misunderstood; but notwithstanding it still remains as the singular spiritual heritage of the nation and the greatest gift of the Negro people.

In this passage, and the essay as a whole, Du Bois examines several themes that have since characterized the study of black music in the United States. The themes that Du Bois identifies here—his contention that Negro folk song was the sole American music; that black music has been mistaken and misunderstood; and that it is the greatest gift of the Negro people—have been applied to volumes of work on black music from the blues, to the spirituals, rhythm & blues, and rap. Among the most celebrated and controversial of his assertions is that music is the greatest gift of the Negro people. The notion that there are distinct subspecies or races of human beings, and that these human beings bring specific gifts or talents to the human species was a popular one among black nationalists at the time that Du Bois was writing his book. This position depended on an acceptance that there are distinct races of human beings, which is ironic, because such a position has traditionally been that of white supremacists. Although Du Bois accepts that there is no scientific proof of the existence of races, he says that differences must be acknowledged. In the *Conservation of Races,* for instance, he writes that we must acknowledge that human beings are divided into races, although, when we come to inquire into the essential differences of races, we find it hard to come at once to any finite conclusion. He says, however, that these socio-historical differences are created by subtle forces that have separated human beings into groups. He argues that there are eight, distinctly differentiated, races, among them, Slavs, Teutons, English (in both England and America), Negroes, romance race, Semites, Hindus, and Mongolians. Each of these races, according to Du Bois, has a specific message, a gift, to bring to the table of the human family. It is from this perspective that Du Bois comes when he says that there are specific gifts that the black race has brought to the human family and that music is the most valuable of these gifts. Du Bois' assertion that Negro folk songs are the sole American musics gained currency and has become commonsense in popular discourse. Many scholars have since pointed out that black music has dominated American popular culture, and particularly musical expression, since the days of slavery. This phenomenon has been the subject of study by scores of scholars and commentators since Du Bois wrote this passage and is the subject of intense debate today (George 1992, Gilroy, Costello and Wallace).

Black music has indeed had an ambivalent position in American society. Like rap, innovative black musicians have been despised, distorted, and reviled by mainstream discourse while at the same time being appropriated by white groups and converted into the standard of entertainment. Nelson George (1992, 1993) and George Lipsitz have documented in detail how black musical forms from the blues, to jazz, rhythm & blues, aka rock 'n' roll, were appropriated by white groups through their access to the cultural industry and avenues of power. Indeed, the first rap song to hit number one on the Billboard charts was made by a white group, the Beastie Boys. This was just like the first nationally acclaimed rock 'n' roll stars, whites, like Elvis Presley and the Beatles, who, in the minstrel style, imitated black artists like Chuck Barry down to appropriating lyrics and body movements (Lipsitz). This trope had ample precedence in popular theater in the South, for instance, where minstrels—whites in blackface imitating slaves—traveled around the region to the delight of their fellow slave owners.

Yet the problem with this perspective is that there is an assumption of racial essence. Musical (or athletic) ability, which we all know is 99 percent practice and hard work, is attributed to some divine or biological gifts or essence. The fact that black scholars, many of whom are opposed to racism, are willing to assert the existence of race, and even celebrate it, is ironic, given that this is the also the position of white supremacists. Among the most eloquent critics of race-based scholarship is Kwame Anthony Appiah, a Ghanaian professor of African and African American Studies at Harvard. In his book, *In My Father's House* (1992), Appiah devotes several chapters to the criticism of the race concept in Black Studies and blames Du Bois in particular for disseminating the "myth." Appiah makes a distinction between racialisms and racism. He says, for instance, that Alexander Crumwell, the father of Pan-Africanism, was a racialist because he believed that skin color reflected the moral and intellectual qualities of the person involved. He refuses, however, to place Crumwell in the same camp with Nazis and South African whites because they, unlike Crumwell or Du Bois, were willing to commit genocide. Appiah says, therefore, that Apartheid and Nazism are examples of racism because they are ideologies which are in place to buttress privilege, while racialists may not be privileged and do not sanction genocide. Appiah, however, insists that the concept itself is the problem and, thus, would place Du Bois among the racialists. Much of the criticism is justified if one were to confine one's analysis to Du Bois' earlier works. However, Du Bois was a copious writer who was not afraid to revise his views and publish his reasons. In his second autobiography, called *Dusk of Dawn* (1940), for instance, he specifically rejects the notion that the concept of race has any scientific basis. In these latter works, influenced much more by anti-imperialism and inspired by the struggle against colonialism in Africa, Du Bois developed a more sophisticated theory of race and racism that has been ignored in the rush to find him guilty of the very racialism that he was fighting. Indeed Du Bois basically comes to the same conclusion as Appiah: that race does not exist as a biological essence but that racism, as an ideology, does exist and its impact continues to be felt.

III. Rap and the Oral Tradition

The Africans who arrived on the shores of the Americas and the Caribbean were not mindless chattel, as the diverse and vibrant cultures of the African diaspora in Europe, the Americas, and the Caribbean testify. Despite the dispersal of the slaves and the amalgamation of ethnicities in the plantation system, the presence of Africa in the syncretic black cultures that formed during the era of slavery is clearly evident. The idea of Africa has been the catalyst for cultural movements that range from the worship of African gods and goddesses in the New World like Voodoo (from Vodun, a West African religion), Santeria (or the worship of West African goddess Jemaja by blacks along the Atlantic coast of South America), the more recent emergence of Rastafarianism with its links to ancient African Christianity, and the Nation of Islam. This Afro-diasporic culture is also reflected in the shared musical and performative traditions. The global reach of reggae music and Rastafarianism in the '60s and '70s, for instance, made blackness a positive sign throughout Europe and the Americas. The assertive black nationalism and back-to-Africa ideology of the rastas "interpolated" black (and colored) youngsters across the globe. In addition to the spread of Rastafarianism across the world, the style of reggae spawned youth subcultures in other continents, including the punks in Europe and rap/hip hop in the United States. However, it is important to note that, although rap is a hybrid of Caribbean and Afro-American musical forms, these are themselves part of the larger Afro-diasporic culture. Out of these various shared traditions, the one that most concerns us here is the oral tradition and, in particular, the trope of "signifying" and its interconnections with rap/hip hop.

The *American Heritage Dictionary* defines "signifying" as: "to denote or make known with a word or a sign or give importance to." Within the black public sphere, however, the concept of signifying has a distinct genealogy that can be traced to the black oral tradition rooted in the culture of the slaves that arrived from Africa. Roger D. Abrahams, author of *Talking*

Black, defines signifying as: "To imply, goad, beg, boast by direct verbal or gestured means. A language of implication" (264). This concept has come to refer to a host of black American language games that teach youth and adults storytelling and practical speaking skills. Both Abrahams and Gates identify indirection as a key element of signifying. "Indirection" is defined as a rhetorical strategy that comments on human behavior through parody, satire, or ritual boasts and insults, among them rapping, toasting, boasting, playing the dozens, jive-talking, talking-shit, talking smart, putting down, sweet-talking.

The term "signify" or "signifying" stems from the tales of the exploits of the trickster figure, "The Signifying Monkey," who has appeared in various guises in the oral tradition of blacks in Africa, the Caribbean and in North and South America. In the Afro-American version, the monkey tricks larger animals than himself and gets them to fight each other.

> There hadn't been no shift for quite a bit
> So the Monkey thought he'd start some of his signifying shit.
> It was one bright summer day the Monkey told the Lion,
> "There's a big bad burly motherfucker livin' down your way."
> He said, "You know your mother that you love so dear?
> said anybody can have her for a ten-cent glass a beer." (Toop, 29)

This kind of rhyming poem is called a toast and has been recorded in the African-American community since the days of slavery (Toop, 29). According to Toop, this version above was recorded at Attica State Prison in New York in the '50s. He describes the toasts as "violent, obscene, and misogynist" and says they have been used to pass time in prisons, factories, the army, or at street corners. In the version quoted above, for instance, the monkey creates a fight between the elephant and the lion through word games. The monkey thus highlights the power of language games. It is also interesting that the monkey does this to pass time between work "shifts."

Henry Louis Gates Jr. traces the origin of the trickster figure to the Fon and Yoruba people of Nigeria and Benin and, in particular, to the divine trickster of Yoruba mythology, Esu-Elegbara: This curious figure is called Esu-Elegbara in Nigeria and Legbaamong the Fon in Benin. His New World figurations include Exu in Brazil, Echu-Elegua in Cuba, Papa Legba in Haiti, and Papa La Bas in the United States. These variations on Esu-Elegbara speak eloquently of the unbroken arc of metaphysical presupposition and a pattern of figuration shared through time and space among black cultures in West Africa, South America, the Caribbean, and the United States (Gates, 5–6).

In Yoruba mythology, Esu is the messenger of the gods and the guardian of the crossroads. According to the Gates study, scholars have identified various characteristics of the trickster figure as: individuality, satire, irony, magic, open-endedness, indeterminacy, ambition, chance, uncertainty, disruption, and reconciliation. Gates says that, within the African-American community, signifying has come to represent a principle of Afro-American linguistic difference. Tales of the signifying monkey, which have been collected/recorded since slavery, represent one of the most significant tropes of the Afro-American oral tradition.

One of the key elements of signifying is the dozens, a game played by black children and adults. Clarence Major's *Dictionary of Afro-American Slang* defines the "Dirty Dozens" as:

> a very elaborate game traditionally played by black boys, in which the participants insult each other's relatives, especially their mothers. The object of the game is to test emotional strength. The first person to give in to anger is the loser. (138)

In addition to the dozens, black youth learned a variety of rhetorical strategies that developed dexterity in the use of language that was not available to white people. As H. Rap Brown, the minister of justice in the Black Panther Party, who earned his name by being a master of black rhetorical games and strategies, puts it: "If anybody needed to study poetry, my teacher needed to study mine. We played the dozens like white people played scrabble. They call me Rap cause I could rap" (26). In his autobiography, *Die Nigger Die!*, Brown says the object of the dozens is "to destroy somebody else with words." An example of H. Rap Brown's dozens is:

> "I fucked your mama
> For a solid hour
> Baby came out
> Screaming, Black Power." (27)

As we have seen, these dozens have their origin in signifying and the oral tradition in general. Formally located only in the black culture, signifying began to cross over into the general public with the advent of radio. In the '50s, for instance, jive talking radio DJ's like Daddy O (Vernon Winslow) of WWEZ in New Orleans and Dr Hep Cat (Levada Durst) of

KVET in Austin took signifying to the airwaves. Dr Hep Cat was known for rhymes like: "If you want to hip to the tip and bop to the top/You get some mad threats that just won't stop."

However, in an ironic twist that reveals the articulation of the Afro-diasporic cultures in the Americas, hip hop, as we know it today, with the rapping, sampling and scratching, first emerged in Jamaica. As I shall show below, these innovations were then introduced to New York by Caribbean immigrants and appropriated by the youth who recognized the potential of sampling beats from popular songs and combining them with their own dozens, toasts, and boasts.

IV. Style: The Meaning of Hip Hop

In its expressivity, its musicality, its orality, its rich, deep, and varied attention to speech, in its inflections towards the vernacular and the local, in its rich production of counter-narratives, and above all in its metaphorical use of musical vocabulary, black popular culture has enabled the surfacing, inside the mixed and contradictory modes even of some mainstream popular cultures, of elements of a discourse that is different—other forms of life, other traditions of representation. (Hall 1992, 27)

In the article quoted above, Hall contends that the black diasporic tradition is characterized by a distinct repertoire that includes three basic elements that are present among communities of African descent in Europe, the Caribbean, and the Americas. The first element is style, which appears as the substance, the subject of the ritual or performance, instead of being the mere husk or wrapping that the culture comes in. Second, in opposition to the "logicentric" (writing/deconstructing) white world, "the people of the Black diaspora have . . . found the deep form, the deep structure of their cultural life, in music." Thirdly, Hall says, these cultures have used the body as "cultural capital" and as "canvases of representation." (27) The emphasis on style, music, and bodily representation is clearly reflected in hip hop culture. It is reflected in the oral presentation of rap and the "body" of hip hoppers with the appropriation of African hairstyles (both the bald heads and the intricate designs on the head are distinctly African), the increasingly popular dreadlocks (Arrested Development), the military fatigues of Public Enemy, and the general way in which the members of the subculture walk, talk, and behave. The rappers are the high priests of the subculture with the global audiences appropriating their body language, dress, and talk. African-American slang, for instance, has become available to the general public at an unprecedented rate since the advent of hip hop.

Like Rastafarianism in the '60s, hip hop "interpolated" mainly black and colored youth in Europe, the Caribbean, and Latin America (where Latino rappers are often black) in the '80s and '90s.

The style of rap is distinct from the parent, African-American culture in several ways. Unlike jazz, the blues, and R & B, there are no bands in the rap scene. The performance aspect of rap is located in the music videos, which are the principal means through which the style of hip hop is disseminated. Because of the perceived threat of violence at hip hop concerts, producers have turned to MTV and pay-per-view television to promote hip hop artists. The rap video is an advertising tool created to sell not only the song but also the clothing styles and attitudes of the rappers. The images portrayed on the videos are designed to sell the rap artist as the high priest of hip hop. The fans copy the modes of dressing, talking, and walking that are demonstrated by the rapper, thus creating a specific style that is different from the style of the parent African-American community, middle-class blacks, and the dominant cultural norms. At the face level, the rappers, the high priests of hip hop, are mostly young black males. Rap videos and lyrics explore the experiences and fantasies of these youth: guns, sex, violence, clothing, money, drugs, cops. Of the few women's rap groups who have successfully entered the rap scene, most are made up of black women.

According to Dick Hebdige (92–96), the dominant/corporate culture tries to contain the challenge posed by subcultures through incorporation that takes two forms: commodification and labeling/domestication. Commodification deals with the conversion of subcultural signs into mass-produced commodities, making them public property and thus deflecting their quality of protest. Thus, the Beatsie Boys (a white group) was the first to reach the top of the Billboard Charts with a rap song. They were followed by a long string of very successful white hip hop artists, like Vanilla Ice who claims to be black because he grew up in an urban ghetto. Or, the Young Black Teenagers, an all-white group who claims blackness is a state of mind.

Labeling allows the dominant group to domesticate or trivialize the "deviant" behavior of the subcultural group. Labeling also allows the intervention of the instruments of law and order (police, courts, and even congressional hearings, in the case of rap). The recent attacks on rappers from presidential candidate and former Senator Robert Dole, Republican bigwig Bill Bennett and conservative blacks in Congress are clearly aimed at the domestication of rap. Both these strategies domesticate subcultural style in an attempt to contain threats to the consensus. This consensus is always contested, however, and the subcultures are never fully contained as the continued production of message rap and roots reggae testify. Subcultures are always in the process of adaptation or negotiation with the dominant class forces in the society. Thus, we have the moral panics and debates over the effect of rap music on children and criminals. Congressional hearings are held, and the music producers are forced to include a warning label on the CD and cassette covers.

Subcultures, therefore, share some of the socio-economic characteristics of the parent cultures, i.e., working-class or middle-class cultures, but also engage in distinct cultural pursuits that are expressed in style—music, dress, and attitudes towards education and work. Hall et al. (1976, 13) say that youth cultures arise as a result of "generation consciousness" that is different from that of the parent culture. This consciousness means that the youth find different ways of "adaptation, negotiation or resistance" in their struggle to transcend the material conditions that their parents live in. This generational consciousness created an identity in the group that was based on the appropriation and use of goods (dress, jewelry, music) from the dominant or parent culture and the use of these goods in different and original ways. Where the parents of hip hoppers were members of the Civil Rights generation, a generation that still had hope, hip hoppers are children of the '80s and '90s, a generation that witnessed the failure of the Civil Rights movement to bring significant change in the lives of the ghetto poor. It is a generation that is marked by hopelessness, and the resulting nihilism is clearly evident in the lyrics and symbols of hip hop.

The consumption patterns of the members of the subculture can be seen as the bridge between them and the dominant culture: the Skinheads, with their working-class, hard, masculine looks; the Teddy Boys in England with their Edwardian dress; the bikers with their leather clothing and tattoos in Europe and the United States; and the hip hoppers with the B-boy (chains, gold teeth) look, the use of military fatigues by Public Enemy or the African style dress and dreadlocks of Arrested Development.

The commodities that the subcultures are associated with can help us understand their attempts at dealing with their circumstances. The highly ritualized and stylized form of hip hop suggests that there is an attempt at solving the race and class problematic that faces the youth. However, this attempt at resolution is pitched largely at the symbolic level. The problematic of a subordinate experience can be lived through, negotiated, or resisted, but it cannot be resolved at that level or by those means.

Hebdige says that there is no subcultural solution to working-class youth unemployment, educational disadvantage, compulsory miseducation, dead-end jobs (17). Subcultural solutions are "imaginary" while the concrete material level remains unresolved.

V. This Imaginary Resolution

The poverty, unemployment, and hopelessness faced by members of a subculture are keys to understanding the response of youth to their material conditions. Subcultural styles may attempt to resist the system, but this resistance is often symbolic and does not challenge the material conditions. Style as resistance, therefore, is not effective in getting the youth out of the lower-class neighborhoods or their poverty and unemployment. It merely represents a different style of adaptation to, or negotiation with, the contradictions of their lives. Thus, the youth in the urban ghettos look to sports, drug dealing, or rap as their ways out of poverty. The only resistance evident is that which is symbolic in nature—lyrics in songs, rearticulation of symbols, using drugs, rebelling against the work ethic, etc. These gestures are a form of resistance, what Hebdige calls a "refusal" (3). Refusal begins with a movement away from consensus. It is the unwelcome revelation of difference which dawns upon the members of a subculture: hostility, derision, white dumb rages. Subcultures are, therefore, expressive forms, but what they express is, in the last instance, a fundamental tension between those in power and those condemned to subordinate positions and second-class lives.

VI. Subcultures Are Experienced As Style

It is the commodities—fashion, motorbikes, hairstyles, tattoos—that groups use to make a statement about their existence. Thus the subcultures are inserted into the consumer culture; they are dependent on the cultural industries for their survival. Their refusal to conform is characterized by a deep contradiction. Indeed, as we shall see, this attachment to commodities is the articulating axis between the hip hop and the dominant/corporate culture. Indeed, the bad boy antics of the gangsta rappers, the ritualized violence and the misogyny in rap videos, can be traced directly to the unholy alliance formed between the subculture and the cultural industries.

Despite these contradictions, however, the countercultural response of the message rap phenomenon has refused to die. Middle-class countercultural rappers like the members of Arrested Development or Public Enemy, continue to provide a critical take on both rap and politics. Thus, hip hop occupies a contradictory space in the cultural milieu.

VII. Twenty Years of Hip Hop

> History is not merely the stuff of imperial dreams from above. It isn't just sanitizing myths written by the few who wield political power. Representing history is within reach of those who seize the opportunity to speak for themselves, those who truly represent their own interests at all costs. The future of our times is being shaped now. History is today. (Dyson 1995, 10)

Representing history, as we have seen above, the protest message of reggae and its outspoken black nationalism was adopted by youth who were experiencing the broken homes, poor schools, unemployment, drugs, and violence that were sweeping the inner cities. Indeed, the earliest groups to be associated with hip hop were the gang subcultures of New York (to be followed later by an even greater association with the gangs of the West Coast). Afrika Bambaata, for instance, a former gang member, formed the Zulu Nation, an association dedicated to promoting the message of black nationalism. Bambaata, who has Caribbean roots, was one of the key elements in the development of rap, both as a DJ and as a producer. Rap, therefore, originated in the underclass of inner-city America in the '70s. However, hip hoppers differed from their parent culture, i.e., the African-American community, in style but not in substance. They were still living in the ghetto, uneducated, and in poverty. The ghetto, therefore, is the articulating axis around which the youth subculture relates to the parent African-American culture. They still face the racial and class oppression that their parents faced, but they choose to deal with the situation in a different way. However, the subculture uses raw materials that are available and affordable. The block parties that characterized the early forms of rap, for instance, required only a set of turntables and amplifiers. As the form grew in popularity, however, and began to be appropriated by the producers and recording companies, the rules changed.

Rap's encounter with the cultural industry was critical in its formation. One of the key differences in the way that the youth deal with their plight is in their relationship to the cultural industries and to technology, i.e., the dominant culture (Hall et al. 1976, Hebdige, Gilroy). Hip hop is a music-based subculture. Rap music and, in particular, rap videos are the medium through which the mores of the subculture are spread. Because of its close relationship to the cultural industry, however, the subculture must come to terms with market forces. As we shall see in the short history below, the story of rap/hip hop is the story of its commercialization in the contact with and reaction to the dominant cultural forces. But, first, let us take a closer look at the socio-economic status of African Americans in the '90s.

VIII. The Ghetto Poor

To understand hip hop, we have to examine its location in the ghettos of large U.S. cities, such as New York, Chicago, Houston, and Los Angeles. Since its inception, rap has evoked black and (lately) Latino ghetto life in its lyrics, video images, and language. As we have seen, rap emerged in the '70s with the upbeat rhythms and attitudes of the disco and R & B era. The street culture of hip hop, with its late night block parties, required safe streets. A comparison of the signifiers of hip hop then and now tells the story. In the '70s and '80s, rap was associated with "Wild Style," "Good Times," "Rappers Delight" "Breaking." In the late '80s and '90s, the signifiers have been "Criminal Minded," "Self Destruction," "Cop Killer," "nigga," bitch," and "hoe." With the advent of gangsta rap, the images and lyrics of the rappers have also changed from boasting to violent images of guns, drive-by shootings, domestic violence, drug-dealing/addiction, and misogyny. The nihilism of the rappers is clearly reflected in the status of the ghetto community in the '90s. Because of the flight of jobs from the cities, the movement of the black and white middle class to the suburbs, and the neglect of social services, like schools and hospitals, the ghetto poor are in much worse shape than they were in the '70s. According to William Julius Wilson, a sociologist at Harvard, New York lost half a million manufacturing jobs, and Chicago, 326,000 jobs, from 1967 to 1987 (Remnick, 25). The pattern was the same throughout the cities of the Midwest and the Northeast. Wilson, who wrote the controversial *The Declining Significance of Race* in 1978, argued that the plight of black Americans can no longer be attributed to racial discrimination alone but also to class forces and "social pathologies" in the African-American community. He said recently that the plight of the "underclass" of black Americans has deteriorated considerably since the '70s:

The social organization of these places changed radically. In those days, the over-
whelming majority of the population was employed—at least seventy percent of
the males. There were all kinds of factories, and now all that's really left is service
jobs. If you're lucky, you can be a hospital orderly, a janitor, or a fast food worker
earning poverty-line wages. (Remnick, 25)

Wilson estimates that the unemployment level has reached 40 to 50
percent in many inner-city communities. This rate of unemployment is
considered at the crisis point by many social workers. Stores have closed;
banks and churches have boarded up their buildings. The only establish-
ments left open in many communities are the bars and liquor stores. Petty
hustling, welfare, prostitution, drug dealing have become a way of life. Of
the 8,500,000 people considered to be the nation's underclass, half are
African Americans. The concept of the underclass, introduced by Wilson in
his study of the ghettos of Chicago, has become a controversial one and has
been used by conservative forces to make the "culture of poverty" argument
that blames the habits of the poor for their plight instead of the structural
constraints of racism and class. A more sophisticated version of the "culture
of poverty" thesis has recently been popularized as the EQ instead of IQ
test. The concept of the underclass, however, as Wilson uses it, referred to
the structural constraints as the cause of the isolation of the ghetto poor.
Wilson says that unemployment is the critical problem in the ghetto and
advocates social intervention in the European mode to break what he considers the critical isolation of the ghetto poor. This isolation from the mainstream work culture leads to problems when the poor go out to seek a job,
Wilson says. The survival skills that are critical in the ghetto (street language, aggression, baggy clothing) disqualify most from mainstream employment. This is the condition of the ghettos throughout the country. The
youth who grow up in this isolated atmosphere have only the television as
a window to the broader society. But the television only reinforces the
devaluation of black life. Recycled stereotypes are the norm while news
broadcasts depict the ghettos in apocalyptic terms. The schools are no better. Teachers and headmasters have given up, resources are few, and school
buildings are falling apart. Many youth grow up in families where none of
the adults work regularly. Even if there were jobs available—decent jobs
that have security and pay well—the youth in the ghetto do not learn how
to function in the mainstream community. Homicide is the number one
killer of black males between the ages of 15–25. There is a higher percent-

age of teen births in the black community than ever before. For every black college graduate, there are 100 incarcerated. A recent (1995) government study showed that one-third of black youth in the 15–25 age group are in the criminal justice system (Remnick, 25). Thus it is no wonder that the lyrics of rappers have become increasingly nihilistic.

The degradation of black life in the society is reflected in lyrics of gangsta rappers who refer to themselves as "nigga," and to their women as "bitch" and "hoe." Although Wilson's analysis of the class dynamics of the black community is perceptive, he ignores the race issue. It is a fact that blacks are incarcerated at higher rates than whites because of racist laws that, for instance, punish crack possession a hundred times more severely than the possession of powder cocaine. It is a fact that black and Latino youth prefer crack cocaine because it is cheaper. Nonetheless, it is the same drug whether it is sniffed or smoked. Yet, the Clinton administration refused to repeal the law and voted instead to build more prisons to incarcerate even more colored youth while their lighter-hued brothers go free. It is also undeniable that the current backlash against Congressional redistricting, welfare, affirmative action, and funding for education is motivated at least in part by racism. This motivation has become clear with the reemergence of white supremacist groups to lead the backlash against the legacy of the Civil Rights era. The Buchanan campaign and the electoral politics of the Christian Right and the Christian coalition are all motivated to a degree by racism. The firebombing, arson, and vandalism that has hit the black churches in the South (fifty black churches burned down since 1995) clearly testifies to the growing undercurrent of racism that pervades the thinking of white America. Thus, the plight of black Americans cannot be reduced to the influence of class factors alone. On the contrary, it is an overdetermined phenomenon where class and race are articulated together and keep the black community in the underclass even after overt/legal racial discrimination is gone.

IX. Three Waves of Hip Hop

According to Ronald Stephens (39), hip hop/rap music can be divided into three waves: the Boogie Woogie Hip Hop Wave, the "Rock 'n' Roll Hip Hop Wave," and the "Hard Core Hip Hop Wave." Groups like the Sugarhill Gang, Grandmaster Flash, and the Furious Five and DJ/producers like Afrika Bambaata have been identified with this stage of the rap music phenomenon which characterized the early examples of rap music in the mid-'70s. At that stage, hip hop was a street subculture of the ghetto youth, who were expressing themselves in a unique style that produced the graffiti, break dancing, the sound system, block parties, rapping MCs, or what we know today as hip-hop culture.

During the early period, most of the rap groups sampled dance music like "Good Times" by Chic, used in the Sugarhill Gang's 1979 "Rappers Delight," which put rap on the international market. As demonstrated by the Gang's hit, the lyrics consisted mainly of toasting, the dozens, and boasting. Before "Rappers Delight," rap and hip hop were exclusively a subculture of the black youth in the ghettos of New York. DJs and MCs distributed their homemade tapes on the street. They promoted the music by hiring youths to stand on street corners and in parks with a cassette player blaring out the music. For years, the mode of dissemination was the cassette tape and the block parties. It took the foresight of Sugarhill records and Sylvia Robinson, a Harlem musician turned producer, to put together an unknown trio called the Sugarhill Gang and record their nonstop boasts over beats taken from "Good Times" by Chic. The record took the U.S. and international charts by storm and launched rap, the ghetto subculture, into the global cultural milieu. Old school innovators, such as Grandmaster Flash and the Furious Five and Afrika Bambaata, were shocked by the recording and the hype that followed it. In no time, both produced their own, much more sophisticated, versions of rap set to sampled dance music.

The old school's relations to the Caribbean (Kool DJ Herc, Grandmaster Flash and Afrika Bambaata all have Caribbean roots) became clearly evident with the emergence of "message rap" with its socially conscious lyrics, reminiscent of dub and Jamaican toasting associated with King Tubby, U Roy, Dennis Alcapone, I Roy, Mtabaruka, and others. In contrast to the commercial and superficial/entertainment trends in the Afro-American music of the time (disco, R & B and funk), message rap adopted the radical black nationalist/social commentary style of the dub poets of Jamaica. In this sense, message rap can be seen as a countercultural response to the problematic of race and class. The message in this kind of rap is ideologically charged and provides a challenge to the hegemonic order that goes beyond the mere "magical resolution" or criminal subcultures of the underclass. Bob Marley's radical rearticulation of blackness, his "return to Africa" ideology and revolutionary stance influenced black youth around the globe.

His eclecticism—the dreadlocks from the Mau Mau war in Kenya; Rasta-farianism, a rearticulation of the back-to-Africa ideology; and reggae music itself, with its mix of R & B and calypso—had a tremendous power to interpolate black subjects around the world. In Kenya, for instance, the Rasta was met with immediate recognition—partly because of the dread-locks borrowed from the Mau Mau, the national colors, and the revolu-tionary black nationalist message. In similar fashion, message rap was met with instant recognition in the streets of Nairobi. Grandmaster Flash & Furious Five, Afrika Bambaata, and message rap in general were adopted by campus radicals and middle-class urbanized youths, while gangsta rap con-tinues to create a following in the cities. The articulations have gone full circle with the rap groups appropriating sounds and lyrics from African artists, e.g., Manu Dibango's Soul Makosa, and from master drummer Babatunde Olatundi's beats.

X. The Organic Intellectuals

Like Bob Marley, Alpha Blondy, Peter Tosh, and other reggae artists, rap groups like XCLAN, Public Enemy, KRS-One, Grandmaster Flash and the Furious Five, The Disposable Heroes of Hiphopcrisy, Ice Cube, Arrested Development, and others serve as "organic intellectuals" in their commu-nity, as they challenge the hegemonic white ideology of capitalism-cum-racism. According to Antonio Gramsci, social groups produce organic intel-lectuals who give cohesion and meaning to the existence of the members. Gramsci insists that all social groups have intellectuals. Every social group, coming into existence on the original terrain of an essential function in the world of economic production, creates, together with itself, organically, one or more strata of intellectuals to give it homogeneity and an awareness of its own function, not only in the economic but also in the social and polit-ical fields (60).

Gramsci says that dominant groups exercise power by both physical force and intellectual or ideological hegemony. Intellectuals, in the tradi-tional sense, function to legitimize the dominant ideology. However, the oppressed produce their own intellectuals who challenge the existing ideol-ogy and create an historic block united around counter-hegemonic ideas. According to Gramsci, the elite attempted to manage consents by making domination appear to reflect the consent of the governed, while the organic intellectuals tried to build historic blocks—a coalition of oppositional groups united around counter-hegemonic ideas (60).

Message Rap, a significant trend in rap music that has lasted from its inception in the '70s to the present, works to counter the dominant racist ideology by the reassertion of the dignity of the African and the revival of black nationalism and its remembrance of Africa. Where the earlier trend of socially conscious rap music, produced by groups like Grandmaster Flash and the Furious Five, focused on reporting the situation in the ghettos, the current trend is not only to report but to assert the dignity of the African American and to suggest counterideologies where the audience can find a new identity. The messages by Grandmaster Flash, for instance, described the plight of the African Americans in the inner cities—the violence, poverty, drugs, and lack of education.

Clearly, these messages are a vivid description of the hazards of growing up in the ghetto. It is also a description that could only be organized by a highly conscious intellectual who has studied the social dynamics closely. Yet, it lacks a vision of the future. There is no prescription for actions that would release the oppressed from their situation. Indeed, in the final analysis, these lyrics could create both anger and a sense of hopelessness since there is no alternative provided. The new generation of socially committed rap artists, however, has a clear vision of a preferred future and the methods through which their community can achieve their aims.

Public Enemy, for instance, uses black nationalist discourse of the Nation of Islam to challenge the hegemonic racist ideology. The use of explicit black nationalist language, the wearing of fatigues reminiscent of the Black Panthers, and their advocacy of the Nation of Islam has led to their being described as prophets of rage. Since 1987, the group has become the spokesperson for a new wave of African-American consciousness shaped in the tradition of Elijah Mohammed, Malcolm X, and Louis Farrakhan (Perkins, 41). The group sees itself as revolutionary in the tradition of Nat Turner, W. E. B. Du Bois, Malcolm X, and the Black Panther Party (Stephens, 39). Indeed they make their connection with the tradition of black nationalism clear in tracks like "Black Voices on the Streets of Watts":

Yeh in the ghetto,
Where niggers fine vine, but aint got a dime,
To defend Panthers against crime..
Let H Rap rap,

Let Huey duey,
Let Bobby Seal deal,
Let Dizzy Gillespie. (Cross, 50)

Despite being attacked and reviled by all sorts of establishment figures and being denied exposure in the media, including black radio stations, Public Enemy continues to enjoy phenomenal popularity. After producing the hit "Rebels Without a Pause," Public Enemy launched a new era in the history of pop music in America. The fact that the group could sell millions of copies of their records, despite their pariah status in radio stations, the mainstream producers, and media, proved that rap artists did not have to dilute their message to conform to the white supremacist culture. Following the example of Public Enemy, rappers could now sell a million records without ever being picked up by pop radio or crossing over, and the artists were becoming aware of the kind of power such independence meant (Light, 862).

The group's lead rapper, Chuck D (Carl Ridenhour), is clearly an organic intellectual in the Gramscian sense. He and the group are very clear about their goals in the African-American community. According to Chuck D, "my job is to build 5,000 potential Black leaders through my means of communication in America. A Black leader is just somebody who takes responsibility" (Azerrad, 32). The uncompromising lyrics of Public Enemy spawned a flood of message rap CDs by groups like the Disposable Heroes of Hiphopcrisy whose raps focus on international relations, class struggle, popular culture, and the socio-economic crisis facing the Afro-American community. Their first CD condemned the Gulf War and was dedicated to K Jones, the first African American conscientious objector from the Iraqi slaughter, and to all others who refused to kill or be killed in the name of the new world order, and to the infamy of those who did and were.

It is Atlanta-based Arrested Development, however, that most reflects the influence of Public Enemy and the radical tradition of the Black Panthers and the Nation of Islam in the '90s.

In contrast to the gangsta image, Arrested Development's male and female members chose to use African-style clothing and dreadlocks. The group is uncompromisingly black nationalist, and their raps explore issues such as homelessness, race, class, gender, the search for spirituality, and the presence of Africa. Their popularity is shown by the fact that they were the only contemporary rap group whose tracks were included in Spike Lee's epic movie *Malcolm X* (1992) and their selection as both the Best New

Artist and Best Rap Artist in the 1993 Grammy Awards. Like the rastas their dress imitates, Arrested Development's rap and video "Everday People" reveal their political agenda calling for cultural purity and withdrawal from the harsh realities of urban America. This is done by juxtaposing rural tranquillity with bleak images of inner-city decay and violence. The group uses a call-and-response style that reflects the black oral tradition and reggae. This moral and spiritual perspective has become popular with rap groups recently. For example, Bones, Thugs and Harmony, who won a Grammy in 1996 for Best New Rap Group, took a spiritual turn heavily influenced by the spirituals.

XI. Despite the Continued Presence of Socially Committed Rap Artists

In the message rap genre, the most popular type of rap continues to be gangsta rap. As we shall see in the next section, message rap does not attract the same corporate sponsorship or attention in the media or the film industry that gangsta rap commands. Thus, the gangstas have developed a crossover audience in the white suburbs and in the global cultural market. This popularity, however, has been accompanied by a foregrounding of misogyny, violence and negative stereotypes of blackness. Despite its blatant commercialism and its nihilism, gangsta rap also reflects the angst of the black American youth and how they negotiate their identity in the hostile racial and economic environment.

XII. Pop Rap and Commodification

The second stage in the '80s identified by Stephens is the Rock 'n' Roll Hip Hop Wave (1). During this stage, the emphasis shifted to the commercialization of rap, with songs shaped around sexual themes, and began to take on the attributes of rock 'n' roll including the grandstanding and the focus on violence and misogyny. At this stage, also, rap music crossed over from having a predominantly black teenage audience to a national audience. This crossover audience, mostly white teenagers, were reached via rap videos and the distribution systems of large corporations, such as MCA Records, Warner Brothers Records, Capitol-EMI Music, Polygram Records, Sony Music (formerly CBS Records, Inc.) and BMG music—all of which are global entities. Only Warner Records, owned by Time-Warner, is based in the United States. Most are owned by transnational corporations, based in

Germany, Japan, the Netherlands, and England. At this stage, rap music production also moved from the electronic age (the Sound System turntables and vinyl) to the computer age where the production of rap is a high-tech studio process of digital sampling and recording. The crossover into the national audience was also marked by the re-presentation of rap on the media with the inauguration of BET's Rap City in 1988, followed in 1989 by MTV's Yo! MTV Raps, and the publication of glossy, advertising-heavy hip hop magazines like *The Source* and *Hip Hop*. Groups like Fat Boys, Kool Moe Dee, MC Lyte, Ice T, Fresh Prince, etc., are characteristic of this period that saw the commercial success of many rap artists. This stage was also characterized by the use of foul language, misogyny, and songs that portrayed women as cunning, deceitful, materialistic, and untrustworthy (Stephens, 36). Run-DMC was also the group that was the most successful in terms of record sales at this stage. The album "Run-DMC" was the first great rap album (Light, 860). The group's next album sold over a million copies, had a video featured on MTV, and established rap firmly as a genre that was to last in the popular culture. Run-DMC is widely recognized as the progenitor of modern rap's integration of social commentary, creatively diverse musical elements, and uncompromisable cultural identification—an integration that pushed the music into the mainstream and secured its future as an American musical genre with an identifiable tradition.

> Nihilism and gangsta rap. We're telling the story of what it's like living in places like Compton. We're giving the fans reality. We're like reporters. We give them the truth. People where we come from hear so many lies that the truth stands out like a sore thumb. (Eazy E, "City of Quartz.")

The violence that occurred at several Run-DMC concerts around the country led to a debate about the relationship between rap and violence and the attempts at censorship. Run-DMC's articulation of a black nationalist position, while at the same time reaching a crossover audience, launched a new wave of hip hop that Stephens identifies as The Hard Core Hip Hop Wave (1). Popularly labeled gangsta rap by the media, this new wave took the misogyny, and the advocacy of violence and nihilism of the rock 'n' roll stage to new heights. At the same time, rap became a global mass media phenomenon under the control of the transnational cultural industry. With signifiers like Cop Killer, Fuck tha Police and Self Destruction, so-called gangsta rap is clearly the most popular trend in the form, and it receives the most attention in the media. The form exposes the artic- ulation of the subculture to the dominant culture represented by the media and the cultural industries. According to Frank Owen:

> When rap became big business, the industry wanted personalities to market. MCs grew to be the focus of the music and their bad boy antics came to eclipse the djs. The djs' job had once been to energize the crowd peacefully. But under the new rules the rappers job was often to incite the crowd with ever more incendiary lyrics from killing cops to brutal sex. Hip Hop was becoming less like dance music and moving ever closer to the shock tactics of punk rock, a trend that heralded the rise of the gangstas. (10)

The logic of the market, therefore, is the key to understanding the rise of gangsta rap. It is critical to note that the foregrounding of misogyny, vio- lence, and other social pathologies in rap emerged simultaneously with the commodification of hip hop. This commercialization process was facilitated by the production of rap videos and their popularization in the media. The power of music videos as an advertising medium reached new heights with the production of the movie-style video "Thriller," based on Michael Jack- son's 1983 hit album. In 1984, rap entered MTV with the Run-DMC video "Rock Box." This video was marked by the Adidas-clad foot of the MC crushing Michael Jackson's white glove. Videos are an advertising medium designed to sell a product or products. The product being sold by the rap videos is the hip hop culture: the clothing, (Run-DMC's endorse- ment of Adidas in the video), the gangsta image, and the stereotypes of blackness. The album "Criminal minded," which featured the KRS-One holding a gun on the cover, launched the use of guns in rap videos, maga- zines, and lyrics. Since this album, rap's association with guns and violence has become a major sales pitch. In a 1991 article, "Rap on Rap: The 'Black Music' That Isn't Either," David Samuels (using statistics from *Billboard*) estimated that rap's audience was mostly white teenagers in the suburbs:

> Although rap is still proportionately more popular among blacks, its primary audience is white and lives in the suburbs. And the history of rap's degradation from insurgent black street music to mainstream pop points to another dispiriting conclusion: the more rappers were packaged as violent black criminals, the bigger their white audience became. (24–25)

Samuels, a writer for the *New Republic,* has been criticized by, among oth- ers, Tricia Rose and Bakari Kitwana for ignoring the underground sales on the streets of cities like Los Angeles and New York, which is the main method of dissemination in the black and Latino communities. Most DJs and MCs push their music through tapes on the street. Some of these tapes even include 800 numbers where orders can be made. These sales have characterized rap since its inception, yet they are invisible in the billboard statistics. However, the weakest aspect of Samuels' argument is the primary position he gives the audience in the shaping of rap music. Although the audience is a critical aspect of the subculture, it is the "corporate gaze," as Bakari puts it, that determines the portrayal of rap stars (18).

While media and corporate industry push the idea (race-baiting) that white teen listeners are fascinated with these images of blackness (black youths as icons of rebellion and coolness; black sexuality and street life as exotic), much of the gaze seems to be coming from the corporate industry itself. Corporate America has preconceived notions of who black youth are and a vision of who they should be, and these images are represented in the style of rap it focuses on, gangsta rap and recreational rap.

The fact is that, since the '80s, corporate forces have articulated themselves to gangsta rap and hip hop culture and taken on the role of patronage. Since this marriage, gangsta rap has come to reflect this corporateness and seems more and more like punk rock. This articulation of rap to the cultural industry has led to the conversion of the music of black youth into a mass-produced commodity. The commodification process (rap videos, hip hop fashions, hip hop films) made rap public property and diffused its protest message. This translation of subcultural style into a commodity freezes the codes and establishes new conventions. Thus we have the conversion of subcultural signs into exotica: X hats, African-style clothing and hairstyles, and baggy prison-issue-like clothing. The protest style of the street is converted into a spectacle in an effort to contain it. This has, of course, been the history of black music from the blues through jazz. This tension between creativity and the market has led to the constant innovation of new styles that have become increasingly "black" in both attitude and identification (as if to thwart appropriation by white groups) since the '50s and the bebop era in jazz. However, this did not deter white audiences and imitators.

Some black critics have insisted that the misogyny in rap should be understood as parody in the tradition of the dozens. During the 2 Live Crew's obscenity trial in 1990, for instance, Harvard's W.E.B. Du Bois Professor of African American Studies, Henry Louis Gates Jr., testified that the sexual violence was not advocated by Luther Campbell's "As Nasty As They Wanna Be?" album. Gates insisted that Campbell was merely signifying. "There is no call to violence here. What you have here is humor, great joy and boisterousness. It's a joke. It's parody, and parody is one of the most venerated forms of art" (Gates, 1990, A3).

The defense of misogyny cannot hold water. The fact is that aspects of the black American tradition (like the Baptist church) have been and are as misogynistic as is the general white supremacist patriarchy in the United States. As we have seen, signifying is part of the black American tradition. Some aspects of signifying, like the dozens, thrive on misogyny as H. Rap Brown's autobiography clearly demonstrates. The disrespect for women, therefore, cannot be excused or dismissed as parody. Indeed, parody, irony, and indirection are strategies used to keep subordinate groups in their place. Using Gates' logic, one could argue that all the racist and sexist jokes and name-calling are mere irony. This amounts to a defense of racist discourses and stereotypes that are an essential part of the structure of domination. Lyrics like Ice Cube's on Too Short's album, "Short Dog's in the House," do not directly counsel violence but are repugnant nonetheless:

> Now stupid little bitches get tossed
> If they don't realize that I'm the motherfukin boss
> Come on down and get your ass pinched
> And if you talk shit, you get your ass lynched
> Cause I'm the b-i-t-c-h-k-i-l-l-a
> Ice Cube's a nigga that's bigga than a nut
> Cause a bitch is a bitch is a whore is a slut. (Kitwana, 51)

The use of the words "nigga," "bitch," "hoe" as a self-reference is one of the clear examples of internalized oppression, a self-hatred that reflects the limiting labels that the white supremacist system has put on black people. As cultural critic Haki Madubuti put it, these words cannot be "de-stereotyped" even if the users are black. Thus, the use of these words by the rappers shows how deeply they have been incorporated into the system and become participants in their own degradation. The advocacy of violence as the preferred means of resolving conflicts within the black community and particularly in gender relations cannot be excused as mere "reality" rap. The fact of the matter is that young blacks are shooting each other at an unprecedented rate. Violence against women is escalating, and the prospects for most black youth in the inner cities are bleak. The only way out of the ghetto seems to be the traditional routes of becoming a rap star or a super-athlete. In this situation, the nihilism expressed in rap music can be seen in the context of what Frantz Fanon calls "horizontal violence," which he describes as reaction of the native to the hopelessness and powerlessness imposed on him by the colonization process. As Fanon puts it: "The native will take all kinds of insults from the colonizer but reach for his knife at the slightest sign of disrespect from his brother" (54).

The artist who most reflects the contested and contradictory image of the gangsta rapper is Ice Cube. Cube's dramatic entry into the rap scene introduced a new and powerful voice into the rap genre. Cube's lyrics reflect the bleak experience of growing up in the ghetto; the gang-banging, misogyny, drug trade, violence. However, he is also capable of reflecting on the relations between the ghetto youth and the dominant culture represented by the police, courts, and prison systems. In "Fuck the police," for instance, in the album "Cop Killer" (NWA—Niggaz With Attitude) Cube depicts the volatile relationship between the inner-city youth and the police and virtually prophesies the beating of Rodney King and the resulting orgy of anger and violence.

> Fuck the police, comin' straight from the underground
> A young nigger got it bad cause i'm brown
> And not the other color, so police think
> They have the authority to kill a minority
> Searching my car looking for the product
> Thinkin' every nigger is sellin' narcotics
> Taking out the police will make my day. (Rose, 129)

Cube was also the author of "Boyz 'n the Hood," which depicted the lives of gangbangers in inner-city Los Angeles with a socking realism. The popularity of the song stems from its frank depiction of life in the ghetto and the slow, heavy track influenced by Run-DMC and put together by Dr Dre and Yella.

> Cruising down the street in my 64
> Jocking the freaks, clockin' the dough
> Went to the park to get the scoop
> Knuckle heads out there shootin' some hoop,
> A car pulls up who can it be,
> A fresh El Camino rollin' Kilo G,

Who rolled down the window and started to say,
It's all about making' that GTA.
Cause the Boyz in the Hood are always hard,
Come talking that trash and we'll pull your card,
Knowin' nuthin' in life but to be legit,
Don't quote me boy cos I ain't sayin' shit.
Donald B in the place to give me the bass,
Say my man JD was a friend of mine,
Til I caught him in my car trying to steal an Alpine
Chased him up the street to call a truce
The silly cluck head pulls out a deuce deuce
Little did he know I had a twelve gauge
One sucker dead LA Times front page.
Cause the Boyz . . . (Cross, 33)

The rap was the basis for John Singleton's hit movie *Boyz N' the Hood*, which portrayed the predicament of growing up in South Central Los Angeles, the eye of the storm. This film also set a precedent for the production of hip hop movies which feature the collaboration of rap artists and black film producers. Like rap, these films depict the reality of living in the ghetto. The grinding poverty, broken homes, drugs, anger and violence, depicted in *Boyz N' the Hood*, set in a background of rap, was an articulate warning of the violence to come on May Day, 1992. The portrayal of the relations of the police with the African-American community is characterized by anger, hatred, fear, and violence. Tre, for instance, is harassed by the police for no reason after he escapes from the scene of a melee between gangs. His reaction to having a gun placed on his head and being threatened with death for no apparent reason except the policeman's hatred of black men is a painful scene of shadowboxing in his girlfriend's house where he expresses his desire to kill an unidentified foe. The constant circling of police helicopters in the neighborhood has been described as a "mobile metaphor of the ominous surveillance and scrutiny to which so much of poor Black life is increasingly subjected" (Dyson, 12). Similarly, the hour-late response of the police to the attempted theft at the Furious and Tre Residence, and to the fact that the thief was almost killed was that it would decrease the number of "niggers" on the street and the cause for worry. This response reflects the criticism leveled at the LAPD for not responding to the riots in the South Central area until hours after they started.

Thus we see gangsta rap reflecting both the reality of growing up black and poor in the '90s but also, at the same time, reflecting the articulation of the form to the cultural industry which leads to the reinscription of racial stereotypes. This contradictory existence has, of course, been the lot of black music since the popularization of black spirituals at the turn of the century. However, the cultural industry is only one aspect of the forces that control the cultural milieu. Equally important in the story of hip hop is the reaction of politicians, clergymen, and the mainstream media to the phenomenon of hip hop. Like the other black musical forms before it, rap has attracted a negative reaction from the cultural elite. Indeed, in the minds of the conservative order, the rapper has come to symbolize all that is wrong with the society. As we shall see in the following section, the reaction of the elite to rap music is a classic case of moral panic where the anxieties of the day are foisted onto a group that symbolizes the other.

XIII. Moral Panics and Folk Devils

The demonization of youth subcultures by the media represents the search for a figure or culture that embodies the "other." The raising of Shakur, Ice T, Snoop Doggie Dog, and gangsta rap in general into the status of an anti-hero or a folk devil by the media over the last few years is evident in the amount of coverage the rap star has received and the association of his antics with the problems facing inner-city blacks as a whole. The moral panic in the wider society in relation to the gangsta rap is evident, for instance, in the dialogue between Shakur, the law, and Vice President Dan Quayle, who attacked Shakur and was promptly answered in rap form. Yet, paradoxically, the anti-hero is given remarkable access to the media, as can be discerned in his appearance in the movies like *Juice* and *Poetic Justice,* his seemingly unrestricted access to MTV, and the media in general. Indeed, the turning of gangsta rap into a commodity fetish has taken a comical turn with the release last Christmas of the rapping Barbie Doll, pagers for "bad" kids, and rapping machine guns. This access can be seen in the context of containment strategies that are used by the dominant culture to incorporate or criminalize members of the sub-culture. This strategy can be discerned in Bill Clinton's use of rap as a racial signifier in his 1992 presidential campaign when he criticized rap star Sister Souljah to symbolically distance himself from black issues and, particularly, from the Rev. Jesse Jackson. Tipper Gore's crusade against rap, its vilification on radio talk shows—whose popularity soared during the Shakur shooting—are only symptomatic of the nationwide perception of the phenomenon. The attacks in the press and by politicians are reflected in the increased instances of rap stars being brought before the courts and charged with obscenity (2-Live Crew), copyright violations, drug and gun law violations, and even murder (Shakur). My contention is that the privileging of gangsta rap in the media—through rap videos, MTV, films and the recording industry, and the active association of blackness with drugs, violence, dysfunctional families, and low IQ—the gangsta image as a reflection of blackness is part and parcel of the hegemonic strategy of criminalization. The anxieties of the dominant culture in a changing cultural and economic landscape often leads to the search for scapegoats. And in the United States, the scapegoats—the "folk-devil"—has predominantly been black.

The gangsta fits neatly into the traditional portrayal of the black male as the "exotic primitive" in American popular culture. This folk devil is evoked at moments of crisis to serve as the bearer of anxieties with immense political value; e.g., the infamous staging of a drug deal outside the White House and the Willie Horton advertisements of the Reagan campaign. As Ishmael Reed puts it: "Mr. Horton seemed to epitomize the image of the Black male projected by the media in the 1980s—that of a roving irresponsible predator." It is clear to me that President Bush's Willie Horton ad campaign was successful because it was created after a decade of black male-bashing in the media. The return of the Democrats to power has not reduced the association of social pathologies with black bodies—Bush posing with crack babies, Clinton posing with a black youth from the inner cities while declaring a continuation of the war against drugs. We see a continuation of the primitive/devil theme in the fascination with the high-profile Mike Tyson rape trial and the baffling coverage of the OJ Simpson murder trial. The art of blaming the other for the social and economic dislocations that the nation has suffered has been perfected by the power brokers throughout the country and can be observed in the use of racial code words such as "family values," "welfare mothers," "crack babies," etc. to delineate the boundaries of the current political "crisis." This technique was effectively used by the religious right as it played a critical role in the right turn that cultural politics in the U.S. has taken since the Republican Convention of 1992. Gangsta rap has a privileged position in this process as the most visible and the most commonly evoked image of the black devil within.

The folk devil—onto whom all our most intense feelings about things gone wrong, and all our fears about what might undermine our fragile securities is a sort of alter-ego for virtue. The association of rap/black culture with drugs and violence reflected in rap videos on MTV shows how, in Stuart Hall's words, "the popular is the site par excellence of stereotyping" (1992, 26). The role of cultural industries in the colonization of public spaces, particularly in this increasingly image based culture and in a community that has been denied other means of self expression, e.g., academia, is clearly evident in rap. The rap music we hear/see—particularly the rap videos on MTV that set the standard—are designed to the specifications of selling/profit and are not a spontaneous cultural expression. In this sense, rap can be seen as an overdetermined phenomenon that reflects both the interest/domination of the cultural industries and also the frustration and creativity of the artist. The relationship of rap to the cultural industries and to the development of new technologies is critical in any serious analysis of the phenomenon.

XIV. Conclusion

Although popular culture is "the scene par excellence of commodification" (Hall 1992, 26), the scene where culture enters directly into the circuits of power, it is my contention that rap is not one homogeneous whole. Some rappers are "organic intellectuals," in the Gramscian sense, providing an invaluable social commentary. They are "organic" because rap is grounded in the Afro-American oral tradition of signifying, the dozens, and more recent roots in the blues, reggae and bebop. This study has shown how rap music developed from the old school message rap of the early '70s to the pop rap of the '80s and finally into the gangsta rap of the '90s. Although these genres emerged consecutively, there is much overlap, so that message rap, or the so-called old school, continues to exist despite the fact that the gangsta rap genre dominates the public version of the form today. Thus, in addition to the essentialist, homophobic, and sexist media industry icons of the gangsta rap phenomenon, the old school tradition of Grandmaster Flash, DJ Herc, Afrika Bambaata, Public Enemy, and the Disposable Heroes of Hiphopcrisy and Arrested Development lives on.

We have seen how the gangsta rap phenomenon has come to dominate hip hop because of its close relationship to the cultural industry (MTV, Hollywood) and the fact that its major audience is white suburban teenagers. This association with the crossover audience has been a critical element in the evolution of rap music from a protest form that emerged in the ghettos of Jamaica and the United States to the global multimedia phenomenon that it is today.

Thus, hip hop is an overdetermined subculture that reflects the material conditions and the racial oppression of the black community but reacts to these conditions in a different style from the parent African-American culture that retains a Christian and conservative ethos. Rap music can be seen as the eloquent response of black and Latino youths to their plight in postmodern America. It not only allows them a means of expression but also provides a way out of the ghetto for the lucky few. In this sense, therefore, rap represents not only the anger and frustration of poor youths but also their aspirations. The fact that the majority of black people occupy a subordinate class position is, however, unaffected by the style of hip hop and even the more radical solution of drug-dealing and gangs. The youth are as poor and undereducated as their parents, and the racial problematic remains despite the subcultural response. Thus, I argue that the style of hip hop can be described as an imaginary resolution of the race and class problematic that the youths face. The attempt at resolution is imaginary in two ways: first, in the way that the youths play out their fantasies in rap videos and lyrics; and, second, because of the fact that subcultural style is reactive (not proactive) in that it does not deal directly with the unemployment, undereducation, and marginalization of the youths but is aimed at resolution at the level of consciousness. Through its close association to the cultural industry—the recording companies, MTV, and the radio stations—rap/hip hop was incorporated into the dominant order through either commodification/domestication or criminalization through labeling and moral panics. The moral panics, reflected in the attacks on rappers from authorities, expose the social and economic anxieties and the breakdown of social consensus that leads to the emergence of subcultures (Hebdige 1979, Gilroy 1993). We have seen how the perceived challenge of hip hop is met with the use of the judicial system and the police and through civic action (e.g., the warning labels on CDs pushed by Tipper Gore). Finally, this study has established the link between hip hop and the broader socio-economic formation and examined the organic relationship that the subculture has to the political and economic structures in the United States.

Bibliography

Abrahms, Roger D. *Deep Down in the Jungle: Negro Narrative Folklore from the Streets of Philadelphia.* Chicago: Aldine, 1970.

Appiah, Anthony. *In My Father's House: Africa in the Philosophy of Culture.* New York: Oxford University Press, 1992.

Azerrad, Michael. "Public Enemy: Rocking the Joint." *Rolling Stone* (1988).

Baker, Houston. *Blues, Ideology, and Afro-American Literature.* Chicago: University of Chicago Press, 1984.

Brown, H. Rap. *Die Nigger Die!* New York: Dial Press, 1969.

Costello, Mark, and David Foster Wallace. *Signifying Rappers. Rap and Race in the Urban Present.* Hopewell: Echo Press, 1997.

Cross, Brian. *It's Not About a Salary: Rap, Race and Resistance in Los Angeles.* New York: Verso, 1993.

Dent, Gina, ed. *Black Popular Culture.* Seattle: Bay Press, 1992.

Du Bois, W.E.B. *The Conservation of Races.* Washington D.C.: American Negro Academy, Occasional Papers No. 2, 1887. Reprinted in Bracey et al., eds. *Black Nationalism in America.* Indianapolis: Bobbs-Merrill, 1970.

———. *Dusk of Dawn: An Essay toward and Autobiography of a Race Concept.* New York: Harcourt, Bruce and Company, 1940.

———. *The Souls of Black Folk.* New York: Gramercy Books, 1994.

Dyson, Michael E. "Performance, Protest and Prophesy in the Culture of Hip Hop." *Black Sacred Music* 5 (1991).

———. "Representin' History." *VIBE* 2 (1995).

Fanon, Frantz. *The Wretched of the Earth.* New York: Grove Press, 1963.

Gates, Henry L. "Rap band members found not guilty in obscenity trial," *The New York Times.* 19 October 1990: A3.

———. *The Signifying Monkey: A Theory of African American Criticism.* New York: Oxford University Press, 1988.

George, Nelson. *Buppies, B-boys, Baps and Bohos: Notes on Post-Soul Black Culture.* New York: HarperCollins, 1992.

———. *The Death of Rhythm and Blues.* New York: Omnibus Books, 1993.

Gilroy, Paul. *The Black Atlantic: Modernity and Double Consciousness.* Cambridge: Harvard University Press, 1993.

Gramsci, Antonio. *Selections from the Prison Notebooks of Antonio Gramsci.* Edited by Quintin Hoare and Geoffrey Smith. New York: International Publishers, 1992.

Hall, Stuart. "What Is This Black in Black Popular Culture?" in Dent, Gina. *Black Popular Culture.* Seattle: Bay Press, 1992.

———, and Tony Jefferson. *Resistance Through Rituals.* London: CCCS Hutchinson University Library, 1976.

Hebdige, Dick. *Subculture: The Meaning of Style.* London: Routledge, 1979.

Kitwana, Bakari. *The Rap on Gangsta Rap.* Chicago: Third World Press, 1995.

Light, Alan. "About Salary or Reality? Rap's Recurrent Conflict." *The South Atlantic Quarterly* 90 (1991).

Lipsitz, George. *Time Passages: Collective Memory and American Popular Culture.* Minneapolis: University of Minnesota Press, 1990.

Major, Clarence, ed. *Juba to Jive: A Dictionary of African American Slang.* New York: Viking, 1994.

Owen, Frank. "Back in the Day." *VIBE* 2, 10 (Jan. 1995).

Perkins, William Eric. 1991. "Nation of Islam Ideology in the Rap of Public Enemy." *Black Sacred Music* 5 (1991).

Reed, Ishmael. "Anti-Hero." *State of the Art: Issues in Contemporary Mass Communication.* Shimkin, David, Harold Stolerman, and Helene O'Connor, eds. New York: St. Martin's Press, 1992.

Remnick, David. "Dr. Wilson's Neighborhood." *The New Yorker* 29 April–6 May 1996.

Rose, Tricia. *Black Noise: Rap Music and Black Culture in Contemporary America.* Hanover: Wesleyan University Press, 1994.

Samuels, David. "The Rap on Rap: The Black Music That Isn't Either." *New Republic* 205 (1991).

Stephens, Ronald J. 1991. "The Three Waves of Contemporary Rap Music." *Black Sacred Music* 5 (1991).

Toop, David. *Rap Attack: African Rap to Global Hip Hop.* London: Serpent's Tail, 1991.

West, Cornel. *Race Matters.* Boston: Beacon Press, 1993.

III
Philosophical Reflections on Contemporary Youth and Popular Culture

Chapter 10
He Ain't Heavy:
Robert B. Parker Revisits *Emile*

Walter P. Krolikowski, S.J.,
Loyola University Chicago

Donald Barthelme wrote "The Abduction from the Seraglio,"[1] almost twenty years ago. Its theme was the changes that setting the story in 20th century America entails if one wishes to retell Mozart's 18th century opera as a Texas country music song. In some ways it is the same story, but, clearly, the new setting arranges the elements in a new pattern. In Barthelme's version, Constanze is a country-music groupie, the Pasha is an enormously successful car salesman, the harem is a Butler building, and the tenor is a disturbed sculptor of massive sculptures of wrought iron. Barthelme's story is just one of many attempts to describe a contemporary situation utilizing a form from an earlier age; metaphorically, the opera plays the part of a *paysage moralisé.*

So, we are not surprised that Rousseau's *Emile* has been revisited in 18th century Spain in the *Eusebio* (1786–1788) by Pedro Montengon, who sets the story in Pennsylvania; in 18th century England in *The History of Sanford and Merton* (1783–1789) and *The History of Little Jack* (1788), both by Thomas Day; in 18th century France in *L'Eleve de la nature* (1764–1791) by Gaspard Guillard de Beaurieu, who sets the story in Virginia. I would maintain that there are at least two retellings of the *Emile* in our own times: in a movie, *The Earthling* (1980), starring William Holden and Ricky Schroeder and set in New Zealand; and in a detective story, *Early Autumn* (1981) by Robert B. Parker, which is set in New England.[2]

Though the earlier authors clearly were imitating and recreating Rousseau's work, each in his own way, we have only internal evidence for thinking the same of the more recent works. In this essay I wish only to explore the connections between the *Emile* and *Early Autumn*.[3] Let us see how his story of *Early Autumn* unfolds and then compare and contrast it with the *Emile*.[4]

I

We begin by looking at a young man badly in need of education.

When we first meet Paul Giacomin, he is fifteen years old. Short and thin, he has dark, long hair in need of a haircut, a long nose, small eyes and mouth, a narrow and sullen face, with hunched shoulders and his head held down. His voice whines, and his fingernails are chewed short. He has no strengths or strength: He doesn't have the strength or agility to get into the high front seat of a Bronco without great difficulty. He's not smart, good looking, funny, or tough; he resembles a bird. All he's got is a kind of ratty meanness.[5] Spenser, a private investigator, says, "The kid is a mess, he's skinny. He seems to have no capacity to decide anything. His only firm conviction is that both his parents suck" (36). Clearly, his parents have never taught him how to act. He has no self-confidence because he's good at nothing, except watching the tube (90). He is not a likely prospect for schooling.

II

Paul's mentor is Spenser, a private detective.

Spenser is not described very fully in *Early Autumn,* but he appears in Parker's other books; as a result many readers already know him before they open this book. In *Looking for Rachel Wallace* (1980), for instance, we are given a thumbnail sketch of him. He is over six feet tall, runs five miles a day, had his nose broken in a fight with Joe Walcott, when Walcott was past his prime, had been a policemen but was dismissed from the force, carries a gun, and drinks only beer and wine.[6] We also know from previous books that he has two friends, Susan Silverman, whom he loves, and Hawk, his dark angel.

In *Early Autumn* he explains his motives more fully. Though he is hired by Patty Giacomin, he does not feel bound to do what she asks even when it is a question of her son (20). His job as a private investigator lets him live life on his own terms.

He feels sorry for Paul because Paul does not know how to act. "His clothes aren't right, and they don't fit right. No one's ever taught him anything" (35). But these are just instances. "No one has taken any time with him. No one has told him anything, even easy stuff about dressing and eating out. He's been neglected" (35).

Spenser carries a gun because there is no harm in being safe. "When you can, it's better to deal with possibilities than likelihoods" (105). He's used the gun to kill people, and he knows that, if he were quicker at killing people, his threats would work better. Why doesn't he kill more? "Something to do with the sanctity of life." But there are no absolutes. "I mean you make rules for yourself and know that you'll have to break them because they won't always work" (70).

He's reading *A Distant Mirror,* which is about the fourteenth century. "I like to know what life was like for them. I like the sense of connection over six hundred years that I can get" (97).

He does not like the country, at least not for long periods of time. "I like cities. I like to look at people and buildings." When Paul asks him whether trees are not prettier, he replies, "I don't know. I like artifacts, things people make. I like architecture" (119). And yet, he is now willing to spend a great deal of time in the country for Paul's sake.

He may be trying to be a Mr. Chips to Paul, but Susan confronts him with his willingness to use blackmail (147). Part of his answer is that he does not see himself as ordinary, and his identity is as important to him as that of parents who "will fight like animals to keep the kid from being taken away" from them (146.) And this identity of his pushes him into spiriting the child away from his parents.

III

Their place of retreat is Kimball Lake, outside Fryeburg, Maine, near the New Hampshire border.

The cabin stands at the edge of a lake on nearly three quarters of an acre of land, woods all around, and at the end of a dirt road. It is secluded, but not the only cabin on the lake. Drinking water comes from a well; the shower uses lake water. The cabin is furnished with a flush toilet, a fireplace, a small electric stove, an old electric refrigerator stocked with beer, and two small bedrooms with metal bunk beds. There is a radio, but no television; there are records, but only of Benny Goodman (95–96).

IV

We learn more about Paul's mother than we do about the father. Patty Giacomin is not wholly to be blamed for what she is. She does not know the
names of prominent sports stars, for example. It's her parents' fault and not
hers, says Spenser. She does not know how to show affection for her son.
"His mother made an awkward gesture of hugging him. But she didn't seem
able to carry through and ending up putting one arm across his shoulders
for a moment and patting him slightly on the back" (94). She is only beginning to know who she is. Being a mother and wife have turned out to be
not enough. "It has taken her a long time to realize the value and need of
self-actualization." But even that is not enough. "She's read all the stuff in
Cosmopolitan and knew all the language of self-actualization, but all she
really wanted was to get a man with money and power" (49). Her husband
thinks this behavior is neurotic, but Spenser, in debating mood, rejoins:
"It's not neurotic. If a man did it, you'd say it was normal" (208).

But Spenser himself thinks that it is neurotic and that the husband is
beneath contempt. Out-of-shape but hefty, Mel Giacomin, in Spenser's
view, wears all the wrong clothes: a gold Banlon turtleneck, beltless green
polyester pants, garish and expensive rings on the little fingers of both
hands (15). He does not fight to keep his boy. At a later point Spenser says:
"Listen to me, Rat Shit, you're talking like you could bargain. You can't.
You do what I say or you take a big fall" (205).

To Paul, his parents seem positive. But Spenser sees it differently:

> That's a clue. Too much positive is either scared or stupid or both. Reality is
> uncertain. Lots of people need certainty. They look around for the way it's sup-
> posed to be. They get a television-commercial view of the world. Businessmen
> learn the way businessmen are supposed to be. Professors learn the way professors
> are supposed to be. Construction workers learn how construction workers are sup-
> posed to be. They spend their lives trying to be what they're supposed to be and
> being scared they aren't. Quiet desperation. (129)

Susan thinks the Giacomins are like all parents, and yet, children survive their parents. But Spenser sees the mother and father hating each other
and using the kid to get even with one another. Kids cannot survive under
such conditions, nor are adoption or an incompetent Office for Children
the answer (36–37). The best that can be hoped for is that the parents stay
away from the kid. Let them pay for his support and his schooling, but stay

away. They are really not interested in the boy, nor do they want him. "Both of you are so hateful that you'll use the kid in whatever way is available to hurt the other" (138).

V

Paul's education begins before he and Spenser leave town and go to Maine. While they talk, Paul is not allowed to play the radio—because they are talking (19). He is asked to choose between staying with his mother or father, but it must not be a mindless choice; he must give reasons (20). He is given a lesson in how to choose when the alternatives look equally distasteful:

> "When all your options are lousy," I said, "you try to choose the least lousy. Apparently you're equally bad off with your mother or your father. Apparently you don't care which place you're unhappy. If I take you back to your father you're unhappy and I get nothing. If I take you back to your mother you're unhappy and I get a hundred bucks. So I'm taking you back to your mother. You understand?"
>
> "Sure, you want the hundred."
>
> "It would be the same if it were a dime. It's a way to think about things. It's a way not to get shoved around by circumstances." (21–22)

Decision-making is to be resolved through that form of utilitarianism some philosophers, like Bruno Schuller, call proportionalism. But in other areas of behavior, different norms are proposed. When Paul does not want to talk about something, Spenser refuses to let go, because Paul had brought it up in the first place. Spenser does not want to hear Paul bad-mouth his mother. Why? Because it's not done (22).

In any case, decisions must be made. Thinking only goes so far. What is controllable may be handled by rational methods, but not everything is controllable rationally.

> "You've had a tough life and it doesn't seem to be looking up. It's time to start growing up. It's time to stop talking and start being ready for whatever comes along. . . . Your way out of a lousy family life is to grow up early and you may as well start now." (74)[7]

Spenser had already made his own decision. He will take over Paul's education. He outlines his plan to Susan, who has asked him what he will teach. "I'll teach him what I know. I know how to do carpentry. I know how to cook. I know how to punch. I know how to act" (90). Susan replies:

"You make it sound simple, but it's not. You don't teach people unless they want to learn. It's not just an intellectual exercise. It's a matter of emotion, of psychology" (90).

Susan is not sure the boy is educable; she's afraid he may be pathological; the chances of success are slight. Spencer replies that he has nothing to lose, and, if things work out, a child has been saved.

The drive north does not begin well: "I plugged a Johnny Hartman tape into the stereo on the assumption that it was never too soon to start his education. He paid no attention" (94).

Paying no attention to Susan's earlier dictum that "you don't teach people unless they want to learn," Spenser announces his unilateral plan to Paul. They are going to build a cabin. On arrival they carry in their equipment and stow it. But "a lot of the things were too heavy for Paul and everything he carried he seemed to handle badly" (96).

They discuss Spenser's friend, Hawk. Like a good liberal, Spenser distinguishes between the public and private person and is content that such a person may be fractionated. "Hawk is not good. He's a good man. You know the difference?" Though Paul does not, he is assured that there is a difference, a difference Spenser will help him learn (99).

Lessons continue the next morning. Paul does not want to get up. Spenser gets him up and showers him. When asked why, Spenser replies:

> "One, you need some structure in your life, some scheduling, to give you a sense of order. Two, I was going to have to do it sometime. I figured I might as well get it over with." (103)

When Paul remarks that Susan is crazy, Spenser rejoins: "I know you don't know any better, but that's against the rules." One should not speak "badly of another person's beloved." Paul's "Sorry" is accepted (103).

A regimen of exercises, stretching and running, is begun, interspersed with didactic lessons:

> "When you're thinking about something important like if your father might try to kidnap you again, it's better to think of what the best thing would be to do if he tried, rather than trying to decide how likely he was to try. You can't decide if he'll try, that's up to him. You decide what to do if he does. That's up to you. Understand?" (105)

Now Paul begins to nod and no longer shrugs. The lesson is spelled out: "A way of living better is to make the decisions you need to make based on what you can control" (105).

When Paul rejects the suggestion that he lift weights, he is asked what he would like to do. On his admission that he doesn't know, he is told that is what weekends are for—to do whatever. But during the week, the regimen will continue. Of course he doesn't know how to do these things, but he will be shown and, in the case of lifting bars that are too heavy for him, helped (110–111).

Resentment in the midst of physical improvement continues; he wants to be left alone. Spencer replies:

> "Because everybody has left you alone all your life and you are, now, as a result, in a mess. I'm going to get you out of it. . . . you don't have anything to care about. You don't have anything to be proud of. You don't have anything to know. You are almost completely neutral." (113)

To Paul's protestation that it is not his fault, Spenser agrees, but adds, "not yet." First, one must be taught; autonomy and responsibility for oneself follow.

The first job is to help Paul be good at something, anything. The plan is:

> "I'm going to have you know how to build and cook and to work hard and to push youself and control yourself. Maybe we can get to reading and looking at art and listening to something besides situation comedies later on. But right now I'm working on your body because it's easier to start there." (114)

Paul sees this plan is, seemingly, not enough; he can't stay in the woods forever. Spenser adds:

> "That's probably so, And that's why, kid, before you go back, you are going to have to get autonomous, yourself. You're not old enough. It's too early to ask a kid like you to be autonomous but you got no choice." (114)

Not surprisingly, such talk reduces Paul to tears. Spenser OK's crying, admits he has cried himself. "You only got up to go" (115.)

And up means moving—slowly—from using one's back and elementary tools to using power saws, even though, even now, the use of power tools would make for more efficient and less costly operations. The point is for work to be like a hobby, where "love and need are one" (118);[8] the point is not simply to be efficient.

Things move forward rapidly. Cokes give way to beers. They go to see a ballet, which Paul likes, even though others, like Paul's parents, would not. Spenser is not afraid to cut them down. They don't know any better.

They don't know what they are, or how to find out, or what a good person is, or how to find that out either. They rely on categories.

> "Your father probably isn't sure of whether he's a good man or not, and he suspects he might not be, and he doesn't want anyone to find out if he isn't. But he doesn't really know how to be a good man, so he goes for the simple rules that someone else told him. It's easier than thinking, and safer. The other way you have to decide for yourself. You have to come to some conclusions about your own behavior and then you might find that you couldn't live up to it. So why not go the safe way? Just plug yourself into the acceptable circuitry." (129)

Since Paul doesn't understand, Spenser tries again:

> "If your father goes around saying he likes ballet, or that you like ballet, then he runs the risk of someone else saying men don't do that. If that happens, then he has to consider what makes a man, that is, a good man, and he doesn't know. That scares the shit out of him. Same for your mother. So they stick to the tried and true, the conventions that avoid the question, and whether it makes them happy, it doesn't make them look over the edge. It doesn't scare them to death." (129)

They are like sleepwalkers, who are afraid to be awakened, unlike Emile, whose sleepwalking is what the tutor wants because he is not ready to look over the edge.

The cabin beings to take shape. Bodybuilding progresses. Paul gets interested in hearing the ball game on radio. It comes to be the time to confront Paul's father, whom Paul says he does not like. Spenser uses that remark to make a point: "'Course it's not that simple. You're bound to care something about his opinions, his expectations. You couldn't avoid it" (150). Then he adds: "But remember, you probably will care. It probably will hurt. It's okay for it to hurt. It's very sensible that it should hurt" (150). As the scene develops, Paul admits it scares him. Spenser says: "I don't blame you. If you're not used to it, it's disturbing. In fact it's sort of disturbing even if you are used to it" (154). Spenser gives Paul an alternative: stay with Susan, an offer Paul rejects: "I want to stay with you." To which Spenser says "We're stuck with each other, I guess" (155).

Spenser sums up:

> "It's the way life is. You don't know what's going to happen. People whose lives work best are the ones who recognize that and, having done what they can, are ready for what comes. Like the man said, 'Readiness is all.'"

VI

What is fifteen-year-old Paul like at the end of his education? He is older than his age group. Physically, he's fit. He can run five miles without strain. He knows how to drink beer and wine. He knows how to order food in a restaurant: he orders pheasant! He has helped build a cabin. He could make his way as a carpenter. He has learned how to work with another, older person. He is free of his parent's influence. He is going to go to a ballet school of his choice. He's ready to try living with a roommate. He no longer needs a "transition coordinator" (176). He is autonomous and can depend on himself.

Is he ready for the coming winter?

VII

Clearly, Paul Giacomin is not a double for Emile. He is too old, has a set of habits which have crippled him as a human being, and hates his parents and himself. But like Emile, if he is to survive in his world, he needs to be educated. He cannot make it on his own. He needs a teacher.

His teacher, Spenser, is not the Rousseauvian tutor; he is not another Jean-Jacques. He is a hired gun, a man with a definite lifestyle which he is unwilling to change. He has a life of his own and friends of his own. But a part of his identity, paradoxically, is to be moved by the sight of suffering, especially by the suffering of the young and helpless: "He ain't heavy; he's my brother." He believes in the sanctity of life. In all these ways he is very much like Jean-Jacques, including his fascination with the past. Jean-Jacques is practically a Stoic reborn; Spenser's present fascination is for the 14th century, when a civilization was in the death throes of the Black Death. He has not saddled himself with a job that will prevent freedom of movement. He can take off several months, if not years, and, though this work goes beyond the call of duty, and to that extent, is a free-will offering, he is being paid by Mrs. Giacomin.

The Giacomins turn out to be the enemy. For Rousseau, as for Raymond Chandler, the enemy is society, especially as exemplified by life in the city, Paris for Rousseau, Los Angeles for Chandler. Living in 1981 has its own distinctive notes: The world is filled with bloodshed; there is fighting in Ulster, China, Angola, Lebanon, Ecuador and Peru. Ronald Reagan is elected president, and John Hinckley shoots him. Cities riot, while science and technology continue to make giant strides in discovering new stars in the heavens and AIDS on earth, cloning fish, and producing personal computers. For Spenser, the city, especially Boston, is his natural milieu, a place he loves, and the society of the '80s is a challenge one is constantly preparing oneself for—dangerous to be sure, corrupt right down to the smallest detail, but the best environment a human being can grow in. One enemy is closer at hand; it is the modern family, in which husband and wife hate each other and use their children as pawns in a game in which they attempt to best each other, in which the adults are simply clones, in every sense, of their parents, who, too, had been failures at parenting.

But both Rousseau and Spenser agree on the country as the best place to carry on an educational enterprise. Rousseau goes to the countryside to get away from the city's influences. Spenser appreciates the countryside's safety features, though it is interesting that Hispanic youths in Chicago find shelter and peace in the central city where gangs do not come. But, where Rousseau uses the resources of the countryside—living in a commune, providing servants and gardens and woods, having an environment in which Emile can learn about the world of nature—Spenser uses the cabin alongside the lake as a getaway from the conveniences as well as the dangers of the city. Voluntarily for Spenser, necessarily for Paul, they are going to follow a regimen which will develop Paul's body and give him some elementary skills to prove to himself that he can depend on his own strengths once he leaves. For Rousseau, the countryside allows Emile to discover the world of nature, which is the humans' world; for Spenser, the countryside allows Paul to discover the world he himself is, both as an individual and in relation to significant others. For both Rousseau and Spenser, the education is a twenty-four-hour-a-day task in which all the activities of the day are educational. Spenser, however, allows for some time off on weekends.

But during the week, education goes on. There is the same emphasis on the physical, rather than the intellectual, in both Rousseau and Spenser. In both, reading is not even a priority. From the beginning, the emphasis is on self-direction, though in the *Emile* the activities are directed in masked fashion by the tutor. Spenser is much more aboveboard. As a result, what is done is frequently unilaterally determined by Spenser, but, in reality, perhaps less frequently than similar activities by the tutor. Spenser forbids certain activities because they are against the rules, while the tutor simply does not allow certain things to happen. What looks like nature being in charge in the *Emile* is unmasked in *Early Autumn* as human interference, but it is paternalistic in both cases.

Direct instruction, therefore, plays an important part even before education in the country begins. But, its end is autonomy, though the means are indoctrination. If one is to become autonomous, education is necessary and necessarily indoctrination. To lift dumbbells at the beginning, someone has to give a helping hand. But certain standards are set: decisions must be rational and open to inspection, even though the decision in the end escapes rationality.

One must become good at something, not simply because the social situation demands it but also because one has no identity without some skills. Both tutors believe this, but, in Rousseau, that process is completed during Emile's time in training while Spenser pushes Paul out of the nest at the end of the novel to begin his training as a ballet dancer. And the explicit point of choosing dancing is that one's skill should be treated like a hobby and never like drudgery.

Travel is a part of education. In *Emile,* it prepares the young man for participation in civil life by having him see the variety of forms that social life can take. Paul is taken to Asia House to see 19th-century photographs of China, which seem to be from another planet and yet human and real— almost as if one has seen the diversity of life without having to travel physically to other places. But, clearly, in both books, there is a sense of the world changing rapidly, and Spenser's use of Shakespeare's "Readiness is all" could have been used by Rousseau as well.

At the end of both books, the student is ready to face his world. Both teachers have been "transition coordinators." But Rousseau goes further. The last half of Book IV and almost all of Book V, which are concerned with religion and marriage, have no counterpart in Parker's book.

VIII

The didactic novel has had a long history. There is a constant fascination with preparing strangers for life in a world they have not created and can change to only a limited extent if at all. There is a constant fascination in helping those who are strangers to themselves find themselves by building their self. There is a constant fascination in finding oneself by helping others find themselves. Jean-Jacques was fascinated in all these ways; so was Spenser. They are both challenges to us all.[9]

Endnotes

1 In *Great Days* (New York: Pocket Books, 1980), pp. 91–95.

2 There is also an anti-Emile by Alfonso Muzzarelli entitled *L'Emilio Disingannato. Dialoghi Filosofici* (2nd ed. 1792).

3 For a more complete look at Spenser, the teacher in *Early Autumn,* a start can be made by reading Doug Robinson, *No Less a Man: Masculist Art in a Feminist Age* (Bowling Green: Bowling Green State University Popular Press, 1994), pp. 37–106.

4 Obviously, there are other influences on Parker. Parker himself points to Dashiell Hammett, Raymond Chandler, and Ross MacDonald. See John W. Presley's "Theory into Practice: Robert Parker's Re-interpretation of the American Tradition," *Journal of American Culture* 12,3 (1989): 27–30 for a discussion of Parker's doctoral thesis. For Thoreau's influence on Parker, see Lonnie Willis, "Henry David Thoreau and the Hard Boiled Dick," *The Thoreau Society Bulletin* 170 (1985): 1–3.

5 Robert B. Parker, *Early Autumn* (New York: Delacourt Press, 1981), p. 37. Henceforth page numbers given directly in the text are references to *Early Autumn.* Paul Giacomin appears in a later book, *The Widening Gyre,* just as Emile appears in an unfinished sequel, *Les Solitaires.* Neither are dealt with in this essay.

6 New York: Dell Publishing, 1980, pp. 2–3.

7 One way of understanding Spenser is to see him as a neo-Weberian. Christian Lenhardt summarizes Weber's theory: "(a) values are on a footing of equality in terms of their validity (value relativism); (b) values are in conflict with each other (value antagonism); and (c) since choices have to be made between values and since we have no rational grounds for making them, the basis for choice is irrational decision (decisionism)." Value rationality is restricted to assessing the consistency of one's values and to a rational anticipation of consequences. Christian Lenhardt, "Max Weber and the Legacy of Critical Idealism," in *The Barbarism of Reason: Max Weber and the Twilight of Enlightenment,* edited by Asher Horowitz and Terry Maley, 37. (Toronto: University of Toronto Press, 1994).

8 Spenser is quoting Robert Frost's "Two Tramps in Mud Time." A favorite poem, it hits off Spenser's wish: "My object in living is to unite/My avocation and my vocation." It also offers some justification for Spenser's taking over someone else's job, namely the parents and the professional teacher. Robert Frost, *Collected Poems, Prose, & Plays* (New York: Library of America, 1995), pp. 251–252.

9 Grateful thanks to Jacqueline Krump, Michael Oliker, Ruth McGugan and Gene Philips for their many suggestions.

Bibliography

Barthelme, Donald. "The Abduction from the Seraglio," in *Great Days.* New York: Pocket Books, 1980, pp. 91–95.

Frost, Robert. "Two Tramps in Mud Time," in *Collected Poems, Prose, & Plays.* New York: Library of America, 1995, pp. 251–52.

Lenhardt, Christian. "Max Weber and the Legacy of Critical Idealism," in *The Barbarism of Reason: Max Weber and the Twilight of Enlightenment,* edited by Asher Horowitz and Terry Maley. Toronto: University of Toronto Press, 1994.

Parker, Robert B. *Early Autumn.* New York: Dalacorte Press, 1981.

————. *Looking for Rachel Wallace.* New York: Dell Publishing, 1980.

Presley, John W. "Theory into Practice: Robert Parker's Re-interpretation of the American Tradition," *Journal of American Culture* 12,3 (1989): 27–30.

Robinson, Doug. *No Less a Man: Masculist Art in a Feminist Age.* Bowling Green: Bowling Green State University Popular Press, 1994, pp. 37–106.

Willis, Lonnie. "Henry David Thoreau and the Hard Boiled Dick," *The Thoreau Society Bulletin* 170 (1985): 1–3.

Chapter 11
Recollecting Honor

Alan L. Soffin,
Delaware Valley College

> "For where old men have no shame, there young men will be devoid of reverence.
> —Plato [1]

> "Be like Mike, drink Gatorade."
> —Bayer Bess Vanderwater advertising agency [2]

"Today, the only consensus on morality . . . seems to be that the United States is experiencing a decay in standards," observed sociologist Norval Glenn, in a *fin de siecle* report to the *Orlando Sentinel.* What distinguished Glenn's survey from the usual report of moral consternation was that its dour assessment "was only moderately less common among younger than older adults." It was, Glenn said, "more than the usual abhorrence by one generation of another's ideas." [3] No surprise, then, that William Bennett's massive *Book of Virtues* becomes a bestseller, that political debate fixates on a breakdown in "family values," that a conservative Congress and a canny administration popularly expand the death penalty for a widened spectrum of crimes, that public school prayer is pressed as a national need, and that a major political party prospers by shaping its agenda to the moral require-ments of fundamentalism. But where does a troubled nation seek the sources of moral decline?

Overwhelmingly, it looks to patent evildoers. Popular culture tirelessly mines the psyches of wife-beaters, child-abusers, addicts, under-aged gun

slingers, rapists, robbers, serial killers and the occasional embezzling finan-
cier for clues to moral decay. Whenever social causes are considered, they,
too, must wear the look of evil. Vivid media portrayals of violence and sex
are skewered, as congressional committees count murders and quiz experts
on the character effects of *grand guignol*. In short, the problem of character
is thought largely to be one of resolve, of *will*—for popular culture believes
we all know right from wrong.

But there is another strategy of inquiry which long ago supposed that
fundamental evil may not be marked upon the brow of criminals nor signaled by the hiss of serpents. Plato's *Republic* hunted moral failure not in
what society deplored but in what it admired. By seeking the reasons for
Athenian decline in the ideas of respected persons like the retired merchant,
Cephalus, the Socratic dialogue suggested that a society sick in its streets
and offices is sick as to what it prizes. In this, the Athenian anticipated the
Nazarene whose attack on failed morality also fell upon the standards of the
well-to-do and visibly virtuous. So, in wondering how drug dealers or
"dead-beat dads" can evidence such unconcern for principled self-respect or,
more simply—if archaically—their personal honor, we might do well to
consider that these miscreants may, early on, have learned such disregard
from the brightest and best in the society around them.

The notion of personal honor merits serious attention. Personal honor
binds respect for oneself to moral integrity. Promises may be kept in business or politics as matters of enlightened self-interest, but, as matters of personal honor, promises are kept apart from calculations of personal advantage. Honor speaks to what we are. To keep a promise out of honor is to
maintain a way of being. In traditional terms, maintaining one's personal
honor means caring for one's soul—a way of speaking which supposes that
our moral condition is real, that it is a portion of our substance. Currently,
any talk of a morally substantial self—one which is more than a system of
drives, impulses, moods, and chemistries (psychological and physiological
substantiality)—is subject either to philosophic dismissal as mysticism or
benign acceptance as poetry. Yet the idea that the self has an existentially
unique or appropriate substance is deeply embedded in practical experience
(so deeply as hardly to be noticed).[4] We all readily agree that a responsible
person is a substantial person, and that no person can be called substantial
who is not responsible.[5] And which of us has not felt empty upon acting

dishonorably, but solid having acted on principle? (Of course, "emptiness" is only a literary expression, and those who have killed themselves to flee their emptiness no doubt died from an excess of metaphor.) All of which is to say that people for whom honorableness is a genuine property of the self will view taking advantage of others as a violation not only of ethics but of themselves. Dishonor constitutes a degradation of their being. Corrected for literalness, *The Picture of Dorian Gray* illustrates (as it were) the point.[6] We are prepared to resist bribery, chiseling, theft, unfair advantage, and the misuse of power when self-respect rests on personal honor, and prepared to do the opposite when self-respect depends upon our prospects for advantage.[7] In this way, a sense of personal honor is the spine of an order which is social, as distinct from one based simply on convenience or the threat of force.

But in an age of positivism, personal honor has the status of an antiquated fiction. Despite the persistence of humanist and sacred traditions, positivism's insistence on a wholly scientific worldview dominates the shaping of contemporary sensibility.[8] (Such cultural inconsistency is nothing new; Gunnar Myrdal's classic, *An American Dilemma,* saw an overarching cultural "conflict between different valuations" as the key to understanding our problems with race.[9]) The evaluative term "hero" has become the value-neutral "role model" of social psychology; the morally significant "human" has been accommodated to the morally irrelevant "naked ape" of anthropology and "organism" of biology (and behaviorism)—despite our being "made in the image of God." Within the worldview advocated by positivism (sometimes called "scientism") only those things for which science can give evidence are real. Unfortunately for moral truths, the evidence of science is confined to sense-experience while moral properties—such as the cruelty of an act or the goodness of an intention—are not sense-perceptible. (An unjust word looks and sounds like a just one; corrective glasses improve our ability to see a behavior but do nothing for perception of its moral quality.) Consequently, moral properties like "obligatoriness" (unlike physical properties such as "hardness") cannot be scientifically established; thus, within science (and therefore, for positivism, within all rational thought), they do not exist.[10] This is why scientific theories can reach no moral conclusions, and why scientists, as scientists, are not ethicists (giving us the literary genre of *Frankenstein,* the mad—because morally blind—scientist whose conditional positivist thought now extends to everyone). Once positivism confines us to a physically sensible world, only physical facts exist. (Here, positivism silently falters because meanings are not physical—are not established on sense-perceptible evidence—so that, meanings, like moral properties, cannot exist and positivism must be without meaning.) But the positivist outlook is too much identified with science to perish from self-contradictions. Without perceptible embarrassment, it simply broadens the physically factual to include thoughts as mentally factual—isn't psychology a science, after all? Because meanings can exist, our norms or standards of right (rational) thinking can exist. But there remains a terrible price. Standards of rational thought (or any way that we mean anything) are real, one must keep in mind, only as mental facts or psychological patterns; they are merely the facts of how we think; their so-called rightness or validity remains unreal. So, it transpires that standards of right and wrong in thought, as in behavior, when looked at objectively (scientifically) are neither right nor wrong. They simply are. In popular culture, then, all arguments come to be viewed as really neither right nor wrong. They are merely psychological facts—the manifestation of each person's psychological belief system (as occasioned in the brain by accidents of upbringing).[11] In popular culture, a theory is "just your point of view." To act against one's advantage for reasons of personal honor would be to weaken one's position for no real reason—one would be, plainly speaking, a jerk. Once science defines reality, the apparent reality of justice or injustice must be considered illusory and renounced ("If you think it's wrong, that's *your* problem!"). In this way, the only thing real about a moral perception is what is factual about it: it expresses (or is associated with) a feeling; it is an attitude, or a "projection." A moral qualm becomes something rather like a headache. "Right" and "wrong" are finally unmasked for what they are: attitudinal tags glued onto physical behaviors by the persuasive force of moral judgments, which are biologically evolved outcries (not truths) that control group behavior in ways (so far) favorable to species-survival.[12]

So it is that, beneath the din of public moral outrage, the properties of honorableness and goodness, when challenged, seem to ordinary people insubstantial—"Where is the scientific evidence?" or "prove it; show me the facts!" Against the urgencies of economic need, inflamed consumership, and the pressures of socio-economic status, thought has no weapon—no ultimately credible account of ordinary moral experience. No wonder culture turns away from reasoning to willed belief—to faith—so as to credit moral experience, and no wonder that religion's "universal" message of selfless love and material renunciation is somehow discovered consistent with devotion to a relentlessly self-interested global economics founded on an ever expanding desire to acquire material things. Worldly power is persuasive, and today's "divine right" accrues neither to churchly nor monarchical thinking but to that of science and technology. The no-nonsense positivism that decried metaphysics ends as the intellectual arbiter of what is real in both popular and academic culture. (Though, for reasons suggested above, positivistically minded academic theorists often find that nothing can be said to be real.)[13] In consequence of positivist thought, whether scientistic or evolved into absolute skepticism, personal honor—because it requires the reality of moral characteristics—takes on the feel of fantasy. Since the self-respect we require cannot convincingly arise from anything we feel or suspect to be fictional, it must be made to rest on something else, something convincingly real. Hence the effective basis of self-respect reduces, at minimum, to the (quasi-physical) fact of social approval and at maximum, to the fact of adulation.[14] As not only moral but all norms become, inevitably, more unreal to culture, the standardless accomplishment of sheer notoriety—the experiential fact of feeling like a "somebody"—replaces honor and "respect" (also a standards-related concept) as the operating measure of substantial or successful selfhood.[15]

Despite being weakened by a scientific world-view, thoughts of personal honor cannot entirely vanish because moral experience and self-awareness exist. We still aspire not to "behave like an animal" or "live like a robot"—expressions which presume the reality of morality and free choice in the teeth of sociobiology, behaviorism, deconstruction, and the rest of positivism's children. We can still recollect that personal honor, socially expressed, requires that we do work worthy of respect, that we are true to our word, and that we never use the love and respect others freely give us for our own interest rather than theirs. If the degree to which we fail these standards is a measure of the degree to which we lack personal honor, then it may turn out that addicts, dealers, and irresponsible youth have the same false basis for self-respect as the insatiable developers, successful corporate raiders, inside-traders and all those who, while reasonably well-off, nonetheless "go along to get along." For whether ghettoized or lionized, all of them base self-respect on grounds devoid of any essential link to moral judgment, deriving self-respect from the facts of peer admiration or increasing group influence. It is becoming a successful self on the principle of becoming a successful baboon, i.e., entirely apart from the moral resoluteness that substantiates one's honorableness as a person.

In a society avowedly devoted to Judeo-Christian ethics, no lesson so morally repugnant could become the cultural norm unless taught by people both admired and successful. Though the socializing process takes innumerable forms, none more brazenly undermines respect for one's vocation, for one's word, and for the admiration and respect others give us than the apparently innocuous, often entertaining, practice of celebrity endorsement. To be sure, endorsement is hardly the most powerful of morally corrosive influences. Nor is it the most fundamental, being driven by a guilt-free ideology of acquisitiveness made rational by a positivist worldview. But the fact that celebrity endorsement can stand uncriticized, indeed, envied and enjoyed, at the very apex of mass communications, reveals just how completely society embraces ideas of self-respect and the uses of achievement that know nothing whatever of honor. *Endorsement is the emblem of contemporary moral amnesia.*

By means of television, beloved athletes, good-sport politicos, jovial coaches, admired thespians, and other media personalities continually enter our homes to define, unwittingly, the higher reaches of success. Journalistic researchers, Tout and Moon, found that, even in the calmer confines of magazine media, not only did endorsement ads constitute 44.4 percent of all ads, but between 1980 and 1986 "the proportion of ads featuring . . . celebrity endorsers increased so that—of all endorsers—11 percent were experts, 14 percent were CEO's, 24 percent were 'consumers', while 51 percent were celebrities.[16] And what greater compounding of success than that Michael Jordan's expected return to the NBA "resulted in an average increase in the market-adjusted values of his client firms of almost $1 billion in stock value."[17] But we do not hear the offstage cadences of agents and hard-balling lawyers when good-time heroes fill the air with portents and memories of childhood fun. This is the atmosphere in which a magazine that calls itself *Sports* can enthusiastically feature articles that compare the relative endorsement potential not of particular athletes but of classes of athletes such as pitchers, quarterbacks and golfers. The endorsement army's ranks are swelled by more serious advisers to the public: the talented coach touts a system for weight loss; the trusted old radio star recommends therapeutic furniture to oldsters for their back problems; the "intellectual" journalist extols the special virtues of a standard brand of coffee; the ordinarily merry face of a famous announcer and television second banana soberly urges an insurance plan on the anxious elderly; a great test pilot recommends the purchase of a particular auto battery; revered athletes appear festooned with brand names, converting their perfected bodies into billboards. People who gain respect for their vocational skills and affection for the entertainment those skills have provided are thus admired for converting that very respect and affection into the currency of personal advantage. A "poster-sized, double-gatefold, pullout poster" of Michael Jordan holding a bottle of Gatorade was supplied to buyers of *Sports Illustrated* on the safe supposition that they would embrace the huckstering image as a kind of gift or "freebie."[18] The power of identification with the celebrity messenger—one of many avenues by which celebrity operates—was recently recognized in a study by Michael Basil. "The fact that identification effects [of Magic Johnson's message on AIDS] were somewhat similar to those [measured] one year earlier reiterates the strength of celebrity effects," Basil declared, describing his results as "consistent with Bandura's Social Cognitive Theory (1986) [that] these effects *depend* on the receiver's identification with the spokesperson" while noting, in addition, the findings of Adams and Greene (1990) that adolescents did indeed identify with celebrities and that [Greene and Adams-Price (1990)] people's beliefs in a celebrity's personality were biased as a result of the identification process."[19] As for the effect of celebrity endorsers on consumption, Atkin and Block, studying the celebrity endorser's effect in alcohol ads presented to young audiences found that "advertisements featuring celebrity figures produce consistently more favorable impact than the non-celebrity ads."[20] In particular, "the use of famous persons to endorse alcohol products is highly effective with teenagers, while the impact on older persons is limited."[21] College students exposed to dummy alcohol ads were more affected by an Al Pacino endorsement than by those of a putative CEO, a wine expert, or a typical consumer.[22] An observation in Brand and Greenberg's study of commercials in the classroom underlines the susceptibility of the young to psychological power, as distinct from reason: "empirical evidence illustrates that while commercials generally are evaluated negatively by adolescents, TV ads can affect the brand preferences of young consumers."[23] The authors cite a study by R. P. Ross, the mere title of which tells the tale: "When Celebrities Talk, Children Listen."[24] Atkin and Block's concluding remarks are equally to the point: "the clear impact [of celebrity endorsement] suggests that young people may be more readily persuaded by a famous name linked to a product."[25] For Atkin and Block, the fact of celebrity influence "indicates that the social implications of this practice should be given closer examination. To the extent that celebrity endorsements . . . encourage underage youth to have a more favorable disposition toward alcohol, there is a basis for concern by responsible advertisers."

But the reason for responsible concern is far broader than underage drinking. It is adult modeling of the moral uses of others—as if we might respect a person who was loved by neighborhood children and then made use of their affection to sell them magazine subscriptions. But, honor has no purchase on our vocational life. If "Deliver me!" was once a cry of religious devotion, it now expresses the pleasure fans experience at being marketed to the highest bidder by their heroes. The total capitalization of vocational achievement, of the love and respect arising from that achievement, thus becomes a model for the meaning of vocational success—a paean to the consummate user that cannot be lost on the young. Since our feelings on this matter have been deadened ("the system works"), some imaginary television scenarios may waken our awareness to the ways in which celebrity endorsements trash work, word, and mutual respect:

The Pope is about to officiate at High Mass. (He pauses, then turns toward us slowly, gravely.) "High Mass is so important. The Lord and the flock depend on a Pope not to stumble." (Now the Pope is seated before an illuminated Book of Hours.) "I pray, of course; (thoughtful hesitation) but I also take No-Doz, just in case. No-Doz never leaves me drowsy." (Smiles paternally, then gives a kindly wink.) "And as we all know, God helps those who help themselves."

(Documentary footage of Martin Luther King flashes onto the screen:) "I have a dream. . . . I have a dream today"; (cut to Andrew Young, standing in his library leafing through a book on the Civil Rights movement. He glances at us.) "Andrew Young here. I knew Martin, of course. Those were momentous times. Exciting days. Now my days are quieter. I still work for equal justice, but I also have time to relax." (Cut to golf course; Young drives ball, turns to camera.) "Leisure's come into my life, but, because I'm still a committed guy, I need clothes that say, 'Hey, I'm with ya'." (Bends over to pick up the tee. We see the "Levi" patch on his jeans.) "That's why Levi's are the jeans for me. (documentary insert of marchers in Selma with Young's voice-over) . . . were when I was on the marches (cut to Young on golf course.) . . . are now. A balanced life. That's my dream . . . and I've got it!" (As he moves off on a golf cart, Martin Luther King's voice-over—"I have a dream.")

(Long shot of Maine house; cuts to shot of ex-President George Bush and former chief of staff John Sununu rocking, side by side in the afternoon sun). Bush: "Haaa . . . haa, wow! Never thought of that. You're right." (Leaning over confidentially) "Truth is, John, YOU should've been the president. How'd you get to be so darn smart?" Sununu: "It's not a matter of smart, Mr. President, it's a matter of work. I read. It's that simple. And one of the things I make sure I read is this." (Sununu hold up magazine) "*Newsweek!*" Bush: "Hey, lemme have a look at that!" (Close-up on Bush's face, eyes widening as he turns pages) "Boy, this isn't dry stuff, John. I mean sports, entertainment, health . . ." Sununu: (suddenly getting up) "Got to catch a plane for the TV show." (Bush starts to return magazine) Sununu: "Keep it, Mr. President. I'll get another copy from Justice Scalia." Bush: "Scalia reads *Newsweek?*" Sununu: "Hey, is Scalia smart? He says it's got more articles than the Constitution, and it's a lot faster read." (Bush laughs) Sununu: (to camera) "Great guy, our ex-president; (winking) . . . great magazine, *Newsweek.*" (close shot Bush, turning pages) Bush: (musing) "*Newsweek,* eh?"

Oh, but these are extreme cases—exceptions! The Pope's, Dr. King's, Andrew Young's, President Bush's and John Sununu's work is too worthy to be used as viewer bait in the pursuit of private gain. Such vocations deserve respect. They are not to be demeaned or trivialized as mere instruments of an individual's or corporation's advantage. But if that is the response, it makes our point: What we respect carries inherent imperatives, and, to ignore these for profit is to demean both the vocation and whomever sells it. (The criticism of Ronald Reagan's breezy, ex-presidential profiteering through public relations appearances in Japan shows that the presidency deserves a level of respect incompatible with merchandising it.) And, what do protestations which reserve respect for a select group of vocations mean for the rest of society's vocations, save that the ordinary work of humankind is undeserving of significant respect—that is, a level of respect sufficient to provide ground for dignity—and that ordinary vocations can be used in whatever way suits personal advantage? Personal honor can find no footing in work when that work embodies no value, no imperatives for respect, so that it rightly can be seen as a cipher—devoid of any standards that might restrain the hand of profit.

Nor is it the case that respected vocations track only with nonprofit vocations like the presidency or religious office. There was public concern over Ernest Hemingway's beer ad as well as Orson Welles' wine commercial. And if the poet Maya Angelou began hawking Avon cosmetics, similar discomfort would (as of this writing) arise. Our concern over treating vocations as mere means to one's advantage tracks with the inherent worth we accord those vocations. The person who might draw substantial self-respect from ordinary work thus confronts an ever drier well despite Sunday-school efforts to proclaim the nobility of labor. Where all might share in the dignity of valuable labor, celebrity endorsement denies that possibility by denying the inherent vocational value on which that dignity depends. The result is that only a few can have what remains as the basis of any convincing self-respect, namely notoriety and cash; an exacerbated inequality of selfhood joins the inequalities of wealth and opportunity already plaguing modern states.

Celebrity endorsement parlays the ordinary market economy requirement that vocational skills be marketed into the elective idea that vocations and vocational accomplishment draw what value they have from being marketed. (When it infects sports, the principle is expressed as "winning isn't everything, it's the only thing.") Thus, vocations are disconnected from the genuine societal needs, the moral imperatives, the personal competencies and the implicit public commitments of its practitioners. Yet these are precisely what justify the existence of vocations, their remuneration, and the respect, admiration, and affection accorded for performing them. Even the "non-serious" vocation of sport has such intrinsic values and corresponding imperatives. The philosopher Robert Novak describes sport as "a form of godliness" and the late social critic Christopher Lasch celebrated its role at length in his *The Culture of Narcissism*, as a (public) "representation of life."[26] Professional sport may thus be justified as communal ritual, as providing an appreciation of human skills, as a model of behavior under pressure, all of which presupposes that its practitioners be truly expert and honest to the game. But the use, for example, of baseball achievement to enrich oneself, as did the well-loved Yankee shortstop, Phil Rizzuto, by encouraging those who admired and loved him as an athlete, to borrow from a particular credit company, violates precisely the implicit compact of mutual respect for a vocation and for the essential relationship of athletic commitment and fandom's devotion which legitimize that vocational pursuit. When vocation, achievement, and the love and respect these engender are treated as abstractions which carry no imperatives of their own so that their importance, like checks, lies in being cashed, we witness a de facto commitment to the principle that everything has a price—the very idea we loath (or regret) when made palpable, as in the television scenarios above. But, perhaps that day is passing: an Associated Press release on endorsements offered to Olympic winners in Atlanta exuberantly proclaimed that "being on a Wheaties box has for generations been confirmation that an athlete has achieved supremacy not only on the playing field but, more importantly, in the marketplace."[27] In today's atmosphere of unlimited aggrandizement (what Plato's *Republic* called the "city of pigs"), the ultimate proof of worth seems effectively to have become that a thing can be profitably sold.

Celebrity endorsement is therefore, sadly, a kind of self-betrayal. For whatever elements of honor as distinct from adulation might rightly accrue to a great practitioner of some art, no grounds for honor exist if one can rightly treat one's task as of no inviolable value. One has only to imagine a great outfielder, upon making a game-saving catch, unfurling an advertisement for a particular brand of hot dogs in order to sense the deflation of his achievement. Something having genuine moral, aesthetic, and vocational import is being treated with an indifference appropriate only to a meaningless achievement—like successfully crossing one's eyes. The endorser bears public witness to the idea that his vocational achievement has not the worth to entail any imperatives (any objective claims on his or her behavior). Lately, the public has implicitly acknowledged this point, feeling somehow betrayed (not simply inconvenienced) by the ease with which professional teams are moved from traditional sites as if the vocation of professional sport did not embody imperatives arising from the good of tradition, loyalty, social symbolism, and community, and so could be treated simply as commodity.

Increasingly, nothing in the work life of humankind needs publicly to be preserved. The daring pilot of experimental craft—even the astronaut—begins to treat work as possessing no imperatives for respect. We have seen a test pilot, renowned for his courage and skill, trade on his accomplishments to persuade us to buy a particular brand of car battery. The dream of environmental mastery, which space flight represents, was similarly devalued by those astronauts who hid stamps on their person for private enrichment upon their return. Even this culmination of an historic human dream, this astounding feat of courage, intelligence and imagination, carried no inviolable imperatives of respect.

Meanwhile the same public which enjoys and envies clever endorsements laments the loss of standards (essentially, the loss of integrity) evidenced by the pandemic of student-cheating that has effectively ended the honor system. With the moral sensitivity that awakens when adults confront the young, adults understand that to be a student is to have a kind of vocation—entailing moral imperatives, historical and social meaning—so that submission to tests of competence is a matter of honor. But students have come to treat their work the way endorsers treat their work: merely as a means to their personal advantage. For such students, the tradition of a school or university could never provide a convincing reason to risk advantage by being honest. Indeed, it is only the inherent importance of religious work, artistic work, reformist work (and, until recently, political work) that continues to shield these pursuits from acceptable use as mere tools. The operative principle, not yet entirely expunged by economic boosterism and popularized positivism, seems to be that any worthy vocation must be valued for its meaning in the human narrative. (In the more familiar context of personal narrative: If someone we love gives us a gift, do we pawn it without compunction and revel in the cash?) In today's atmosphere of anarchic self-aggrandizement and the privatization of all public trust, General George C. Marshall's refusal to publish an autobiographical account of his public service on the ground that one ought not profit from the performance of one's duty would be thought not simply foolish, but actually unintelligible.

As the generations learn from their heroes and exemplars that few (and ever fewer) vocations are sufficiently demanding of respect not to be regarded as our personal tools, a profoundly antisocial (indeed, antireligious) lesson is taught: We cannot trust each other's stewardship of our common life. For we recognize that, were the Pope to use his religion, his religious office, and his personal reputation in an attempt at purely personal gain, he would prove his willingness to dishonor religion. His stewardship of religious imperatives could no longer be trusted. Were Andrew Young similarly to dishonor Martin Luther King's vocation and the Civil Rights reform movement, clearly, no one could trust his accounts of it or of his participation in it. A hypothetical Bush-Sununu endorsement of a magazine would present public officers whose respect for the moral significance of public work would be plainly weak. Only fools would trust their devotion to the public interest. (Imagine a president exiting a NATO meeting to sell autographs and original documents to the highest bidders.) And, if every vocation from plumbing to garbage-removal creates part of the public good and is part of the public trust, then the happy acceptance of celebrity endorsement sets a general tone of vocational irresponsibility which cannot but destroy public trust. (But, as we know, our dispiriting level of litigiousness is the fault of the legal profession.)

The not wholly expired idea that vocation has inviolable standards is what lies behind the abhorrence of prostitution. It is not that sex is bad; it is that the selling of the body denies its role as an aspect of oneself. Only if the human body entailed no imperatives of treatment or respect could it be justly treated as a commodity. But the body does have moral meaning and moral implications (hence, the pejorative "flesh-peddlers"). It is the denial of inherent moral import that permits vocations and vocational achievement to be peddled. Because this denial is repellent to awakened conscience, it is, of course, accomplished by indirection. Thoughts must be turned away from unreal, insubstantial principles to factual, real consequences so that endorsement can be handled merely as a question of engineering:

"Your Holiness, the Church is too remote from people as it is. The idea that you have troubles and needs and that you try to deal with them, even in mundane ways . . . that's just a helpful truth. And since when is it a sin to make a good living? Do you go around the world knocking capitalism? Look, this commercial will do more to help spread capitalism in the poverty areas that really need it than any books by economists ever could. Showing the faithful that you know how to make a little money will put them in a self-improvement frame of mind."

"Andy, do you realize how many young people don't even know that Martin Luther King ever had a dream? At least, with this ad, kids will ask who he was. They'll learn a little. And what was Reverend King trying to do in the Movement toward the end except stick up for the black man's right to make money on an equal footing with the white man? Don't you realize how many black kids are going to say, 'Hey, there's a black guy cashing in just like the white guys do. A black man can be famous and rich as any white dude'? And tell me what's wrong with the message of buying pants that still connect with the common man? And that bit about the balanced life, Andy—is that good advice or what?"

"C'mon, George. You mean to tell me that just by getting a magazine—a magazine you admit is a good one—you're going to sully the Office of the President? Get serious, George, if Nixon didn't bring it down, or Harding, what are you worried about? Nobody thinks the President is a saint! You're just a regular guy. It makes the President human; everybody likes to make an extra buck. What are you, God? So you get behind a good newsmagazine, make a few dollars—part of which you can give to charity—and the United States Government is not going to be hurt. You know it. I know it. And more kids will read a decent magazine. And, next election, can you imagine the Democrats beating up on your support for our candidate because you like *Newsweek* or because you're doing the same thing the great basketball and baseball stars do?"

Few styles of rationalization fall more familiarly on the contemporary ear than the free-form utilitarianism which treats vocations as without inherent ethical substance because nothing has inherent ethical substance. Only because we do retain a sense that work, things, relationships, statements, and actions actually possess inherent values—values peculiar to each—do we refuse to sell the White House, the original Constitution, and, as yet, our state and national parks in order to reduce taxes or encourage entrepreneurship. When we squirm at a Pope selling No-Doz we know the Pope would be ignoring what religion uniquely is and therefore what imperatives or obligations must govern its practitioners. None of the ideals and obligations pertaining to one's work, one's word, and one's public responsibilities restrains our fictional Pope. The world is his oyster, not God's. The willingness to sell one's word is an act devoid of personal honor, a sellout of mutual trust—the first condition, as we have noted, for any social life. Even the meanest criminal organization knows the need for the honest word—reserving some of its most dreaded punishments for members who speak falsely to the group. The point is symbolized in the taking of oaths, a pledge of mutual trust absolutely inconsistent with the selling of one's word. If it were true that mutual trust were consistent with commercial endorsement, one could logically ask to be paid to take an oath of fealty.

Even in this heyday of salesmanship, the giving of one's word is still the closest approach moderns make to the traditional pledging of one's "sacred honor." Indeed, it remains common moral sense that if one's word is for sale, oneself is for sale. The depth of our self-deceit in respect of celebrity endorsement is signaled by comparing its acceptability with the unacceptability of selling the human body. Sell the bodily self and you commit a (generally) illegal act, which is (generally) considered shameful. But sell your word or your reputation on national television, and not only do you break no laws, but in a self-professed, Judeo-Christian culture that preaches the preeminence of spirit over body, you will enhance your reputation in addition to your income.

There was a time when to learn that a person's word was for sale was to uncover a scoundrel. A person who sold his word or his standing had no honor. No longer is the person in the crowd who cries out, "Yes, doctor, I'll take another bottle of that snake-oil, cause it sure done me good!" decried as a shill whose identification once meant shame and undermined belief in the product. Today's shill has been ushered onto the stage while the "doctor" stands by to take orders. "Do you love me?" asks the image of the smiling shill. "Don't you admire me?" implies the image. "Don't you respect my talents and my reputation?" Don't you feel I'm your friend? Am I not a great kidder and helper of children?" And today's crowd responds, "This is my hero, my friend, my entertainer. Besides, this is exactly what I would do if I had a great reputation." For a shill is not a shill among shills.

This harsh observation is supported by the way popular rationalizations identify with the endorser's point of view. A favorite is to point out that the viewers realize the celebrity doesn't necessarily believe what he or she is saying. The idea seems to be that we don't condemn insincerity if we are understood to be aware of it. Worse, we praise it to the degree that it is well done: "Great commercial!" That is, we approve of insincerity on the basis of excellent technique. (When values are not real, effectiveness is all.) But the celebrity is not picked as an actor; acting ability is a plus. The celebrity is picked essentially for his or her actual (real life) credibility or reputation. ("[Arnold Palmer] has such credibility now; people just believe him."— advertising agent on the effectiveness of the golfer's paid endorsements.)[28]

So actual insincerity is rationalized away as if it were theatrically performed insincerity where an actor's ability to be convincing would rightly be a thing to enjoy. But, of course, the endorsement is not a play, it is a practical action seeking to affect the practical choices of an audience. It is a moral phenomenon, not an aesthetic one. It appears we are so enamored of celebrity, and so identified with cashing in that the patent disrespect shown us and the patent willingness of the hero to be a shill must somehow be made all right. "Wouldn't *you* say a cereal makes you strong or this is the best battery if someone offered you a million dollars?" is the common, defensively aggressive retort to criticism of endorsement. But when people think it a kind of trump to argue (in essence), "Wouldn't you forget about honesty and sell your word and your reputation if someone paid you enough and no one really got hurt?" then, they need not analyze the minds of criminals for clues to moral decline.

Rationalization is further evidenced by the argument that the commercial is perfectly harmless because viewers all know "this is a paid endorsement (is really insincere)." But it is well-known to these arguers that advertisers would never spend millions on endorsements if awareness of the celebrity's insincerity prevented the endorsement from significantly affecting the choices of viewers. The protestation "I know this is just a commercial (an insincere or ungrounded message)," therefore, fails as an argument that endorsing is, despite massive spending, an inconsequential act and therefore not a violation of honor or trust. When it is not a convincing piece of direct, insincere recommendation, celebrity endorsement amounts to manipulation by seduction.

Nor is it any less a rationalization to argue that appearing in a commercial without saying "buy this" or, perhaps, saying anything at all, is to do something morally different from giving one's word. If the commercial were a commercial for drugs, or assault weapons, or teenage smoking, no celebrity who was paid to allow his or her face just to appear in such a commercial would escape responsibility as an advocate of that message. Few remarks better signify the comfort with which selling oneself and one's vocation is widely accepted than the justification publicly given by— William Smithburg, the CEO of the Quaker Oats Company, for hiring Michael Jordan. "Because he is respected everywhere as a leader in sports and a proven performer," said Mr. Smithburg (as reported in the *Washington Post*), "Michael is perfect to represent Gatorade." Consonant with

Smithburg's scrupulous regard for mating an advocate's credentials with his advice is the additional revelation that "Mr. Jordan was willing to swap beverages [ending a two year relationship with Coca-Cola] because Quaker was willing to offer a multiyear contract . . ." Perhaps the brightest and best idea of personal honor was enlarged by exposure to higher learning: "This year," *The Post* noted, "Nike, Inc. will give Nevada-Las Vegas's Jerry Tartanian, Georgetown's John Thompson, and 54 other college basketball coaches endorsement contracts worth more than $4 million, top-of-the-line merchandise valued at $600,000, and invitations to a five-day, all expenses paid outing in Colorado Springs." Of course, should coaches' exemplary earnings falter, perhaps the new exemplars will be statesmen and stateswomen such as former Governor Cuomo of New York and vice presidential candidate Geraldine Ferraro who, along with the late Speaker of the House, Tip O'Neill, have already done commercial endorsements, laying their names, their words, and their vocations on the line for cash. (The foregoing examples were cited before Senator and ex-presidential candidate Robert Dole appeared in a commercial for a credit card company in which he "returned" to Russell, Kansas—the small town he once held out to the nation as a symbol of old-fashioned character—to be "welcomed" by gray-haired war "veterans" and warmed by a patriotically flown American flag, so that against a background of heroism, gratitude, loyalty, friendship, community, and the private life he has publicly spoken of with love, he could be challenged by a "store clerk" for identification in order to use the nationally known credit card he wasn't selling us but just good-naturedly kidding about. (He must have been kidding, since consumer debt is dangerously high, and the credit card he happened to be hawking didn't have the lowest interest rate.) Of course Dole would have refused any attempt to make use of his mother's grave; some things are worthy of respect! Unlike the people we have to watch out for who throw up their hands and say, "Layoff! I didn't do nothin', officer!" Dole's face has never appeared on any Post Office listing of con artists.

Much hand-wringing goes on over the defacing of public buildings and spaces, over our failure to put nature and our planet above personal gain, over journalism's drift to the easy sell of sensation rather than the difficult sell of sound reportage, over the influence of money on legislation, over the collapse of educational honor systems, over the need to lock every door, the need to police every industry and profession; in short, over a general decline in America's sensitivity to ethics. But ethical sensitivity and integrity don't (often) pay, at least not for the individual whose economic survival or success is perpetually threatened or in doubt. If, typically, they did pay, ethical problems would diminish in a hotly competitive marketplace; the need for regulation would be lessened, not increased. So tradition wanly reminds us, "virtue is its own reward." But it cannot be its own reward where personal honor or integrity are consistently ignored in the practices of pop culture's elite. And without felt concern for the soul, without the visceral conviction that personal honor is real and is actually part of one's substance, ethics are impediments to self-realization—rules of the game to be respected by enlightened self-interest only when the referee is watching. Morality does not work unless what one has to lose is one's self.

So it is that a nation in decline may be said to suffer from its heroes— a difficult notion to confront in that it tells us we suffer from ourselves. Hence, "know thyself," for exploitation has become impalpable. Popular culture enjoys its endorsements, its own exploitation providing it's fun— letting companies advertise cost-free on its shirts, its hats, its shoes, its automobiles. But we cannot pine for the lost days of honor while we tolerate the treatment of our work, our word, and the love, respect and trust accorded us as commodities in a world of up-front, profit-making fun. Honor cannot exist when sold; it can only, when sold, be sold out. And when the "best" sell it out, what can we expect of the least?

"In the kingdom of ends everything has either a price or a dignity. Whatever has a price can be replaced by something else as its equivalent; on the other hand, whatever is above all price, and therefore admits of no equivalent, has dignity." —Immanuel Kant[29]

Endnotes

1   Plato, *The Dialogues of Plato.* Vol. 4, *The Laws,* Book V, B. Jowett, trans. (New York: Bigelow, Brown & Co., 1919), p. 427.

2   Stuart Elliot, "Advertising," *The New York Times,* August 9, 1991.

3   Norval D. Glenn, "Whatever Happened to Morals?", special to the *Orlando Sentinel,* pp. G1+. (The author is Ashbel Smith Professor of Sociology in American Studies at the University of Texas at Austin.)

4   In passing: When someone asks "Is that your own idea?" they cannot mean "Is it in fact in your mind?" Plainly, it is. For an idea to be one's own, part of oneself, it must be accepted through rational assessment. This apparently minor point is the tip of the iceberg; the self's substance is essentially normative.

5   Here it is common to exclaim "mere words!"—as if to choose one's words were not to choose one's thoughts. Well-established usages are never "mere." Language is experience made sane, the text of hard-won understanding. (The tragedy of the "feral" or cruelly isolated child shows how crucial is the link between mind and its objectification in language.) See, especially Frederick Will, "Thoughts and Things," *Proceedings and Addresses of the American Philosophical Association* 42 (1968–69), pp. 51–69.

6   Against Oscar Wilde's image of the decaying sinner's soul one might offer the humane slogan "hate the sin but not the sinner" or the wise admonition to condemn a child's acts ("cheating is wrong") but not the child ("you're a cheat"). But the language for engendering character differs from language for describing it; the truth is: one becomes what one does.

7   The term-limits movement to eliminate the possibility of political careers reflects the tension between trustworthiness and personal advantage—though, like this essay, not that between honor and fanaticism.

8   Joseph Wood Krutch's *The Measure of Man* (Indianapolis: Bobbs-Merrill, 1954) provides an excellent critique of the positivism permeating Western culture.

9   Gunnar Myrdal, *An American Dilemma*, vol. 1 (New Brunswick, N.J.: Transaction Publishers, 1996), p. lxxix.

10 For the same reason, the positivistically minded philosopher David Hume decided in his *Treatise on Human Nature* (part IV, section vi) that the self did not exist; one has no sense-perception of one's self. See David Hume, *A Treatise on Human Nature*, Part IV "Of the Skeptical and Other Systems of Philosophy," Section VI "Of Personal Identity": "nor have we any idea of *self* . . . for from what impression could this idea be derived?" Though here we state the matter over-simply, we claim to state the spirit and its implications rightly. Thus Hume in Section VII, "The Conclusion of this Book," confesses to a philosophical "melancholy and delirium" which "fortunately. . . . Nature herself suffices to [cure]"; that is, the experiences of ordinary life dispel "these [philosophic] speculations [that] appear so cold, strained, and ridiculous that I cannot find it in my heart to enter into them any further." Here Hume epitomizes the contemporary cultural dichotomy between a philosophy of moral unreality and the experience of moral life. See esp. pp. 140–43 in *The Essential David Hume*, Robert Paul Wolff, ed. (New York: The New American Library, Mentor Books, 1969).

11 In capitalist culture it is acceptable to think that the beliefs we live by are just the effect of social conditions, so long as no one argues that what we think results from economic conditions. That would be Marxism; "belief-system" theory is "psychology." (Belief-system theory takes quite sophisticated forms so as not to seem a matter of psychology; note, for example, Alvin Plantinga's "Rationality and Religious Belief" where belief in God can be "properly basic [properly unchallengeable]" and one's thinking rests on a foundation of believing: Steven M. Cahn and David Shatz, ed. *Contemporary Philosophy of Religion* [New York: Oxford University Press, 1982], pp. 255–77.)

12 Being favorable to species-survival seems for some to reinstate the soundness of morality, while speaking scientifically, but that is only because "goodness" has been covertly and illegitimately reintroduced by thinking species-survival is good. For science, there exists no property of goodness, or any other value property.

13 The positivist path to an empty reality is not new. David Hume early on "proved" in the *Treatise* (Part III, section xiv) that causation (causal necessity) was not real because it could not be perceived by the senses. Thus, ironically, what was essential to science in sense-perception was used to deny what was essential to (most) science in explanation. Thus scientism becomes the "black hole" into which all reality, including itself, eventually disappears.

14 As to the possible other fact of direct self-approval: "I am the greatest" or "I love myself," its existence in the end depends on the fact of other people's attitudes, or else veers toward psychosis and away from any model of what, for society, self-respect might plausibly be.

15 Along with standardless notoriety come other manifestations of standardlessness such as the denial of any difference between high and low culture, fine art and entertainment; standards are "elitist." As for the standardless self, its reality is psychological and bodily, so that self-improvement centers on feeling good about yourself and being in shape.

16 Patricia A. Stout and Young Sook Moon, "Use of Endorsers in Magazine Advertisements," *Journalism Quarterly,* 1990, Fall, v67 n3, pp. 536–46; see esp. p. 544 and p. 542. (Earlier TV studies [Friedman, Termini, and Washington, *Journal of Advertising Research,* 6, 1977 pp. 22–24] reported celebrity TV endorsement up from 15 percent of ads to 20 percent between 1975 and 1978.)

17 Lynette Knowles Mathur, Ike Mathur, and Nanda Rangan, "The Wealth Effects Associated with a Celebrity Endorser: The Michael Jordan Phenomenon," *Journal of Advertising Research,* May/June 1997, v37 n3, p.67–93; see esp. p.67.

18 "It's Official: Michael Jordan Is Now Promoting Gatorade," Stuart Eliot, The Media Business, *The New York Times,* Friday, August 9, 1991.

19 Michael. D. Basil, "Identification as a Mediator of Celebrity Effects," *Journal of Broadcasting and Electronic Media,* 1996 Fall pp. 478–95; see esp. pp. 491, 481. See also Albert Bandura, *Social Foundations of Thought and Action: A Social-cognitive Theory* (Englewood Cliffs, N.J.: Prentice-Hall, Inc., 1986), esp. p. 54; C. Adams and A. L. Greene, "Secondary Attachments and Adolescent Self-concept," *Sex Roles,* 22 (February 1990): 187–98; A. L. Greene and C. Adams-Price, "Adolescents' Secondary Attachments to Celebrity Figures," *Sex Roles,* 23 (October 1990), 335–47.

20 Charles Atkin and Martin Block, "Effectiveness of Celebrity Endorsers," *Journal of Advertising Research,* February/March v23 pp. 57–61, pp. 60. ("Summing all 18 semantic differential scales, the total celebrity score of 76.7 is significantly higher than the noncelebrity score of 72.3.")

21 Atkin and Block, p. 60.

22 Atkin and Block, p. 57.

23 Jeffrey Brand and Bradley S. Greenberg, "Commercials in the Classroom: The Effect of *Channel One* Advertising", *Journal of Advertising Research,* January/February 1994 v34 n1, pp. 18–27.

24 Brand and Greenberg, p.19; see also R. P. Ross, "When Celebrities Talk, Children Listen," *Journal of Applied Developmental Psychology* 5, 3, (1984), p.185–202.

25 Atkin and Block, p. 61.

26   Michael Novak, *The Joy of Sports* (New York: Basic Books, Inc., Publishers, 1976),
      p. 27; Christopher Lasch, *The Culture of Narcissism* (New York: W. W. Norton & Com-
      pany, Inc., 1978), p. 109.
27   *Inquirer* Staff, "Suspense is over in cereal thriller," *The Philadelphia Inquirer* (5 August
      1996), D.9.
28   Bill Brubaker, *The Washington Post* (Washington, D.C.), March 11, 1991, pp. A1+.
29   Immanuel Kant, *Grounding for the Metaphysics of Morals* (1785), James W. Ellington,
      trans. (Indianapolis: Hackett Publishing Co., 1981), p. 40.

Bibliography

Adams, C. and A. L. Greene. "Secondary Attachments and Adolescent Self-concept." *Sex
    Roles* 22 (February 1990), 187–98.

Atkin, Charles, and Martin Block. "Effectiveness of Celebrity Endorsers," *Journal of Adver-
    tising Research* 23 (February/March 1983): 57–61.

Bandura, Albert. *Social Foundations of Thought and Action: A Social Cognitive Theory.* Engle-
    wood Cliffs, N.J.: Prentice-Hall, 1986.

Basil, Michael D. "Identification as a Mediator of Celebrity Effects (Magic Johnson and
    HIV Prevention Campaigns)." *Journal of Broadcasting and Electronic Media* 40 (Fall
    1996): 478–95.

Brand, Jeffrey, and Bradley S. Greenberg, "Commercials in the Classroom: The Effect of
    Channel One Advertising," *Journal of Advertising Research* 34 (January/February 1994):
    18–27.

Brubaker, Bill. *The Washington Post* (Washington, D.C.), March 11, 1991, pp. A1+.

Elliot, Stuart. "It's Official: Michael Jordan Is Now Promoting Gatorade." *The New York
    Times,* 9 August 1991.

Friedman, Termini, and Washington, *Journal of Advertising Research,* 6 (1977): 22–24.

Glenn, Norval D. and Ashbel Smith. "Whatever Happened to Morals: Individuals Are Set-
    ting Their Own Standards and Blurring the Lines Between Right and Wrong," *The
    Orlando Sentinel* (30 June 1991), pp. G1+.

Greene, A. L. and C. Adams-Price. "Adolescents' Secondary Attachments to Celebrity Fig-
    ures." *Sex Roles* 23 (October 1990): 335–47.

Hume, David. *A Treatise on Human Nature* in *The Essential David Hume,* Paul Wolff, ed.
    New York: The New American Library, Mentor Books, 1969.

Inquirer Staff. "Suspense is over in cereal thriller," *The Philadelphia Inquirer* (5 August 1996),
    D.9.

Kant, Immanuel. *Grounding for the Metaphysics of Morals* (1785), James W. Ellington, trans.
    Indianapolis: Hackett Publishing Co., 1981.

Krutch, Joseph Wood. *The Measure of Man.* Indianapolis: Bobbs-Merrill, 1954.

Mathur, Lynette Knowles, Ike Mathur, and Nanda Rangan, "The Wealth Effects Associated
    with a Celebrity Endorser: The Michael Jordan Phenomenon." *Journal of Advertising
    Research* 37 (May/June 1997): 67–93

Myrdal, Gunnar. *An American Dilemma,* vol. 1. New Brunswick, N.J.: Transaction Pub-
    lishers, 1996.

Plantinga, Alvin. "Rationality and Religious Belief." In *Contemporary Philosophy of Religion,* Steven M. Cahn and David Shatz, eds. New York: Oxford University Press, 1982.

Plato. *The Laws,* Book V. In *The Dialogues of Plato.* Vol. 4., B. Jowett, trans. New York: Bigelow, Brown & Co., n.d.

Ross, Rhonda P., et al. "When Celebrities Talk Children Listen: An Experimental Analysis of Children's Responses to TV Ads with Celebrity Endorsement." *Journal of Applied Developmental Psychology* 5 (1984): 185–202.

Stout, Patricia A. and Young Sook Moon. "Use of Endorsers in Magazine Advertisements." *Journalism Quarterly* 67 (Fall 1990): 536–46.

Will, Frederick. "Thoughts and Things," In *Proceedings and Addresses of the American Philosophical Association* 42 (1968–69): 51–69.

Chapter 12
A Schematic Analysis of Popular Culture, Adolescence, and Sport: Surprising Implications for Education and Our Democratic Future

Philip L. Smith,
Ohio State University

Culture with a capital "C" has traditionally been defined as Platonic-like in nature. Meaning and value are assumed to be ultimately transcendent, owing little or nothing of their construction to ordinary human beings. The thinking here goes something like this: "If Culture were dependent on circumstances, or contingent in any way on ordinary people, it would lose its intellectual and moral authority. Authority is grounded in objective and immutable truth. Only those who understand this and possess the talent and training to recognize the truth in tradition and law are fit to shoulder the burden of leadership and decide how power should be exercised."

Culture of this kind has never been easy to establish, not only for obvious political reasons, but because it is hard to translate general cultural mandates in specific and concrete situations in a relevant and consistent manner. The usual model for this has been to regard general cultural mandates as core, abstract principles that are embodied in tradition, reflected in social conventions and sustained by the legal and moral practices of ordinary people in their daily lives. High culture represents the purest form in which these principles are known and celebrated. Low, or "popular," culture, defined by the mundane practices of ordinary people in their daily lives, is an attempt to understand and appreciate general cultural mandates from "the ground up," so to speak.

It is not perforce to disparage these practices or the people who engage in them to characterize popular culture in this way. Rather it is to recognize the need everyone has to face to live life in particular circumstances. The problem is how to do this in an acceptable way, given the great distance between high and low culture and the variable conditions of human experience. Popular culture tends to develop its own internal dynamic precisely because the translation of general cultural mandates is so problematic. Operating idiosyncratically, it begins to resist and undermine higher authority. When higher authority initiates corrective action, an adversarial relationship is created that fosters the further development of popular culture's internal dynamic as a mode of resistance.

By various means and degrees, ordinary people begin to show animosity towards virtually every symbol of higher authority. There comes a point when popular culture can no longer be described as a loyal, although perhaps misguided, attempt to honor the core, abstract principles of Culture with a capital "C." Popular culture has been transformed by its own internal dynamic into a hostile alternative both to the principles of culture and to the very idea of a Platonic-like model for conceiving of meaning and value. On the alternative model, meaning and value are relativistic, worldly, and highly personalized.

This picture of popular culture can be seen as either positive or negative. Viewed as positive, it portrays schematically the development of Western-style democracy, from Athens and Rome, through the Renaissance, Reformation, and the Enlightenment, to the present, where, at the end of the 20th century, a fashionable number of intellectuals have proudly proclaimed that, at least philosophically, we have finally purged ourselves of the idea of cultural hegemony and can openly oppose its exploitative consequences. We fully recognize that individual human beings must be given their due as ends in themselves and that lasting community can only be found in respectful association with natural diversity.

The negative view of popular culture sees it as a reflection of adolescence, understood to be a necessary but dangerous stage in human development that goes from infancy to adulthood. Without adolescence, maturity could never be achieved. The danger is that it combines growing independent power with unreasonableness. The emergence of independent power during adolescence may be largely a physiological phenomenon, but to some extent it represents an allowance from an enlightened adult community, recognizing the need for individuals in this phase of life to test their talents against reality. The rejection of externally imposed modes of control is essential for the final leap to maturity, whereby a higher authority can be understood and appropriated as a valid extension of an independent and rational self.

If, by some measure, adolescent rebellion is to be accepted as normal in the course of healthy self-development, it might still be asked, "How much development is that?" The danger inherent in adolescence is that coupling self-assertion with immaturity can be a recipe for disaster. Lacking the guidance of a strong cultural authority would seem to be no less detrimental for individual development than being oppressed by it. How can the right balance be found?

The feeling of being alone in a hostile world is typical of adolescence. Moreover, it is unclear to the adolescent who should bear the responsibility for this. Is it one's own fault? Would embracing the authority of the adult world help the problem or worsen it? Adults would like to believe that, given sufficient time and a decent education, an adolescent will be brought back in line with reasonably prudent social conventions. Popular culture prepares the individual for the possibility that social conventions may never be prudent. It encourages individuals to believe, for a variety of reasons, that one must always be ready to fend for one's self. Assuming this attitude, the distinction between "acting out," which suggests an untutored, perhaps malevolent, immaturity (epitomized by adolescence), and "acting up," which suggests a more reasonable and courageous response to troubling circumstances, becomes fundamentally problematic.

Herein lies the difficulty: If popular culture regards this distinction as fundamentally problematic, by what light does it guide adolescent development? Adolescence, it would seem, is an idea that itself was born of popular culture and reflects the same kind of immaturity that is found in its source. In this regard, it is similar to our modern conception of democracy, which is also a product of popular culture. Democracy is not driven by a logically consistent vision of a good society. And adolescence cannot be contrasted with a reliable image of a mature person. Because popular culture relativizes, materializes, and individualizes meaning and value, it cannot establish any substantial or generalizable authority for the normative ideas that it generates. It lacks an internally coherent structure that would allow ideas like democracy and adolescence to be explicated and justified a priori. Its sole basis for understanding ideas, for discussing and defending their meaning and value, is human experience. It was, as I recollect, Charles Peirce, the father of pragmatism, who acknowledged human experience as "the most mendacious witness there is, but it is our only witness, and all we can do is put it in the sweat-box and torture the truth of it as best we can."[1] Peirce believed that, ultimately, truth resides outside of human experience. It is only that human experience, seriously examined, is our only way to know the truth. John Dewey, the more influential philosopher of pragmatism who followed Peirce, did not believe that truth could be kept apart from experience, even in this modest way. Neither does popular culture. So, where does that leave us?

The increasing dominance of popular culture in the world today explains why the institutions and practices associated with high culture are in such rapid decline. High culture pillars like philosophy, theology, opera, museums, and libraries are seen by popular culture as being out of touch with reality, disrespectful of actual human experience, or both. However, what reason is there for believing that popular culture can protect itself, and us, from the degrading effects of the hyper-demanding, sensation-seeking, self-indulgent postmodern personality without reverting to the assumptions of high culture? To suggest that ordinary people can do better at managing their affairs than their high culture counterparts only begs the question. How is this possible? Lacking external standards, or special mental powers, the only tool available to popular culture for interpreting experience is self-assertion, the quality of which is to be judged by two criteria: (1) its objective and practical developmental outcomes, and (2) its capacity to sustain interest and motivation.

An illustration of how self-assertion can be put to good use can be found in the area of sport. Sport begins as play. As play moves away from purposeless self-expression and adopts the characteristics of socially constructed, rule-governed behavior, games emerge. Games become sport when interaction becomes competitive, and rules not only regulate activity but begin to define its meaning and value for anyone who participates in the sport. Eventually, the sport develops a practice that has its own integrity. Understanding this practice is more than an intellectual act, more than a behavioral expression or display of skill, and more than having any particular feeling or attitude. It involves all these things, and, thus, is like a culture unto itself. As with any culture, it has its own reality. Not everyone who engages in the practice necessarily understands or cares about it. At some point, the practice must resist challenges to its integrity, and the stewards of the sport must be prepared to sanction or exclude those who do not sufficiently understand or respect it.

Notice, too, that, as with popular culture, there is no assumption that the practice of a sport is anything except the human construction of those who partake of it. The sport may serve a host of extrinsic, even conflicting, ends. It may be commodified as a business, consumed as a form of entertainment, or indulged in as egotistical self-expression. But, if the practice is like a culture, maintaining its own standards and encouraging the pursuit of its own internal good, its meaning and value is not merely in the eye of the beholder. It is something to live up to and honor. At the same time, it is something to experiment with and to modify when conditions warrant, since, after all, it is a human construction, for which its stewards are reasonable.

The challenge of developing and maintaining sport practices that mature and enrich those who engage in them is, in one way, easier now than ever; in another way, harder. It is easier in that sport practices can no longer be constrained or trivialized by high culture. As a dimension of popular culture, they are simply too powerful. It is harder, because the control of these practices is increasingly in the hands of those who do not understand or respect them, and who, themselves, seem to need the guidance the practice is supposed to provide. How this circumstance has come about is a long and ugly story. Yet, sport practices survive and prosper today as never before. In this, there may be a lesson for other areas of popular culture. The self-assertion they promote is participatory, objective, and practical. They involve the body and spirit, equally with the mind, in building practices that are as exhilarating as they are developmental, which is something even volatile adolescents can understand and respect.

Endnote

1   I read this statement years ago and committed it to memory, but am now unable to locate the original even in Charles Sanders Peirce, *Collected Papers,* 8 vols. (Bristol: Thoemmes Press, 1998). It is plausible that Peirce could, would, and/or should have said it.

Bibliography

Bloom, Alan. *The Closing of the American Mind*. New York: Simon and Schuster, 1987.

Harrington, Michael. *The Politics at God's Funeral: The Spiritual Crisis of Western Civilization*. New York: Penguin Books, 1983.

MacIntyre, Alasdair. *After Virtue*. South Bend: University of Notre Dame Press, 1981.

Peirce, Charles Sanders. *Collected Papers*. 8 vols. Bristol: Thoemmes Press, 1998.

Putnam, Hilary. *Realism with a Human Face*. Cambridge: Harvard University Press, Cambridge, 1990.

Rorty, Richard. *Contingency, Irony, and Solidarity*. New York: Cambridge University Press, 1989.

Taylor, Charles. *Sources of the Self: The Making of the Modern Identity*. Cambridge: Harvard University Press, 1989.

———. *The Ethics of Authenticity*. Cambridge: Harvard University Press, 1992.

Toulmin, Stephen. *Cosmopolis: The Hidden Agenda of Modernity*. Chicago: The University of Chicago Press, 1990.

General Editors: Joseph & Linda DeVitis

As schools struggle to redefine and restructure themselves, they need to be cognizant of the new realities of adolescents. Thus, this series of monographs and textbooks is committed to depicting the variety of adolescent cultures that exist in today's post-industrial societies. It is intended to be a primarily qualitative research, practice, and policy series devoted to contextual interpretation and analysis that encompasses a broad range of interdisciplinary critique. In addition, this series will seek to provide a pragmatic, pro-active response to the current backlash of conservatism that continues to dominate political discourse, practice, and policy. This series seeks to address issues of curriculum theory and practice; multicultural education; aggression and violence; the media and arts; school dropouts; homeless and runaway youth; alienated youth; at-risk adolescent populations; family structures and parental involvement; and race, ethnicity, class, and gender studies.

Send proposals and manuscripts to the general editors at:

> Joseph & Linda DeVitis
> College of Education and Human Development
> University of Louisville
> Louisville, KY 40292-0001

To order other books in this series, please contact our Customer Service Department at:

> (800) 770-LANG (within the U.S.)
> (212) 647-7706 (outside the U.S.)
> (212) 647-7707 FAX

or browse online by series at:

> WWW.PETERLANGUSA.COM